Islamic Studies

Level 9

Mansur Ahmad, Husain A. Nuri

weekend Learning

ISBN: 978-0-9818483-1-0

Library of Congress Cataloguing in Publication data available upon request.

First Edition: 2009
Cover Design: Mansur Ahmad
Illustration and layout: Mansur Ahmad and Husain A. Nuri

WeekendLearning Publishers
5584 Boulder Crest St
Columbus, OH 43235

www.weekendlearning.com
email: weekendlearning@gmail.com

Preface

The concept of a series of Islamic Studies books was conceived in 2002 when both of us were teachers and/or principals of two weekend schools in two different states. We used several excellent textbooks or reference books for the schools. However, as teachers soon we realized there was no single textbook available that could meet our classroom needs. Some of the available books have too many or too few lessons for an academic year. Some lessons are too long for a class hour, some are too short. Some lessons are too difficult for the age; some are too basic for higher classes. Some books are written without a 12 year curriculum in mind. The lessons in higher grades, therefore, did not develop from the knowledge base of the prior years. Sometimes, extra emphasis was placed on one topic at the cost of other important topics. We thought a balanced knowledge base was, thus, lost.

We always felt there ought to be a way out. We began writing the lessons ourselves to meet the needs of our schools. We involved other teachers. For the next two years, we conducted classes based on the lessons we prepared. In the meantime, both of us met other principals and teachers across the country. We wanted to find out how they teach Islamic Studies and what their major concerns were. Most of the principals and teachers we talked to, expressed their inability to find or develop a good curriculum. If they had a curriculum they could not find lessons to complement the curriculum.

This survey prompted us to develop a functional, comprehensive curriculum for weekend schools in the West. We wanted to have a curriculum that would include everything Muslim students growing up in the West would ideally need to know. We wanted to include topics based on the life experiences of students growing up in the West. Muslim children growing up in the US, Europe and Australia are facing diverse challenges and conflicting pressures at schools and at friend circles. They are constantly influenced by mainstream youth culture. We wanted lessons to address their issues from their perspective.

The curriculum alone would not be of any use unless there were lessons based on the curriculum. The lessons had to be age appropriate, suitable for typical class duration of most of the schools. As we continued to write and edit lessons over the next two years, we made the curriculum increasingly meaningful.

In 2007 we published pre-printed coil bound versions of these books. More than thirty schools in the US and UK used the books. We also received large number of inquiries from many other schools. Based on the suggestions, comments and reviews received from many of these schools, we have edited the books and made changes as appropriate.

We are thankful to Allāh for giving us the ability to write these books. We pray to Allāh to accept our labor and make us successful in communicating the message of Islam. We hope Islamic schools and home schools in the USA and other countries will find these books useful. Any mistakes or errors in the books are our fault. We will appreciate receiving meaningful comments and suggestions to improve the series.

رَبَّنَا تَقَبَّلْ مِنَّا ۖ إِنَّكَ أَنتَ السَّمِيعُ الْعَلِيمُ ﴿١٢٧﴾

"Our Rabb! Accept from us, you indeed are the all-Hearing, all-Knowing." (2:127)

March 1, 2009

Mansur Ahmad
Husain A. Nuri

Table of Contents

How to use this book effectively
Instructions for the teachers and the parents

The lessons for the Level Nine Islamic Studies book expand and elaborate understanding of Islamic history, morals and principles for students growing up in the West. The purpose is to make students understand the connection between the *deen* and the *dunya*. Sensitive issues like peer pressure, dating, alcohol and gambling, violence in Islam, food laws and moral building lessons like 'ibadah, indecency and family values are addressed. Nonetheless, the length of each lesson is kept within a reasonable limit so that teachers can cover the material within an hour or less.

We strongly recommend teachers read the lesson before coming to the class. Please give a thought on the delivery of the content of the lesson. If needed, bring index card with highlights or sequence of discussion written down. In most lessons, the teacher should explain the content of each paragraph rather than reading out the lesson. Make good use of marker board to jot down the discussion points and sub-headers of the lesson. Help the students understand the perspective of the time-line or map if provided in the lesson. Ask questions frequently to reinforce learning and make frequent eye contact with the students. Keep a track of time so that the lesson gets covered within the allotted time.

For maximum benefit, each lesson should be completed in one class hour. We recommend that a test be conducted after every fifth or sixth lesson. weekend**Learning** has designed an MS-Excel based user-friendly program to record homework and exam scores. It will become handy when report cards are prepared. For this program as well as for question bank, ready-to-print exam and homework questions, obtain a CD from the publisher.

Homework:

Teachers are requested to assign regular homework and also grade these regularly. For this grade, the time commitment for homework is about 10-15 minutes per lesson. It is strongly encouraged that parents supervise the student for the homework. A parent's regular supervision of homework will indicate education is valued.

Teaching Respect:

From an early age, students should be taught to show respect to Allāh, His Prophets and Angels. The teachers and parents are requested to mention the following:

Whenever the word Allāh appears in the book, please add the glorification "*Subhāna-hu wa-Ta'ālā*."

Whenever the word Muhammad, or other words indicating Muhammad, e.g. Rasulullah, the Prophet, or Nabi appears, please add the prayer, "*Salla-llāhu 'alaihi wa Sallam*." We have used (S) in the book to remind the prayer. Whenever the student comes across the names of a prophet or an angel, please add the prayer "*Alai-hi-s Salām*". This is noted by (A). The students should be taught to add the prayer "*Radi-allāhu 'an-hu*" for a khalīfa or a male companion of the Prophet (S). For a lady companion, the prayer "*Radi-allāhu 'an-hā*" should be used. These are noted by (R) or (ra).

Suggestions:

Please provide suggestions, corrections, ideas, etc., to improve the book by sending an e-mail to the publisher at *weekendLearning@gmail.com*. It is a combined effort of the publisher, authors, teachers and parents to prepare our future ummah. May Allāh guide us all! Amin.

classwork**weekend 1**

Signs of Allāh in Nature

Objective of the Lesson:

The Qur'ān encourages people to look at the nature to understand the signs of Allāh. The students will analyze a few selected verses of the Qur'ān to understand how Allāh wants us to look at the signs. Also, they will study the meaning of the words *'ayat'* related to the signs of Allāh.

The simple definition of "sign" is something that indicates the presence or existence of something else. For example, a dark cloud is a sign of imminent rain. Smoke is a sign of fire. Many police cars and ambulances with flashing lights are a sign of an accident. New leaves on a tree are a sign of arrival of spring. Falling leaves are a sign that autumn has started. The presence or existence of one thing tells us about the presence or existence of another thing.

Let us apply the above definition and these analogies of signs to know more about Allāh. We cannot see Allāh, but as we declare faith in Islam we believe that Allāh exists. From a critical point, this might be a blind faith. Allāh does not encourage us to follow a blind faith. He asks us to learn about Him through His signs. Everything in the universe is a sign of Allāh. Therefore, when we see presence or existence of trees, flowers, mountains, rivers, stars, oceans, etc., we should be able to conclude that someone created all these.

However, the above analogies are not enough for someone who does not believe in Allāh. For such a person, presence or existence of trees, flowers, mountains, rivers, stars, or oceans, is not enough to convince in the existence of Allāh. This person fails to connect a sign with its cause. For example, on seeing many police cars with flashing lights, he may conclude something different than what most people would conclude. He might be right. He might also be right if he had concluded a smoke was not caused by fire; the smoke may have been by a chemical process that did not result in fire. However, to conclude that trees, flowers, mountains, rivers, stars, or oceans simply happened on their own, without Allāh creating them, would be a wrong conclusion. Therefore, in the Qur'ān when Allāh talks about His signs, typically He concludes with a question such as "will you not understand," or "do you not see," or "perhaps you will pay attention."

Meaning of Āyah: Each of the messages in the Qur'ān is an indication or a hint of Allāh. For this reason each verse is called a sign of Allāh. The Arabic term for sign is *āyah*. The word *āyah* is used in the Qur'ān over four hundred times.

الٓرٰ ۚ تِلْكَ اٰيٰتُ الْكِتٰبِ الْحَكِيْمِ ①

Alif Lam Ra. These are the Āyah of the Book, full of wisdom. (10:1)

الٓرٰ ۚ تِلْكَ اٰيٰتُ الْكِتٰبِ الْمُبِيْنِ ① اِنَّآ

اَنْزَلْنٰهُ قُرْءٰنًا عَرَبِيًّا لَّعَلَّكُمْ تَعْقِلُوْنَ ②

Alif Lam Ra. These are the Āyah of the perspicuous Book. We have indeed revealed it— a Qur'ān in Arabic, that you may understand. (12:1-2)

Purpose of signs: The purpose behind any type of sign is to convey a message. A street sign conveys a message about the street or traffic rules. Similarly the signs of Allāh, whether these are verses of the Qur'ān or anything in nature, convey a message. The Qur'ānic *āyah* primarily appeal to our three faculties—hearing, sight and understanding. When a Muslim reads the Qur'ānic *āyah*, he or she understands the meaning through use of these faculties. However, when non-believers read the *āyah*, they may not or do not want to grasp the meaning. For most people, an octagonal red traffic sign means to stop, but many people do not 'see' it or ignore its presence. The Qur'ān clarifies the purpose of the signs as follows:

اِنَّ فِيْ خَلْقِ السَّمٰوٰتِ وَالْاَرْضِ وَاخْتِلَافِ

الَّيْلِ وَالنَّهَارِ لَاٰيٰتٍ لِّاُولِي الْاَلْبَابِ ﴿١٩٠﴾

Surely in the creation of the heavens and the earth, and the alternation of the night and the day, there are Signs for the possessor of understanding. (3:190)

Types of signs: Although the word *āyah* means a sign, it has different shades of meanings. It also means miracles by the prophets, and books of Allāh. In short, the word *āyah* can be used for anything and everything, as everything is a sign of Allāh. In Arabic usage everything is an *āyatullah*.

There are two basic types of signs:

1. Prophetic signs
2. Natural signs.

Prophetic signs were the ones brought by the prophets. These signs can be further divided into two types: a) oral or written revelations, and b) physical miracles. Similarly, the natural signs can be further divided into two types: a) external—relating to the world around us, and b) internal—relating to ourselves.

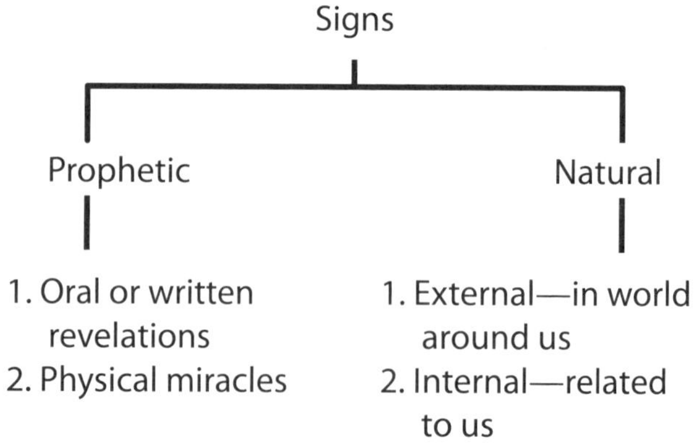

Some prophetic signs: All the prophets received signs from Allāh. Their teachings and the Books that they delivered were signs of Allāh. The victory of Muslims in the battle of Badr is a sign of Allāh.[3:13] When Musa (A) came with a clear sign, his opponents called these as magic or enchantment.[28:36] Both 'Isa (A) and his mother are signs to the mankind.[21:91, 23:50] The rescue of Ibrāhīm (A) from fire is a sign of Allāh.[29:24] Some other signs of Allāh that we find in the lives of the prophets are the rescue of Nūh (A) in his ark,[29:15] the she-camel that Sālih (A) showed to the Thamūd,[17:59] and the silence of Zakariyyāh (A).[19:10]

While the signs of Allāh are abundant in the nature, we can experience many religious signs even today. During visit to Makkah, we can see many signs.[3:97] The spread of Islam all over the world is also a sign.[41:53]

Even the evil-doers are signs to us. The destruction of the townships of Sodom and Gomorrah is a warning sign to the mankind.[15:75] The preservation of the body of Pharaoh is also a sign for any oppressor.[10:92] Therefore, the Qur'ān stimulates us to think about the signs of Allāh that are abundant around us:

And in the earth there are Signs for the convinced, and in yourselves. Will you not then see? (51:20-21)

And of His Signs is the creation of the heavens and the earth, and the diversity of your tongues and your colors. Certainly in this there are indeed Signs for the learned. (30:22)

Signs to science: Many people assume that science and religion cannot coexist. They derive such assumption as their religious teachings contradict science, and some of the descriptions in their religious texts cannot be supported by science. Science is defined as knowledge or a system of knowledge that covers general truths or the operation of general and natural laws. Since Allāh created the universe, and He has set up the laws of its function, truly speaking science is the laws of Allāh. In our scientific practice, we define science as observation, identification, experimental investigation and theoretical explanation of any phenomenon. We can explain many phenomena to some extent, but cannot fully explain how and why something happens.

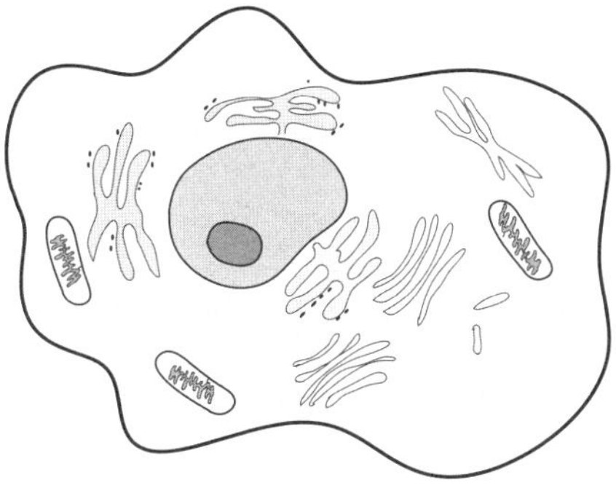

Allāh is invisible, and we cannot see Him. For this reason, many prominent scientists believe that God does not exist as they cannot observe God in a laboratory. They refuse to accept the presence of God, as their theoretical explanation is limited. Some scientists will accept the presence of God, but will only term Him as Nature. When they observe cells divide or electrons flow, they will call it as an act of Nature. Calling Allāh as Nature does not undermine His almightiness. Allāh wants us to think about Him and understand His power from His signs in the universe.

When Allāh asks us to think about the signs in nature, He is asking us to fully investigate His creations by our scientific methods. If we are not arrogant, our scientific studies will only convince us that a Supreme Power does exist who controls everything in the universe.

Why we need revelation: No doubt, Allāh's signs are everywhere. Mere looking and watching at the signs without right guidance will put us in jeopardy.

For example, by looking at the planetary position, an astrologer tries to foretell about the future. He cannot understand anything about God by looking at the planets. When some polytheists look at the power of sun, they begin to worship it. Some take a river as a goddess, and some take animals as gods. They see the power of an object, but fail to understand that a Supreme Power created the sun, rivers and animals. With right guidance, we can avoid falling into the grave error of worshipping the created. Trying to read the signs without prophetic guidance is like trying to understand a speech without knowing the language.

To properly understand the signs of Allāh in nature, we should listen to the words of the prophets. The Qur'ān is the word of Allāh, revealed to the Prophet (S). By accepting Muhammad (S) as our guide, we can begin to understand the true meaning of the signs of Allāh.

From the Prophet's life: A hadīth reports that Prophet (S) was walking with some of his companions when he met an old woman who was turning wool into thread using a spinning wheel. He greeted her and began speaking to her. He wanted to know the reason for her faith in Allāh. She explained that the spinning wheel does not turn unless there is a hand to turn it, and the heaven cannot turn unless there is someone turning it.

Turning away from sign: The signs of Allāh are instruction to us. If someone does not pay attention to the signs of Allāh, that person conceals the truth. Denying or ignoring the signs is a negative quality of human being. Only the transgressors conceal the truth. In this regard the Qur'ān says:

> *And We indeed have revealed to you manifest signs; and no one rejects them except the miscreants. (2:99)*

> *And those who belie Our signs are deaf and dumb in utter darkness. Whom Allāh pleases He leaves him to wander; and whom He pleases He places him upon the Right Path. (6:39)*

> *.... We shall soon requite those who turn away from Our signs with an evil chastisement, because they have been turning away. (6:157)*

For a Muslim the proof of *tawhid* is the signs in nature. The word *tawhid* means declaration of oneness of Allāh. The Qur'ān encourages us to study the nature, appreciate the diversity in nature and look for uniformity in nature. Allāh wants us to 'read' the signs in nature and understand the existence of One God. The more we understand the 'signs' the more we will know about God.

homework**weekend 1**

1. What is the basic meaning of the word 'sign' as mentioned in the lesson?

....

2. What are some of the meanings of the word "*āyah*" as mentioned in the Qur'ān?

....

3. In verse 3:190, the change of day and night is considered a sign of Allāh. In a few sentences, describe some majesties of Allāh that we can understand from this sign.

....

....

....

....

4. What are the three faculties to which the Qur'ān frequently appeals? Name them.

....

....

5. What are the two types of prophetic signs? Name them.

a. .... b. ....

6. In verse 30:22 three signs of Allāh are mentioned. What are the three signs?

a. ....

b. ....

c. ....

7. Read verses 11:96. Based on reading the lesson, what type or types of signs did Mūsā bring with him?

....

8. Read Sūrah Al-i-'Imran, verse 13, which discusses about the battle of Badr. As a sign of Allāh, what did the Muslim soldiers see in their enemies?

....

9. Read verses 12:109 and 23:80. At the end of each verse, there is a question posed to a particular faculty. Which faculty do these verses appeal?

....

10. Read verses 10:67, 16:65 and 30:23. In each of the verse, there is a question posed to a particular faculty. Which faculty do these verses appeal?

....

Ponder Over the Qur'ān

Objective of the Lesson:

The Qur'ān is not just about memorizing and reading. We need to ponder over its message. Allāh instructs us to open our hearts and think deeply about its teachings. Only through intelligent, analytical study we can understand and appreciate the inner meanings of the Qur'ān.

The Qur'ān, a relatively short book, has extraordinary amount of knowledge. Allāh told us that if the entire oceans were ink and the entire trees were pen, we would not be able to finish writing the word of our Rabb.[18:109]

The scholars of Islam study the Qur'ān, verse by verse, word by word, letter by letter, to understand Allāh's expression. They explained the meaning of the Qur'ān as they understood. However, no scholar would dare to limit the meanings of the Qur'ān to what he understood, or say that the Qur'ān has exhausted its meaning. Learned scholars of Islam freely admit that they know merely a few drops from the Qur'ānic ocean.

The scholars of Islam understand that knowledge is a dynamic process. It advances in every age, in every generation. One of the reasons Allāh wants us to ponder over the Qur'ān is that with advancement of knowledge our understanding of the Qur'ān will become more refined and relevant to the time.

In the Qur'ān, Allāh repeatedly encourages us to follow Islam. Interestingly, He does not want us to follow Islam blindly. He wants us to ponder over the message of the Qur'ān. The more we ponder on the Qur'ān, the more will we learn. The knowledge in the Qur'ān is not limited to religious rituals; it contains knowledge of every aspect of life.

Call to ponder: Unless we understand the message, the Qur'ān will remain an ordinary book to us. If our rational mind is locked and heart is sealed, the true teachings of the Qur'ān will not make much sense. For this reason the

Qur'ān frequently appeals people to think, reflect and ponder.

أَفَلَا يَتَدَبَّرُونَ الْقُرْآنَ أَمْ عَلَىٰ قُلُوبٍ أَقْفَالُهَا ﴿٢٤﴾

What! will they not then ponder on the Qur'ān, or is it that they have locks on their hearts? (47:24).

The interrogative mode of the verse tries to shake up our stagnant mind and awaken us to undertake serious studies of the Qur'ān. The verse did not use the word seal, as sealing is a relatively permanent, irreversible arrangement. A lock can be opened with the right key. Moreover, this lock is not an external one, it is on the heart. The owner of the heart can unlock if there is sincere intention.

Four words about pondering: Four words are used while encouraging us to ponder on the Qur'ān. These words are *dhakara* (to remember), *fakara* (to think), *dabbara* (to ponder, reflect) and *'aqala* (to use understanding).

Dhakara or remembering is of three types. The first type is when we *dhikr* or remember Allāh in our heart. We remain aware or conscious of Allāh all the time. We feel that Allāh is watching us all the time, He is with us, and therefore we do not do anything that will displease Him. The second type of *dhakara* is to remember Allāh using our tongue. We recite His name and praise His glory. The third type is to remind others about Allāh. When we remind others about our duties towards Allāh and His creations, we also remind ourselves.

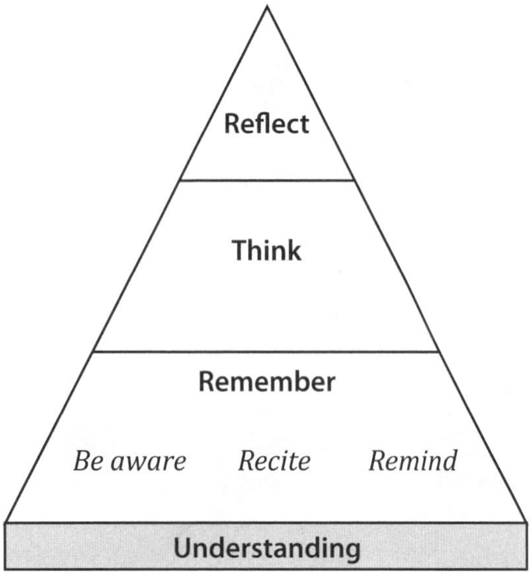

A higher level of remembering about Allāh is *fakara* or to think. Thinking is more than remembering. When we do *fikr* or think, we analyze any information that we may have. When we see creations of Allāh, we can analyze their attributes and try to see how they connect to each other. In verse 30:8, we are asked to think about ourselves. A systematic way of analysis may be called critical thinking. Thinking is not always positive. Someone may think in a positive direction, while others may be indulged in evil thoughts.[74:18]

The highest level of pondering is *dabbara* or reflecting on the message of Allāh. When we are at the level of performing *dabbara*, we are deeply studying the words of Allāh. Such reflections can be done when we are actively studying the ultimate source of knowledge, the Qur'ān. This is not the type of study that analyzes mathematical problems, chemical equations, or physical properties of elements. When we do math or solve chemical equations we think. Reflection on the Qur'ān is the highest form of thinking, as there is no limit to the knowledge in the Qur'ān.

All the remembering, thinking and reflecting will be successful if we use proper *'aqala* or understanding. Allāh has revealed the Qur'ān in Arabic so that the people of Arabia could understand (*ta'qilun*).

إِنَّآ أَنزَلْنَٰهُ قُرْءَٰنًا عَرَبِيًّا لَّعَلَّكُمْ تَعْقِلُونَ ﴿٢﴾

We have indeed revealed it—a Qur'ān in Arabic, that you may understand. (12:2)

With this understanding, the Arabs were able to spread the message of Islam. For a good *'aql*, we must use all our faculties, such as hearing and sight.[10:42-43] Those who do not want to hear the truth, or speak the truth are the ones who do not have the *'aql*.[8:22]

Who should ponder: Although pondering on the Qur'ān or on the messages of Allāh is the highest degree of thinking, it is not restricted to only those who are scholars or the enlightened. Everyone, at their own levels, should try to reflect on the Qur'ān. The more they reflect on the Qur'ān, the higher will be their level of understanding. Allāh even encourages the non-Muslims to reflect *(dabbara)* on the Qur'ān, and receive guidance as they will see that the Book has no discrepancy:

أَفَلَا يَتَدَبَّرُونَ الْقُرْآنَ ۚ وَلَوْ كَانَ مِنْ عِندِ غَيْرِ اللَّهِ لَوَجَدُوا فِيهِ اخْتِلَافًا كَثِيرًا ﴿٨٢﴾

Do they not then ponder over the Qur'ān? Had it been from anyone except Allāh, they would surely have found in it a great deal of discrepancy. (4:82)

How to ponder: When we try to ponder on the Qur'ān we must seek help from Allāh. He is the Teacher of the Qur'ān, and can guide us to the right conclusion. Some people hesitate to ponder on the Qur'ān thinking that the Book is too difficult, or that they may end up with a wrong conclusion. Allāh has stated that He has made the Qur'ān easy for everyone to understand and remember its teachings.[44:58, 54:17, 22,32,40] Without adequate knowledge or without proper intention, we can become misled, so it is important that we seek refuge with Allāh against the Shaitān when we begin to read and think about the Qur'ān.[16:82] If we are guided by Allāh, there is no chance that we will corrupt the meaning of the Qur'ān.[85:22]

We can start with only a few verses of the Qur'ān. A slow, regular step-by-step method of studying will lead us off the ground. If you have access to a scholar, it is helpful to listen to the scholar. In addition to the listening, you must put your own effort of *dabbara* or reflection. If we do not know Arabic, a compromised way of reflecting will be to study from a reliable translation. However, it is best to study the Qur'ān in Arabic. Use an index to reflect on a topic of the Qur'ān. A topic or theme may be mentioned in different parts of the Qur'ān. Reading the related verses on a topic can give a clearer understanding of the position of the Qur'ān. We should follow the best understanding.[39:18,55]

What to ponder: The message of the Qur'ān being so vast, it is virtually impossible for anyone to thoroughly ponder on all the topics of the Qur'ān. We can begin with any topic that interests us or an issue that bothers us. It may relate to social life, inter-personal relationship, legal decrees, or even scientific truths. Whatever is the issue, we will find enough material in the Qur'ān to ponder over. Allāh instructs us to "read from the Qur'ān what is easy for you."[73:20]

When to ponder: While the Qur'ān encourages us to ponder, it discourages us to become reclusive monks. We should be part of a society and fully contribute to its needs. Yet, we should ponder on the Qur'ān on a regular basis.[35:29] We are never too young or too old to ponder on the Qur'ān.

Why reflect or ponder? We may wonder why it is important to ponder over the Qur'ān, is reciting the Arabic Qur'ān not enough?

This question leads us to understand who we, the human beings, are and what makes us different from other animals. We cannot run as fast as a horse, we cannot swim as well as a fish, we cannot fly like a bird, and we are not as strong as an elephant. Our brain and intelligence made us superior over other animals and we are the *khalīfah* of Allāh. We are also blessed with a structured language. If we want to be good human, we should use our greatest strength, which is our brain.

كِتٰبٌ اَنْزَلْنٰهُ اِلَيْكَ مُبٰرَكٌ لِّيَدَّبَّرُوْٓا اٰيٰتِهٖ وَ
لِيَتَذَكَّرَ اُولُوا الْاَلْبَابِ ﴿٢٩﴾

A Scripture We have revealed it to you abounding in blessings, that they may ponder over its verses, and that the possessors of understanding may reflect. (38:29)

If we fail to use our brain, i.e. fail to ponder over the Qur'ān we symbolically become like cattle:

— hearts they have they do not understand with these, and eyes they have they do not see with these, and ears they have they do not hear with these. They are like cattle; rather they are more astray. They are themselves the heedless ones. (7:179).

You will find similar message in other verses too.[25:44; 47:12] We should therefore use our brain, remember the Qur'ānic guidance, and reflect over the verses. The Qur'ān is a Book of eternal guidance and it is the last of all the Divine Books.[3:40] However, our understanding of the book is limited to the extent of our knowledge. As our knowledge expands, so will our understanding of the Qur'ān if we contemplate over it.[39:29] With better understanding, we will be better at applying the Qur'ānic principles to uplift our life in this world and in the *akhira*.[2:5,201; 7:156]

Think about an animal or a bird that refuses to do what it is naturally and instinctively required to do but does not do. Think of a bird that does not want to fly or a fish that refuses to swim. Will these animals be successful? If we do not exercise our brain, what will happen to us?

Inquisitive prophets: One way to ponder over the Qur'ān is to ask questions. Ask questions to yourself, ask questions to others who know. Sometimes you will not find an immediate answer. Sometimes you will find answers that seem to have satisfied your current question. Even then, keep the doors and windows of your mind open. It is possible that your level of understanding will improve with advancement of your knowledge and you will find the answer or even a better answer.

The Qur'ān has several examples that prophets were not afraid of asking questions. Ibrāhīm (A) received knowledge and wisdom while he was still a young person. In spite of being a prophet of Allāh, he was not sure how Allāh gives life. Therefore, he asked.[2:260]

In another example, Mūsā (A) asked Allāh if he could see Him.[7:143] In yet another example Zakariyyāh (A) prayed to Allāh for a son. Allāh assured him that a son would be born to him and his name would be Yahyā (A). Even after getting the assurance, Zakariyyāh could not convince his heart. He asked Allāh as to how would it be possible.[19:10]

The Qur'ān is logical, and the arguments presented in the Qur'ān are clear. If we truly have to benefit from the Qur'ān, then we have to understand the messages of the Qur'ān. We have to use our all senses in deciding a path, be it Islam or a path away from it. Our brain, intelligence and other senses are truly gifts of Allāh that we need to use. We will be questioned if we have used all our faculties in making our decision.

homework**weekend 2**

1. Can a person completely understand the Qur'ān? Briefly explain your answer.

....

....

2. List a few reasons that Allāh want us to ponder on the Qur'ān.

....

....

3. According to this lesson, what are the three types of *dhikr*?

   a. ....

   b. ....

   c. ....

4. At what point should I stop pondering over the Qur'ān?

   a. When I have learned everything.
   b. When I cannot learn any more.
   c. When I become graduate from this school.
   d. I should never stop pondering over the Qur'ān.
   e. When I start teaching others about the Qur'ān.

5. Read verse 13:3. List the natural objects mentioned in the verse that can help us to think (*fikr*) about the Allāh and His messages.

....

....

....

6. If the Qur'ān was not divine, what was the most likely thing to find in it? Read verse 4:82 to answer.

....

7. Based on verse 47:24 who do you think placed the lock on the hearts of those who do not ponder over the Qur'ān?

....

....

8. Read verse 29 from sūrah Sād. The verse says Allāh wants us to ponder over the Qur'ān. What is specifically mentioned in the verse because of which we should ponder?

   a. Warning.
   b. Blessings.
   c. Teachings of the best kind.
   d. Promise of Jannah.
   e. Revelation through Jibril.

9. In sūrah *al-Furqān*, Allāh says a type of people will be rewarded with high places in *Jannah* because when they heard the divine message they did something. Read verse 25:73 then circle which of the following choice is correct.

   a. They fell down in prostration.
   b. They circulated the message to others.
   c. They did not sit down idle.
   d. They did not become deaf and blind.
   e. They did not give false evidence.

10. List some examples from the lives of prophets that they were not afraid to ask.

   a. ....

   b. ....

   c. ....

classwork**weekend 3**

Preservation and Compilation of the Qur'ān

Objective of the Lesson:

The Qur'ān was revealed gradually over twenty three years, yet it was compiled systematically, accurately and entirely. Students will study the process of preservation and compilation of the Qur'ān and analyze the factors that were in favor and against the process.

It is important to know the way the Qur'ān was compiled and preserved at the time of Prophet Muhammad (S) and later. This lesson gives an insight about what happened to the Qur'ān during the time of the Prophet (S) as he received the revelation over twenty three years and what happened after he passed away. Prophet (S), although not skilled at reading or writing, ensured the revelation he was receiving was being recorded i) properly, ii) completely, iii) promptly, iv) orderly, v) accurately and vi) consistently. We need to understand the mechanism he employed to compile and preserve the revelation and whether or not these mechanisms could work. Today we will review the entire process of compilation and preservation of the Qur'ān. In doing so, we will also address a frequently raised question whether the Qur'ān we read today is the same Qur'ān revealed to the Prophet (S). Why is this question raised? What are the evidences for or against it?

Reason for the doubt: Many non-Muslims express doubt about the accuracy and precision in compilation and preservation of the Qur'ān done at the time of the Prophet (S). They believe the present day Qur'ān is not the same Qur'ān revealed to the Prophet (S). Our analysis will indicate otherwise.

The non-Muslims express doubt about the Qur'ān as they are uncomfortable about the credibility of their religious book.

After the time of Mūsā, the Torah was erased from Jewish memory for several decades when they were held captive in Babylon. After about 70 years of captivity, when they were released from bondage, they recollected the Torah from their memory and wrote it down. Until about 100 C.E., the Torah was edited and re-edited several times by the Rabbis. The Qur'ān speaks about these changes in many verses. The Talmud, a human compilation of book of codification, was prepared around the same time. Obviously the Jewish scholars feel embarrassed when the present day Torah cannot be accurately and correctly referred to the 'original' Torah revealed to Mūsā.

The Bible, as we see today, is not the original Injīl revealed by Allāh to 'Isā (A). The Bible contains individual books written by various human authors, many of them did not live during the time of 'Isā and many were not his direct disciples. Many other books were not included in the Bible, these are still available in museums.

Adverse factors in preservation of the Qur'ān : In the Qur'ān verse 15:9 states:

إِنَّا نَحْنُ نَزَّلْنَا الذِّكْرَ وَإِنَّا لَهُ لَحَافِظُونَ ⑨

Surely We ourselves revealed the reminder and We most certainly are its Guardian. (15:9)

Notice the emphasis added in the verse: *We most certainly are its Guardian.* When Allāh proclaims He is the guardian of the Qur'ān, He has surely preserved the integrity of the text from all type of material degradation either by human or by nature, intentional or otherwise. The Qur'ān speaks of itself as a well-guarded tablet (*lawh mahfūz*).[85:22] This means, among other things, the Qur'ān is protected from any physical and material changes ever taking place, at any period of time, and at the hands of zealous followers or wicked antagonists.

The language of the Qur'ān plays an important role in preservation of the Qur'ān. The language in which it was revealed must remain in use. Disuse of the language would be an adverse factor in preservation of the Qur'ān. Allāh has assured the language in which it was revealed to remain in vogue and should never go into disuse as happened with Latin, ancient Greek, Sanskrit, Aramaic and many other.

Some other adverse factors during the time of revelation of the Qur'ān were little literacy in Arabia and inadequate means of preserving written record. Early Muslims overcame both these adverse factors by memorizing the entire Qur'ān. Large number of the companions and their followers in each generation continued to memorize it. At the same time, written copies of the Qur'ān were meticulously made, circulated and preserved. Earliest available copies of the Qur'ān are preserved in museums in Istanbul and Tashkent. Comparison of the present day Qur'ān with the early copies shows the text in the present day Qur'ān is accurate and correct.

Evidence of compilation of the Qur'ān : Although illiteracy among the Arabs was one of the adverse factors, skill of writing was nevertheless known to them. Many Makkan and Madīnan people knew writing. The internal evidence about writing down the Qur'ān can be noticed in the very first set of revelation where the use of pen is mentioned. The Prophet (S) was asked to "recite" and he was told that Allāh taught men the use of pen. This symbolic allusion is significant.

Other internal evidences are the Qur'ān speaks itself as a book (*kitāb*)—which indicates it is a book in writing, it is complete and it is a volume rather than loose sheets. In the Makkan revelation, verse 56:78-79 says: *in a book well preserved, none can touch it except the purified one.* This clearly shows, even at that early phase of revelation, passages of the Qur'ān were available in written form and it was in common use.

Well authenticated Tradition of the Prophet (S) indicates when 'Umar went to kill his sister for accepting Islam, he heard her reciting the Chapter 20 of the Qur'ān, and then he wanted to see or hold the Qur'ān in hand. This also confirms that the revealed portion of the Qur'ān was already in written format. In another Hadīth compiled by Bukharī, it is reported that the Companions were forbidden to travel to enemy's land with a copy of the Qur'ān. This also indicates written copies of the Qur'ān existed at the time of the Prophet (S).

Compilation at the time of the Prophet (S): There are numerous evidences that show the revelations were written down immediately or soon after the Prophet (S) received one. Abu Dāwūd reported on the authority of 'Uthmān that it was customary for the Prophet (S) that whenever a verse was revealed, he summoned one of the scribes to write it down in the chapter where such and such verses occur. During the process of revelation, many unfinished chapters existed at one given time.

Scribes of the Prophet (S): One of the most famous scribes to write down most of the revelations was Zaid ibn Thābit. In the absence of Zaid, several other companions were engaged,—both in Makkah and Madīnah. Among them, some prominent were Abū Bakr, 'Umar, 'Uthmān, 'Alī, Zubair Ibn 'Awām, 'Abdullāh ibn Sa'd, Ubbay ibn Ka'b. As many as forty different scribes wrote down at least one or more of the verses under direct supervision of the Prophet (S).

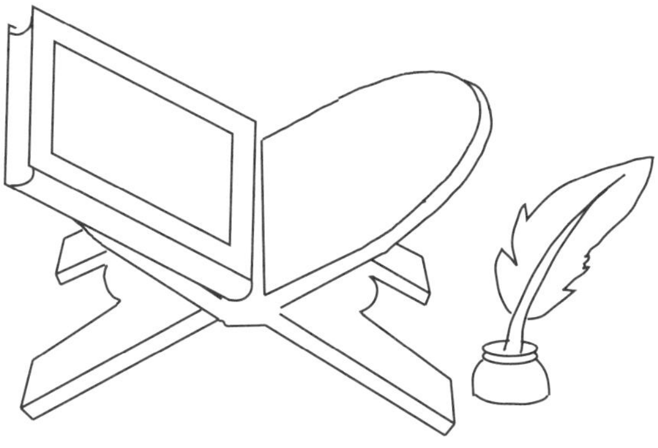

The need of writing down the revelations was so important that during the migration of the Prophet (S), pen, inkstand, and writing materials were among the essential things carried.

Role of Abū Bakr: After the Prophet (S) passed away, Abū Bakr was appointed as the khalīfa of the Muslim community. He ruled for only 2 years and then passed away. During this short period of time, despite turmoil among the community, Abū Bakr realized the need to collect all chapters of the Qur'ān and bring them under one volume.

The whole Qur'ān was already written down as manuscripts, but the manuscripts were scattered and stored with several companions. At the instruction of Abū Bakr, 'Umar publicly announced that whoever possessed any portions of the Qur'ān, directly received from the Prophet (S), should bring it. These manuscripts were accepted after two witnesses attested to their authenticity. Zaid and other companions who memorized the Qur'ān verified the manuscripts for authenticity. Even then, until someone bore witness that he heard the text of the manuscript directly from the Prophet (S)'s mouth, they were not accepted as 'authentic.' Such was the precaution against any error.

When these manuscripts were collected in one place, it was only a single compiled volume without additional copies. When Abū Bakr passed away, this volume was transferred to the custody of 'Umar and upon his death the volume was transferred to the custody of 'Umar's daughter Hafsa. She was one of the widows of Prophet (S).

Variations in Reading: At the time of revelation of the Qur'ān there were seven different dialects among the Arabs, of which Quraish dialect was the finest and richest. During the time of 'Uthmān when Islam was wide-spread in Arabia, different tribes started reciting the Qur'ān in their own dialect. Some words in Quraish dialect meant a different thing when pronounced in another dialect. 'Uthmān was afraid if people in far corners of Arabia started reading the Qur'ān in their own dialect, they would misunderstand the messages. Apart from Arabia, the people in newly conquered territories, e.g. Armenia, Syria, Iraq, etc., had variations in the reading of the Qur'ān. The differences were primarily in the nature of *qirā'at* or modes of recitation.

Role of 'Uthmān Ibn Affān: 'Uthmān realized that if such minor differences in pronunciation were allowed, one day the Qur'ān would have wide variations in text and interpretation. To prevent this 'Uthmān ordered all private copies of the Qur'ān, including parts of a sūrah in collection with individuals, should be burned. All companions of the Prophet (S) supported 'Uthmān in burning the 'unauthorized' copies.

Now with all private copies burned, 'Uthmān had another responsibility—making the "official" copy of the Qur'ān available. He collected the authentic copy made during the time of Abū Bakr and had additional copies transcribed from it for circulation. Once again Zaid ibn Thābit was engaged to make the transcriptions. Later twelve other scribes were appointed under direct supervision of 'Uthmān to make more copies of the Qur'ān. All these twelve scribes were, at one time or the other, scribes with the Prophet (S). These official copies were later sent to the governors in territories occupied by the Muslims.

All later day Muslims learned, memorized and made additional copies of the Qur'ān from these official copies circulated by 'Uthmān.

Important to note that the *tashkeel* or vowel marks in the Qur'ān was not added yet. These would be done by 'Ali. The addition of the vowel marks helped the non-Arabs to properly pronounce the Qur'ān.

Interesting Facts

- Images of several pages of an early copy of the Qur'ān, written in gold leaf in kufi script, can be accessed at the web site of the Shreidan Libraries, The Johns Hopkins University. The link is http://goldkoran.mse.jhu.edu.
- A 700-year old hand written copy of the Qur'ān has been restored and housed in Jiezi Masjid in Xunhua, China. This is the oldest known copy of the Qur'ān in China.
- Aurangzeb, although the emperor of the largest Mughal empire, led a simple life by exchanging money for volumes of the Qur'ān that he himself would copy.
- In Christianity, the criticism of the authenticity of the text of Bible has been a recognized field of study for last several centuries. The following text is from a dictionary of the Bible: "The Bible did not fall from heaven as a ready-made book. It was written by men; men also have copied it. God has not been pleased to protect the text miraculously from all corruption. The autographs inscribed upon perishable papyrus, and not preserved with any special care, soon disappeared. Each copy brought into existence intentional or unintentional changes in the text. Even attempts to correct errors produced new mistakes." (A Standard Bible Dictionary. Editors: M. W. Jacobus, E. E. Nourse, A. C. Zenos. Funk and Wagnalls Company, 1909. p 580)

homework**weekend 3**

1. At the time of revelation the Qur'ān, what are the six important aspects of recording that were addressed?

....

....

2. What are the two places where the earliest copies of the Qur'ān are preserved in museums?

   a. Istanbul and Cairo.
   b. Istanbul and Tashkent.
   c. Tashkent and Madīnah.
   d. Tashkent and Damascus.
   e. Damascus and Jerusalem.

3. When the Qur'ān states that it is secured as *lawh mahfūz,* what does this mean?

....

....

4. The content of previous scriptures were changed mostly by their own followers. Read verse 18:27, and then comment if people had changed the original Qur'ān as revealed to Muhammad (S).

....

....

5. Explain why 'Uthmān b. 'Affān burned the other copies of the Qur'ān.

....

....

6. Write some of the adverse factors in preserving the Qur'ān at the time of Prophet (S).

....

....

7. Due to scarcity of writing tools, early Muslims developed a system to preserve the Qur'ān with full integrity. With all the recording and archival media available today, Muslims still widely employ the same system. What is this system that does not require pen and paper?

....

8. Why did the Prophet (S) use scribes to record the revelations?

....

....

9. Verse 56:78-79 says: *in a book well preserved, none can touch it except the purified one*. This is a proof that the Qur'ān was being written down at the time of revelation. According to the lesson what type of proof is that?

   a. Internal proof
   b. External proof

10. Read Sūrah Al-Hijr, verse 9. Who is the guardian of the Qur'ān? What is the title (in Arabic) of the Qur'ān used in this verse?

....

....

'Ibadat: *Some Easy Ways To Do It*

Objective of the Lesson:

Each religion has different forms, rules and objectives of religious worship. In Islam, the formal ways of doing 'ibadat is obviously doing all the rituals, such as salāt and fasting. However, there are many other 'ibadat, for example every good deed is an act of worship. This lesson discusses the meaning and significance of 'ibadah and shows some of the ways we can do 'ibadah at every moment in our lives.

Worship is an integral part of all religions. Merriam-Webster Dictionary defines "worship" as reverence offered to a divine being or supernatural power. The mode, objective, and rules of worship are different from religion to religion. Furthermore, the 'object' to whom the devotees worship may be different. For example, the object of worship for idol worshippers is one or many idols. Some people worship natural powers, celestial objects, inert objects, animals, plants, or living or dead human beings. Many religions assign specific places for worship and prohibit other places. Many religions prescribe that worship should be performed at one given time in a day or a week. In some religions worship is done only under the leadership of a priest. In some religions some worship is restricted only to males or sometimes only to females.

The Arabic word for worship is *'Ibadah*. Islam takes the meaning of 'ibadah to a level uncommon in other religions. Islam projects entire life of a person as an act of worship. Worship in Islam establishes a bond between the Creator and His servants. In Islam all men, women, boys and girls recognize their Creator as One and show all forms of devotion to the Only Creator. They submit to Him with their body and mind to declare there is none worthy of worshipping except Allāh. By this declaration Muslims dissociate them from idolatry.

The simple meaning of the word 'ibadah is to worship. The word is derived from the root *'abd* which means servant or slave. If we relate the meaning of the word 'ibadah to its root, we can translate the word as 'to serve' or 'to be a servant' or 'to be a slave.' Since a Muslim worships Allāh, his 'ibadah means to be a servant or a slave of Allāh and do what He asks him to do.

Being a servant: In ordinary sense a servant is a person who serves his master. He can be a servant for his master, the master's wife and the family. Thus, he can have several human masters at the same time. Strangely enough, both the master and the servant can together be servants of another master. Thus, there can be a chain of master-servant relationship. At any point in this relationship, these masters and servants can have their own god as their master. If they happen to be Muslims, they have Allāh as their ultimate master.

In contrast to such servant and master relationship between two people, to be a servant of Allāh requires absolute submission to Allāh. Under such relationship, the Master is Supreme—there cannot be any other chain of command above the Master. He is the Master of all the masters. The Qur'ān says:

إِن كُلُّ مَن فِي السَّمٰوٰتِ وَ الْأَرْضِ إِلَّآ اٰتِي الرَّحْمٰنِ عَبْدًا ﴿٩٣﴾

There is nothing in the heavens and the earth but that comes to the Merciful as a servant (19:93).

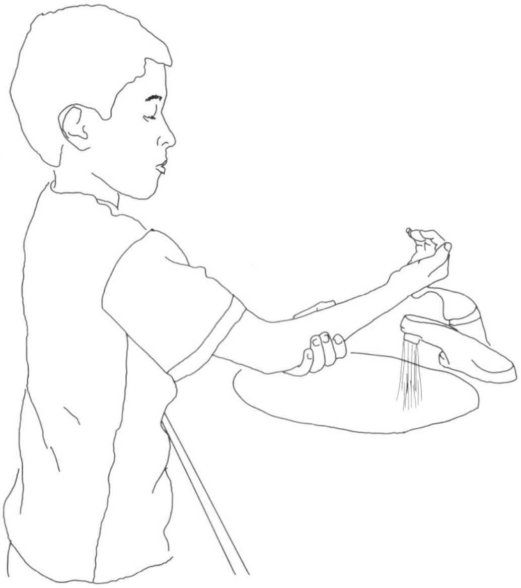

In a wider sense, everything in the entire universe are slaves of Allāh. They are His "slaves" because they cannot and do not disobey Allāh. On the other hand, human beings have the freedom of choice and they are free to accept or reject Allāh. For that reason, we have used the term "servant." Now with this understanding, let us see how the servant can worship His Lord.

Worship is a right of Allāh: Muslims understand worship as a means to please Allāh. Worship is a right exclusive to Allāh. No one else has any right to be worshipped. As Allāh is our Creator, He has the only right to be worshipped or served:

وَمَا خَلَقْتُ الْجِنَّ وَ الْإِنسَ إِلَّا لِيَعْبُدُونِ ﴿٥٦﴾

And I have not created the jinn and the mankind but that they should worship Me. (51:56).

This verse states that our sole objective should be to worship Allāh alone. Allāh has directed us to eat the permitted foods, support our families, and help the neighbors. Therefore, all these and similar mundane activities, if done properly, becomes forms of worship. If we eat permitted food only, we are following the commands of Allāh, and thus we are worshipping Him. The servant is expected that he or she will follow the orders of the master.

Intention and motives: Similar to eating permitted food, if we speak nicely to someone, because Allāh likes fair speech,[2:263] we are worshipping Allāh. However, if we speak nicely to please the other person only, we are not worshipping Allāh. Our motive behind every action should be to please Allāh. If we stay away from everything that Allāh prohibited and do only those things that Allāh permits us to do, we are doing 'ibadah. Therefore, Islam considers eating, drinking, sleeping, working, doing household chores, even simple innocent recreation and games become acts of 'ibadah if these are done with good motives. Thus, whenever you do a good deed or avoid an evil for fear of Allāh, you are doing an 'ibadah.

Scope of worship: Unlike any other religion, the scope of worship in Islam is vast. Worship in Islam is not limited to a set of few prescribed duties, nor are the worship limited to those duties to be performed at specific time or occasion. In Islam every good deed that has been done to please Allāh is an act of 'ibadah. The Prophet (S) was instructed to declare the following verse:

Say: "Surely my salāt and my sacrifice and my living and my dying are for the sake of Allāh—Rabb of all the worlds." (6:162)

Since our every activity is required to reflect a state of submission, our every good deed is a reflection of 'ibadah. If we think only performing the salāt or paying the zakāt will make us good Muslims, we should think again. Doing these rituals mechanically, without letting these activities change our behavior, will not make us righteous. In fact, Qur'ān condemns the one who performs salāt,[107:4] but refuses to do charity or turns away the orphans.

While ritual prayers are needed, true form of righteousness is not attached to the rituals alone:

There is no virtue in that you turn your faces towards the East and the West, but virtue is in him who believes in Allāh and the Last Day, and the angels, and the Books, and the Nabis; and who gives wealth out of love for Him to the near of kin, and to the orphans, and the needy, and the wayfarer, and the beggars, and to those in captivity; and who establishes the Salāt, and pays the Zakāt; and the fulfillers of their contract when they make a contract; and those who persevere in hardship and affliction, and during the panic. These are those who have verified the truth; and these are themselves the pious. (2:177)

Lawful enjoyment: It is possible for a person to excel as a truly good Muslim while he or she is fully enjoying the pleasure of the worldly life. Without saying 'no' to any of the permissible pleasure, a person can advance spiritually from one stage to another. Islam does not recommend abstinence from the legitimate pleasures of life—provided that such pleasure does not cross the limits of Islamic rules and does not violate the code of ethics. The Qur'ān tells us:

"And seek by means of what Allāh has given you the home of the Hereafter, and do not forget your share of this world, and do good as Allāh has done good to you, and do not seek making mischief in the land. Surely Allāh does not love the mischief-makers." (28:77)

Good company: Selecting good friends equates to following one of the commands of Allāh. Wasteful and idle talk can take us away from doing the right duties. Again, doing right deed is a worship. Allāh says:

And when they hear idle talk, they turn aside from it and say: "For us are our deeds, and to you are your deeds;— 'Salam be upon you'! We do not follow the ignorant." (28:55)

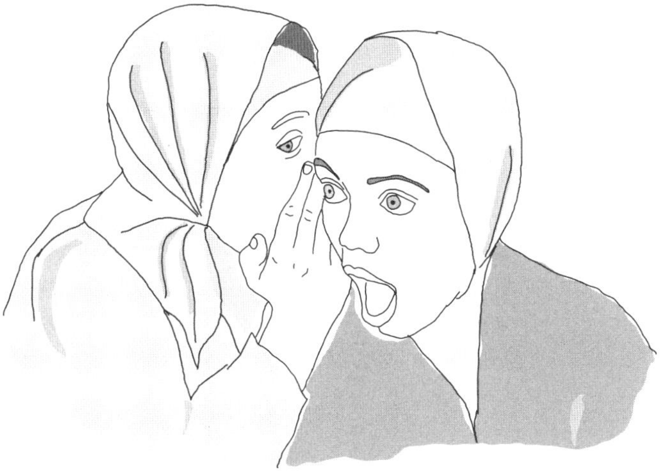

Easy ways of worship: The easy ways of worship are easy enough. Do things that please Allāh and avoid those that displease Him. A person can turn everyday activities into acts of worship by seeking Allāh's pleasure through these activities. In order for the daily activities to be counted as 'ibadah, we should meet the following conditions:

a. Our action must have good intention.
b. Our action must be lawful and morally good.
c. Our action must not prevent us from doing our religious duties.

Worship is free from intermediaries: Some acts that appear to ease the 'ibadah actually violates worshipping Allāh. Some people erroneously think that if one can employ a 'saintly' person as an intermediary, the 'ibadah will be easier and more likely to be accepted. An intermediary is a person who acts as an agent. He tries to establish link between two parties. Often the intermediaries require payments or fees to be paid to them when they provide the 'service' of setting up the link. In real life sometimes such an arrangement is necessary to make the system work.

However, Islam has carefully removed any need of an intermediary when it comes to worshipping the Rabb. Islam establishes direct link between man and his Creator. An intermediary is not required, it is in fact a serious form of sin.[2:48; 6:70]

Worship at every place: In order to make 'ibadah meaningful and effective, Islam has eliminated the need of intermediaries and removed the need of a specific place as "the only" place of worship. Islam recognizes any clean place, one's own home, bed, open ground, masjid, back of an animal, or a ship, is good enough for the performance of 'ibadah. Hajj is the only 'ibadah that has rituals done in specific places in and around Makkah.

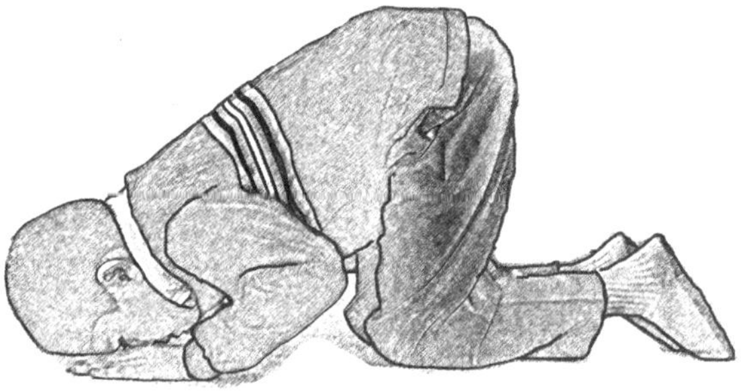

homework**weekend 4**

1. Read Sūrah Az-Zumar, verse 11. How should we perform our 'ibadah?

....

2. The word 'Ibadah is derived from a root word. What is the root word and what is its meaning?

Root: .... Meaning: ....

3. Read verse 16:36. What are the two things the prophets told their people?

....

....

4. Verse 2:177, included in the lesson, cites several factors as virtue. When we make a contract, what should we do to attain a virtue? In case of hardship, what should we do to attain virtue?

a. When we make a contract, we should ....

b. When we are in hardship, we should ....

5. If a person is dedicated to doing 'Ibadah what should he/she do about the enjoyment of this life?

....

....

6. Read Sūrah Al-Baqarah, verse 48. Explain how helpful will an intermediary or an intercessor be for us on the Day of Judgment.

....

....

7. Why is everything in the entire universe slave of Allāh? ....

8. What are the three conditions that should be fulfilled to make everyday activities become 'ibadah?

a. ....

b. ....

c. ....

9. To attain the best form of 'Ibadah, should we give up worldly enjoyments? Please explain in the space below.

....

....

10. Which of the following choices is correct about worship in Islam?

a. All forms of devotion is due only to the Creator.
b. Devotion is directed to the prophets.
c. Islam encourages only ritual forms of worship.
d. Islam limits rituals and encourages good deeds.
e. Islam limits worship to five specific prayers of the day.

Human Beings: *Are We Truly Superior?*

Objective of the Lesson:

Allāh made us, the human beings, superior over all other creations; but do our activities always reflect our superiority? This lesson analyzes some of the key aspects of being "human" and highlights the factors that make us superior and factors that make us inferior. The lesson also analyzes the implication of being superior.

Human beings are one of Allāh's finest creations.[95:4] They are unique in many ways. They have certain characteristics that make them special. Human beings are the most intelligent creatures, and their position is above the rank of angels. In spite of being superior creations, many times these 'superior' creations can be inferior to other creations. Superiority of human being is our birth right, but sometimes we squander the right and shamelessly choose to become inferior.

To understand what makes us superior and what makes us inferior, we need to go back to the creation of Adam.

Creation of Adam: Allāh created human beings as a vicegerent or representative on the earth. Allāh created Adam with His 'own hands'[38:75] and blew into him His own spirit. Before the creation of man, the angels were doubtful whether human beings will live up to the expectations.[2:30] Their doubt was dispelled when Allāh taught Adam names of all things.[2:31] The term 'names' plays a significant role in the Qur'ān. Allāh mentioned *"And to Allāh belong all the finest Names..."*[7:180] Allāh's names are not mere names, they are His qualities. Similarly, when Adam was taught the names of all things, he did not simply learn the names, but also understood the inner qualities and attributes of each name.

By teaching the names Allāh gave Adam power over the things he learned.[22:65; 31:20] All other creations know the 'names' of only certain things – i.e. they know the qualities of things that matter to them. Even angels know the names of only a few things. Allāh gave human beings power over the creation by making them understand the qualities and attributes of everything. This responsibility is enormous. When people violate the power and fail to honor the responsibility, they cease to be "human being". The lesson header asks: *are we truly superior*? The answer is it depends.

Abilities of animals: When we compare ourselves to animals, we realize that animals have many abilities better than us. The fastest Olympic sprinter will not be able to catch a running cat, we cannot fly like a bird, cannot walk nonstop as far a distance as a migratory bird flies, or cannot swim like a fish. The animals and birds thus have many specialized abilities.

Although animals can do many things better than human beings, there are several things that animal cannot do. These abilities separate human beings from animals. We will discuss only few of these abilities of human that differentiate them from animals. These are freedom of choice, speech, creativity, wearing clothes, relationship and responsibility.

Freedom of choice: Unlike animals, human beings have the ability to "choose" an alternate course of action. All the animals follow their own instinct. They cannot distinguish right from wrong. Human beings are the only animal that give less importance to their instinct, instead follow their God given ability to choose an alternate course of action. If they had followed their instinct more, they would have no problem in following Allāh—the Creator. For the Qur'ān says:

وَمَا خَلَقْتُ الْجِنَّ وَالْإِنسَ إِلَّا لِيَعْبُدُونِ ٥٦

And we have not created the jinn and the mankind but that they should worship me. (51:56)

However, we see people worship false gods and associate with Allāh. They think they are intelligent enough to find alternate ways of worshipping.

Choice of worshipping of Allāh is the single-most criterion that separates human beings from animals. Although animals worship Allāh in their own ways,[24:41] they do not have the ability to refuse worshipping Allāh. Human have the ability to refuse to accept Allāh as the deity to worship. In spite of that, they remain under the rules of Allāh. Allāh made the rule that one has to breathe to survive. A staunch *kāfir* cannot break this rule, or does not even think of changing this or similar rules. When human beings decide not to worship Allāh, they do not become free, rather they become rebel. They remain under the dominion of Allāh, but choose to violate some rules. The choice of human is limited to the matter of faith and some actions that they can take. They cannot choose their parents, place and time of birth or postpone their death, or select their race, skin color and so on.

Unlike animals or plants, human beings are able to recognize *tawhid*. Since animals or plants do not recognize, they are not liable to answer to Allāh, therefore, they will not be judged. On the contrary, only human beings will be judged because they have the original human nature—called *fitrah*—that was innate in them. Human beings were created knowing that "there is no god, but God." Prophets were sent to remind people about this *fitrah*. Therefore, to associate others with Allāh means to go against the *fitrah*.

Speech: The ability to express a thought by speech or by writing is exclusive to human beings, True, many animals make sounds that deliver some sense of emotion, but these are not structured languages. A penguin can identify its offspring by its characteristic sound, and a whale can locate its partner using a single pitch of sound made miles apart. We do not have such abilities. However, we have the ability to speak, and the speech can be truthful or false. For animals, they cannot speak falsehood; therefore their expression should be treated as truthful. A dog will not wag its tail when it is going to attack. If we resort to falsehood, and intentionally try to misled people by our speech or writing, we have lowered ourselves below the level of animals.

Animals do not use their behavior to express pride. Male members of some animals, such as lions, try to overpower other males mainly to control their group. Humans use speech to show pride, to raise one's rank above other, or use speech to humiliate others. The Qur'ān teaches us to be humble, and treat others as similar to us. Whenever we are proud, we have lowered ourselves below the levels of animals.

Animals that live in a group trust their leader. A flock of migratory bird will form an echelon, a V or J shape of flight. All the birds in the echelon trust their leader, as the leader does not break the trust. Humans, on the other hand, use their speech to make promises and often break a promise. Interestingly, the leader of the echelon is not permanent. As the leader gets tired, another bird moves ahead to occupy the tip of the echelon. This is teamwork in birds. Many times we lower ourselves when we refuse to share our power and

authority. Rasulullah (S) showed that he was a leader that people could trust. He also consulted with others in many matters, and did not act like an authoritarian. The lives of the Rightly Guided Khalīfas also show similar excellent traits, appropriate for human beings.

Creativity: In one way human beings are different from animals is that they can create or develop things. A bison of today lives the same way as another bison that lived 5000 years back. Human beings use their gift of intelligence to improve their living conditions. We make and develop things that should make our lives better, not worse. However, people also create things that lower them in their position. Some people fabricate an idol and start worshipping it. This is the lowest of the low that a human being can slip. Some people make and use intoxicants which degrade the gift of thinking. Some will create things that are used to destroy other people. Most animals will not attack others unless hungry or threatened.

Covering up: As animals do not have the ability to make anything other than their nests, they cannot make or wear clothing. Human beings can make clothing, and these clothes allow them to cover their shame and survive in difficult weather. However, many people degrade themselves and use clothes to expose their bodies rather than to cover. Allāh instructs us to dress modestly, and to cover our body parts. People become inferior to animals when they decide to promote their body instead of using their intelligence.

Relationship: Interpersonal relationship is of much higher order in human society. In the Qur'ān, Allāh has specific directions for our relationship with the opposite gender. The Qur'ān has clear direction as to who we can marry and who are beyond the limits. Any relationship must be socially accepted through the institution of marriage. This is not so for animal kingdom. Some human would lower the moral standards to develop relationship outside the institution of marriage. In doing so, they are only fulfilling their animal urges.

Animals do not undergo moral downfall, human beings are susceptible to suffer moral downfall. This is beautifully illustrated in the following verse:

> *And certainly We have produced for Gehenna a large number of jinn and men;— they have hearts but they do not understand with these, and they have eyes but they do not see with these, and they have ears but they do not hear with these. They are like cattle; rather they are more astray. They are themselves the heedless ones. (7:179)*

Responsibility: Allāh created human beings to be His *Khalīfa* or vicegerent.[2:30] A khalīfa is a representative of another being. The office of representative is to follow the directives and uphold the interests of the one who is being represented—in this case Allāh. Human beings have the awesome responsibility of being Allāh's representative.[35:39] In other words, the primary task of human beings is to act on behalf of Allāh.

Human beings are created to be the khalīfa on the earth. However, man may decide to forego this responsibility and degrade himself to a much lower level. Animals are not khalīfa, thus they have fewer responsibility and expectations. Some types of animals are more responsible, while some types are less. A dog can be trained to do some task, and it will continue to perform the task even in the absence of his master. If a dog is trained to bring sheep back home in the evening, it will do this task every evening. However, a cow or a camel may not be similarly responsible. If you use a camel for plowing your land for many years, it will still not proceed to farmland by itself to fulfill its responsibility.

The roles of most animals are to eat and breed. Unless you train or use an animal for different role, it will limit its acts to eating and breeding. However, human beings take up more responsibility and go beyond their physical needs. One of the primary responsibilities of the human beings is to contribute to the society that they live in. While animals may take care of their offspring, they usually do not take care of other adults in their society. Many types of animals do not even live in any society. Some animals pair up with a member of opposite gender only for procreation. Human beings, on the other hand, live in a society. Their responsibilities go beyond taking care of their immediate family. We are responsible for caring of the needy, as well as guiding others to the right path. If we see someone is being mistreated, we should prevent the misdeed. An animal may not try to prevent an attack on one of its herd members. Animals may not have sense of community, or need to participate for the betterment of the community. Some human beings also do not fulfill the responsibility towards the community. They remain selfish, and are happy if their own need is satisfied.

In conclusion, we can say human beings can be superior or inferior depending upon what we do and what we worship. It is true we are designed to be the best of the creation. Superiority over the creation is a gift from Allāh. However, we often squander this gift and fail to live up to the expectations. We cease to be human beings. It is an enormous failure. We should exert our best to live up to the expectations and never fail to represent Allāh on the earth. The following verses from sūrah Ibrāhīm points out the sad reality of human beings:

> *Allāh is He Who has created the heavens and the earth, and He brings down water from the sky, then He produces by it fruits as a provision for you. And He subjected to you the ships that they may sail in the sea with His command, and He makes subservient to you the rivers. And He makes subservient to you the sun and the moon, both moving precisely; and He makes subservient to you the night and the day. And He gives you of everything that you ask Him for. And if you were to count the favors of Allāh, you will not be able to count them. Surely human being is indeed great wrongdoer, very ungrateful. (14:32-34)*

homework**weekend 5**

1. What did Allāh teach Adam? Read verse 2:31 to answer.

....

2. In Sūrah At-Tin, you will find the following verse. Write the meaning of the verse in the space below.

لَقَدْ خَلَقْنَا الْإِنسَانَ فِي أَحْسَنِ تَقْوِيمٍ ﴿٤﴾

The meaning of the verse is: ....

3. Write any three ways that people use their speech to lower themselves below the levels of animals.

a. ....

b. ....

c. ....

4. Read verse 24:41. What does the verse tell us about the salāt and praise by the animals and the birds?

....

5. We have freedom of choice to worship Allāh. List a few rules of Allāh that even a staunch *kāfir* cannot refuse to obey.

....

6. Give any two examples of human creativity that degrade their position.

a. ....

b. ....

7. The *fitrah,* the innate human nature or natural disposition is provided in every soul. Read verse 91:8, and then write what does the *fitrah* allow us to recognize?

....

8. What is one thing that Allāh gave to human beings but not to other animals?

a. Ability to think.
b. Ability to remember.
c. Ability to recognize each other.
d. Freedom of choice.
e. Freedom to live as long as they like.

9. Select all the choices that make a man below the level of animals. This man:

a. does not care about others in the society.
b. tries to become a leader of a group.
c. makes and stitches winter clothes.
d. has intimate relation with a woman outside marriage.
e. can make lengthy speeches.

10. Write a short paragraph about our responsibilities, as *khalīfa* on the earth, to our fellow beings.

....

....

....

....

....

....

Islam and Violence: *Dispelling a Myth*

Objective of the Lesson:

Some of the Qur'ānic verses related to war, oppression, fighting for justice and retaliation are misunderstood by many when they read these verses without the context. As a result Islam is viewed as a violent, militant religion. This lesson discusses some of the areas that cause misunderstanding among the Muslims and non-Muslims.

Can a religion promote violence? Can a religion that advocates peace be violent? This question has recently surfaced after several Muslims committed acts of violence and terror in the name of religion. Their action led the Western world blame that Islam, as a religion, promotes violence. Prior to the sporadic violence, the world has already witnessed decades of upheavals in the Middle East, the blame for which was entirely and unfairly placed upon the Palestinians. The world has also witnessed several 'Islamic' movements that resorted to violence. The Western world, particularly the media, quickly concluded that Islam is a radical faith and it sponsors violence. This notion was further strengthened by scores of malicious non-Muslim writings. The fuel to this notion was amply provided by some Muslims as they justified their terrorist action based on the way they understood the teachings of the Qur'ān and the sayings of the Prophet (S).

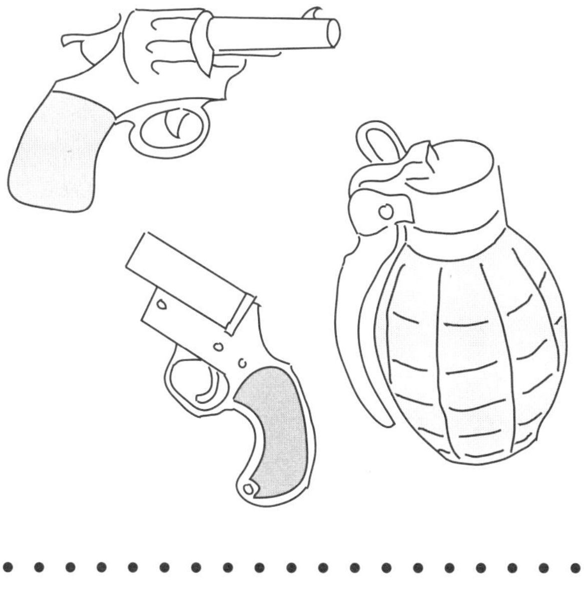

Is Islam really a militant, violent religion that promotes hatred and killing? In this lesson we will investigate the origin of such notion and dispel the misunderstanding. Muslim youths need to understand the correct interpretation of the verses that are used by the Western press to malign Islam on one hand, and militant Muslims to promote their violent agenda on the other.

Violence in history: In the light of the recent events it may seem that Islam has always been violent. When people conclude in this manner, they forget or ignore their own history. Over the course of history, Christianity and Judaism promoted more violence than present day radical Muslims have perpetrated. Yet based on the recent history, the blame for terrorism is squarely placed upon all the Muslims. It remains that no forms of aggression, whether it is done by Muslims, Christians or Jews are acceptable.

Misinterpreting the Qur'ān: It is quite easy to handpick a few verses from the Qur'ān, interpret these without the context and conclude that Islam promotes violence. In fact, this is how most of the non-Muslim writers and the Western media are depicting Islam.

We will discuss some of the verses which are often misquoted. Non-Muslim readers causally read these verses and present much distorted image of Islam.

Analysis of verse 2:190: Often the Western media pick the first part of the verse 2:190 that states *"And fight in the way of Allāh..."* and use this section as a proof of Qur'ān's endorsement of violence. The complete verse is as follows:

وَقَاتِلُوا فِي سَبِيلِ اللَّهِ الَّذِينَ يُقَاتِلُونَكُمْ
وَلَا تَعْتَدُوا ۚ إِنَّ اللَّهَ لَا يُحِبُّ الْمُعْتَدِينَ ﴿١٩٠﴾

> *And fight in the way of Allāh against those who fight with you, but do not transgress. Certainly Allāh does not love the aggressors. (2:190)*

Casual reading of the verse appears to indicate Islam has given free permission to fight against anybody. If you read carefully, the verse is not asking the Muslims to launch an attack on the non-Muslims. They are asked to fight *against those who fight with you*. Obviously, others have already attacked the Muslims and the Muslims are asked to respond. The phrase *against those who fight with you* does not mean undue hostility of the Muslims in a peaceful environment, rather it points to an already hostile environment created by the aggressor. The Western readers are puzzled why the Qur'ān would permit fighting, but they fail to realize the permission to fight was given only as self-defense. Whether or not the Qur'ān gave this permission, people in every religion in every period in time would fight if they are attacked. It is a natural instinct.

The religion of Islam is the only religion claiming to be a complete guidance for man's spiritual and temporal welfare. Therefore, it is important that the religion will tell its followers as to how they should respond when their basic civic rights are violated.

The critics of Islam ignore the second half of the verse where it says: *but do not transgress. Certainly Allāh does not love the aggressors.* Even when Muslims are required to fight against their aggressors, they are asked to refrain from exercising undue aggression. Islam never permits rough, senseless and excessive show of strength. On the contrary, in the examples of non-Muslim countries we can find exceedingly high level of undue aggression by using weapons of mass destruction or undertaking mass ethnic cleansing.

Analysis of verse 2:191: Another verse, when casually read, seems that Muslims are encouraged to violence—kill the enemies wherever they find.

وَاقْتُلُوهُمْ حَيْثُ ثَقِفْتُمُوهُمْ وَأَخْرِجُوهُمْ مِّنْ
حَيْثُ أَخْرَجُوكُمْ وَالْفِتْنَةُ أَشَدُّ مِنَ الْقَتْلِ ۚ
وَلَا تُقَاتِلُوهُمْ عِنْدَ الْمَسْجِدِ الْحَرَامِ حَتَّىٰ
يُقَاتِلُوكُمْ فِيهِ ۚ فَإِنْ قَاتَلُوكُمْ فَاقْتُلُوهُمْ ۗ
كَذَٰلِكَ جَزَاءُ الْكَافِرِينَ ﴿١٩١﴾

> *And kill them wherever you find them, and turn them out from where they have turned you out; for, persecution is worse than killing. But do not fight with them near the Sacred Masjid unless they fight with you therein; but if they fight with you, then fight with them. Such is the reward of the Unbelievers. (2:191)*

The critics of Islam imply that Muslims are duty bound to kill their neighbors, colleagues or anybody they can find. Far from it, the verse lays down a war strategy in the context of war already thrust upon them as noted in verse 2:190.

The magnitude of attack and level of persecution is indicated when the aggressors expelled the Muslims from their places of living. Under such circumstances, Islam permits the victims to regain their places of living by evicting the aggressors. The places could be a individual homes, or a neighborhood or a country. The verse further states any act of persecution (*fitnah*) is considered worse than actual act of killing. The aggressors created *fitnah* by violating the social, political, or religious rights of the people they attacked.

Fighting is not allowed in the sacred territory of the Ka'bah. However, if the enemies disrespect the sanctity of the Ka'bah and launch attack near its territory, the Muslims cannot remain silent. The verse permits the Muslims to fight *if they fight with you* in the sacred territory. Such messages throughout the Qur'ān indicate that Islam does not promote aggression, but gives people the right to defend them if they are attacked.

Analysis of verse 9:5: Many critics of Islam often misquoted verse 9:5. This verse is sometimes mentioned as the 'sword verse' although the word 'sword' is not present. These critics raise an alarm by citing this verse out of context.

فَإِذَا انْسَلَخَ الْأَشْهُرُ الْحُرُمُ فَاقْتُلُوا
الْمُشْرِكِينَ حَيْثُ وَجَدْتُمُوهُمْ وَخُذُوهُمْ
وَاحْصُرُوهُمْ وَاقْعُدُوا لَهُمْ كُلَّ مَرْصَدٍ ۚ فَإِنْ
تَابُوا وَأَقَامُوا الصَّلٰوةَ وَآتَوُا الزَّكٰوةَ فَخَلُّوا
سَبِيلَهُمْ ۚ إِنَّ اللّٰهَ غَفُورٌ رَّحِيمٌ ۝٥

So when the sacred months have passed, then slay the polytheists wherever you find them, and capture them, and besiege them, and lie in wait for them at every ambush. But if they repent and keep up the salāt and pay the zakāt, then leave them alone on their path. Surely Allāh is most Forgiving, most Rewarding. (9:5)

However the permission to fight in this verse was given in the light of those who have cancelled the peace treaty against the Muslims.[9:4] During the pre-Islamic era and during the development of Islamic era, annulment of a peace treaty between two tribes was nothing but declaration of open war. We should remember that during the time of the Prophet (S) there was no formal government or a nation. The Muslim community itself was the nation. When this nation was attacked, they were required to defend them by launching a counter attack.

With or without this Qur'ānic instruction, a Muslim community or a nation is expected to react exactly the same way a non-Muslim community or a nation would react if they were attacked or war is waged against them. During the World War II, when Germany attacked other European nations, they had to defend themselves. The German government was the attacker and other nations were engaged in a defensive war.

The critics of Islam often quote the second half of the verse to imply that non-Muslims were converted into Islam with a great degree of force. This message must be reviewed in conjunction with several other fundamental ordinances of the Qur'ān that say: *there is no compulsion in religion, the Right Path has indeed been made distinct from the wrong* (2:256; also see 6:105; 10:99; 18:29; 27:92; 42:15; 73:19; 76:29). Keeping this in mind, the only way the captives in war could be prevented from reverting to hostility upon their release was to make them embrace Islam. Such conversion in Islam was purely a war strategy and should not be viewed as a general approach during peace time.

Nowhere does the verse 9:5 say that the captives were to be converted. Three conditions are mentioned about the captives: if they (a) repent, (b) keep up salāt, and (c) pay the zakāt, then they should be left alone.

The condition of professing faith in Islam is clearly absent. Mention of salāt and zakāt may have misled the critics into believing that the captives were converted into Islam and then left alone. Even before the advent of Islam, the Arabs were accustomed to performing the salāt and paying the zakāt, just as Ibrāhīm, Ismā'īl, Mūsā, Jesus and their disciples were mandated.[10:87, 19:31,55; 21:73] By sincerely expressing repentance for waging war and then by showing adherence to their form of salāt and zakāt, the captives would have rightly demonstrated change in their evil intentions.

Bible on violence: There are several verses in the Bible that permit its followers to be violent. Just as Qur'ānic verses should not be taken out of context to understand its message, similarly the verses from the Bible should not be taken out of context. Below are some of the verses only for the academic interest:

> *Your eye shall not pity, life shall be for life, eye for eye, tooth for tooth, hand for hand, foot for foot (Deut. 19:21)*
>
> *Now if the city will not make peace with you, but make war against you, then you shall besiege it. (Deut. 20:12)*
>
> *You shall strike every male in it with the edge of sword, but the women, the little ones and livestock and all that is in the city, you shall plunder for yourself. (Deut. 20:13-14)*
>
> *You shall utterly destroy them....just as the Lord your God has commanded. (Deut. 20:17)*
>
> *Now therefore, kill every male among the little ones, and kill every woman who has known man intimately. But all the girls who have not known man intimately, spare for yourselves. (Num. 31:17-18)*

Terrorism: In last several decades, the world has witnessed terrorism by many political, religious or ethnic groups. Sometimes, Muslim groups initiated terrorism, and at other times Muslims were victim of terrorism. Terrorism is use of force or violence against people or property to cause fear, and often to achieve a political or ideological goal. Mostly, terrorism is an act against civilians. The Qur'ān says:

وَ لَا تَبۡغِ الۡفَسَادَ فِی الۡاَرۡضِ ؕ اِنَّ اللّٰہَ
لَا یُحِبُّ الۡمُفۡسِدِیۡنَ ﴿۷۷﴾

...and do not seek making mischief in the land. Surely Allāh does not love the mischief-maker. (28:77)

The Qur'ān repeatedly teaches Muslims to promote peace, justice, and prohibit evil. Allāh surely does not love those who make mischief. The Qur'ān teaches us that force should be used only as the last resort. It teaches us to maintain and help grow normal relationship with all the people and to promote peace. Even during conflict, Muslims are required to show initiative of peace and honor peace treaty. Muslims are allowed to fight only in their self defense when enemies have already attacked them.

homework**weekend 6**

1. Write who are at fault for circulating the idea that Islam promotes violence?

....

....

2. Answer the following based on the verse 2:190:

   a. When is a Muslim allowed to fight? ....

   b. What should be the limit of fighting? ....

3. Under what circumstance are Muslims allowed to fight near the Sacred Mosque?

....

....

4. Read verse 42:41. Then answer the following:

   a. Who has the right to defend? ....

   b. Are the defenders subject to blame? ....

5. Read verse 42:42. Then answer the following:

   a. Who are the people that are should be blamed? ....

   b. What will these people receive in return? ....

6. What is the main reason that Qur'ānic verses allowed Muslims to fight? In order to:

   a. promote Islam.
   b. get rid of the non-Muslims.
   c. terrorize the world.
   d. defend them when attacked.
   e. oppress the enemies.

7. The following text is part of verse 2:256. The write meaning of this section of the verse in the space below:

لَآ إِكۡرَاهَ فِي ٱلدِّينِۖ قَد تَّبَيَّنَ ٱلرُّشۡدُ مِنَ ٱلۡغَيِّۚ

....

....

8. Based on verse 2:191, what is worse than the actual act of killing?

....

9. The Qur'ān does not promote aggression, but if attacked by enemies Muslim should not do something. Read Sūrah al-Anfal, verse 15, and then write down what is prohibited.

....

10. Which religious book (s) tells their followers to engage in war as needed?

a. Only the Qur'ān.
b. Only the Bible.
c. Both the Qur'ān and the Bible.
d. The Qur'ān, the Bible and the Torah.

Peer Pressure

Objective of the Lesson:

Everybody experiences peer pressure to some extent in their life. Some peer pressure is good and many are bad, particularly when people yield to the pressure without applying reason and good sense. This lesson discusses how to identify peer pressure and how to make a right decision – during every period in life.

All of us experience peer pressure in one form or the other. Not only the youths face peer pressure, adults too face it in different ways, from different groups, and at different times. Scientists who study human behavior pattern may define peer pressure in a highly technical manner, but for simplicity we can define peer pressure as: when friends persuade you to do something that you do not do or do not want to do. An example would be that you are about to take a decision, but others get involved, they influence and pressure you to make a different decision. You feel obliged to make your friends happy and be one of them. You feel obliged to adopt their behavior or attitudes. You feel that you have to fit in.

Although you may get more acceptance from your peer by fitting-in, you will earn more respect if you take the right position. Your peers may make fun initially if you take the right position, but eventually they will acknowledge that you are good, trustworthy and have good character.

You should avoid peer pressure not simply because you are a Muslim youth. Every person, whether Muslim or non-Muslim, should try to avoid peer pressure.

Good and bad peer pressure: The advises of your parent or teacher are not peer pressure, as they are not your peer. A peer is one who is your friend, partner, coworker, teammate, or someone of your age. Your parents have their own peer group, but they are not your peer. Some peer pressure are bad and some are good. Sometimes you learn from your peer and they learn from you. Peers can have positive influence on each other. Sometimes you may like a friend who is always good in sports or does well in class and you want to be like him or her. By interacting with a good group, maybe you got a brilliant idea about your school project. Positive peer pressure is good, but the danger of negative peer pressure is enormous.

Soft peer pressure: Soft peer pressures are those that you do not learn from your peer, but from those who look like your friends. For example, youths in TV shows are not your friends, but you imitate their behavior, style and attitude. You do not interact with them, but they indirectly influence you by their language, clothing or actions.

Why do you give in: The main reason youths give in to peer pressure is they want to be accepted by their friends. They like to fit in. They worry that unless they do things that their friends do, they will make fun of them. Sometimes they just do it because they are curious to try something new that their friends are trying. The most common excuse is that 'everyone is doing it'. As a result youths give up their judgment, value, common sense and do what others are doing.

Sometimes lack of better judgment draws you to peer pressure. For example, some of your friends are doing a dangerous trick, but fortunately nothing bad happens. Now others start believing that since nothing bad happened, nothing bad will happen. So they all join in. Drinking alcohol is bad for both Muslims and non-Muslims. When some youths start drinking, others may not see the immediate danger. They begin to consider it as a normal behavior and they give in.

We can summarize some of the main reasons we give in to peer pressure:

a. Lack of confidence
b. Low self respect
c. Fear about the peer group
d. Fear of getting rejected by the peer group
e. To show off or to improve the position in the group
f. Close ties with an influential bad buddy
g. Lack of values and knowledge about *deen*
h. Reaching for a 'glamorous' life

How to avoid peer pressure: Two effective ways to avoid peer pressure are:

a. trusting your good sense or common sense, and
b. trusting your belief about what is good and what is bad.

While peer pressure is everywhere, it is also possible to avoid negative peer pressure. If you think escaping is difficult, then you may have to start slowly but strongly. Prepare some appropriate responses that you would need under certain types of peer pressure. Have your responses ready and stick to your position.

Peer pressure usually comes in a nice, friendly and exciting way. Most of the time peer pressure will tempt you to some kind of excitement. For example, drinking alcohol or trying drugs promises unknown excitement. These are some of the most common temptations you will have to face in your life. When temptations come, you have to be prepared with your answer. Have your answers ready with you, and speak out your answer. Stick to your answer. You do not have to criticize or condemn the invitation, but make your decision known to your friends. Do not give a reply that puts you in a position where friends can continue putting pressure on you. Make sure when you say "no" to something, you mean it.

Example situation: After a sports event, someone opens a bag full of beer cans. They start to distribute the cans. Since this was a surprise act, you could not avoid being in the situation. Your first response should be: "I do not drink," and then walk away. If they continue to insist, then your response could be: "No thanks! Drinking is against my values."

This situation and timing may not be right to give a discourse on religious teachings, but you should not hesitate to clearly express your position.

A du'a against bad peer pressure: In Sūrah Al-Kahf, we see an example of the options of a rightly guided people when the community was exerting a bad peer pressure on them. To avoid the pressure, they walked away—to a secluded cave. They also prayed to Allāh to help them in this situation:

رَبَّنَآ ءَاتِنَا مِن لَّدُنكَ رَحۡمَةً وَهَيِّئۡ لَنَا مِنۡ أَمۡرِنَا رَشَدًا ١٠

Our Rabb! give us from Yourself mercy and provide for us in our affair a right course. (18:10)

Let Allāh help you: Your best help under any difficult or challenging situation can come from Allāh. So let Allāh help you. But Allāh does not help unless you help yourself. When you feel peer pressure to do something bad, you have to take the initiative to walk away from it. Leave the rest upon Allāh. Once you have complete confidence upon Allāh and your values and beliefs, you will experience wonders in life. Know your boundaries and never try to cross it. You should know what pleases Allāh and what displeases Him.

Choosing friends carefully: Since peer pressure comes from friends, you must choose friends carefully. We will become like those with whom we spend most of our time. It is narrated that Prophet (S) once said: *A person is likely to follow the faith of his friend, look carefully whom you choose to befriend* (reported by Ahmad). When the Prophet (S) was asked who to befriend with, he replied: he who helps you remember Allāh and reminds you when you forget Him.

Ask yourself if you feel uncomfortable and unsafe with a particular friend. Are the friends asking you to overstep your limits? Are the friends violating your belief about what is good? If the answer is "yes" to any of the questions, cut down your interaction with such friends. You do not have to be loyal to them. You will find they were never loyal to you, they are now looking for someone else to be their companion.

from**hadith**

Prophet Muhammad (S) said: "Seven kinds of people will be sheltered under the shade of Allāh on the Day of Judgment. They are: a just ruler, a young man who passed his youth in the worship and service of Allāh, one whose heart is attached to the mosque, two people who love each other for the sake of Allāh, a man who is invited to sin but declines, saying 'I fear Allāh', one who spends his charity in secret, without making a show and one who remembers Allāh in solitude so that his eyes overflow (with tears)."

Prophet Muhammad (S) said: "The most enviable of my friends is a believer with little property who finds pleasure in prayer, who performs the worship of his Rabb well, who obeys Him in secret, who is obscure among men, who is not pointed out by people, and whose provision is a bare sufficiency with which he is content." - Al-Tirmidhī.

homework**weekend 7**

1. The best way to avoid bad peer pressure is to remember the teachings of Islam. Read verse 43:36, and then identify who becomes the friend of a person that forgets Allāh.

....

2. Write three reasons a person gives in to peer pressure?

a. ....

b. ....

c. ....

3. Read verse 20:85. Who was the evil man who had exerted peer pressure on Children of Israel into calf worshipping?

....

4. According to the lesson, what are the two things that can help you in avoiding peer pressure?

a. ....

b. ....

5. Briefly describe a scenario where you felt peer pressure and describe how you overcame it.

....

....

....

6. What answer would you have ready with you in order to resist peer pressure?

....

Choices We Make

Objective of the Lesson:

Allāh has given human beings an important attribute called 'choice.' Our ability to 'choose' from various alternatives makes us the best of the creation. We can choose to be a good Muslim, and choose not to be a good Muslim. The choices we make in our life makes us who we are and what will happen to us in this life and in the Afterlife.

A simple definition of choice is the act of choosing from alternative of beliefs, lifestyle and behavior. Every living being has some ability to make choices. Some of the choices are determined by their natural instinct, therefore, in true sense these are not choices. For example, a cow 'chooses' to eat grass, it will not 'choose' to eat meat, since eating grass is its nature. Similarly a lion will not 'choose' to eat a full meal of grass leaving aside a game animal it has killed. A cow may choose to eat a full meal of grass in normal condition, but it will avoid eating at all when sick. Similarly, if a lion has already eaten a full meal, it may 'choose' not to eat meat from a game of another lion. Such choices are purely within the limits nature has set for each animal.

When we compare such a 'choice' of an animal to the choices we make, we can find interesting results. Similar to animals, we too have natural instinct. Therefore, it is normal that we would do most of the things that nature wants us to do. But unlike all other animals, we can choose to go against nature.

Choice comes with responsibility: Everyday we make choices. Some are small and others are big. Some are routine choices requiring little planning. Some choices are good while others are bad. Regardless of what choices you make, all choices come with a price tag. The price of choice is responsibility and accountability. You are responsible for the choice you make and then you are accountable for the choice.

Based on the choices we make, our life becomes good or bad. If we carefully made the right choice and then carry out the responsibility associated with the choice, the result will be good. If we made a bad choice, we are responsible for the choice, and the consequence of the bad choice will be bad.

Our choices shape our life: Choice is power. As mentioned earlier, choice is an act of selecting from among alternatives. If you do not have power, you cannot choose from the alternatives. When you make major choices in life, you are exerting major power. The major choices you make in your life shape the future course of your life. Your future will not come by the matter of chance. Each choice leads to a consequence and life's major choices will have major consequences.

Choice is a gift from Allāh: When Allāh created human beings, He gave them a unique feature—the ability to choose between alternatives. The angels and animals do not have this ability. Human beings have the ability to choose from alternatives in life whether it is about faith, food, lifestyle or place of living. We may abuse the gift of choice by making wrong choices in life and pay the price. Similarly we may best use the gift of choice by making good and intelligent choices and live happily.

Choice and circumstance: Sometimes people see themselves as the victim of their circumstances. They fail to realize that their own choices played a role in creating those circumstances.

Some of our daily choices appear to be inconsequential and some have serious bearings. How can we make sure that we are making the right choices in the matters that mean the most to us? Here are a few suggestions:

Beware of where the road leads to: Before making any major decisions, make sure you understand where the road leads to. It is not difficult to see the end of many of the roads that you may choose to walk on. If you choose to try drugs, it is not very difficult to see where the road will lead you to. If you choose between a course of study between medicine and law, you know very well what you will become at the end of your study. If you have an aptitude to become an artist, and you choose mathematics as your field of study, obviously you will land on the wrong field. Sometimes not acting on a good choice is also wrong.

أَلَمْ نَجْعَل لَّهُۥ عَيْنَيْنِ ﴿٨﴾ وَلِسَانًا وَشَفَتَيْنِ ﴿٩﴾
وَهَدَيْنَٰهُ ٱلنَّجْدَيْنِ ﴿١٠﴾

Have we not made for him two eyes, and a tongue and two lips, and pointed out to him the two highways? (90:8-10)

In most cases it is better to choose a road that has been tested to be successful by others. In the matter of faith, it is always prudent to walk on the path that has been tested by others. In sūrah Fātihah we ask Allāh to help us choose between two alternatives. One alternative is the path of wrong and the other is the path of righteousness. We admit that the Straight Path was tested by

others—the path of those upon whom Allāh has bestowed His blessings. This path was tested to be the good path by prophets and righteous people.

Make choices based on faith: Many a times in life you will have to choose between different options. Under such circumstances make choices based on your faith. If your faith is strong, you will always get support and blessings from Allāh. When you face difficulties in life, your faith binds you together and shows you the right direction.

Do not make choices based on emotion: Sometimes we are forced to make choices based on emotions. The best approach will be if we do not make decisions purely based on emotion. An emotional decision sometimes turns out to be a bad and regretful one.

Beware of the Limits: It is important that all of us stay within the limits or boundaries. A child will be in danger if he or she crosses the safe boundaries and walks on the street. A fish will be in danger if it jumps out of the water, which is its limit. We too have our limits or boundaries. Allāh clearly instructed us to stay within the limits and not to cross the boundaries (2:173,187,190,229,230; 4:13,171; 5:77; 9:112; 58:4; 65:1).

These are the limits of Allāh so approach them not. (2:187)

These limits are with reference to different social, political, ethical, financial and spiritual circumstances. The limit is not compressing, it is sufficiently large and it accommodates everything needed to lead a good life. We are given the freedom to overstep the boundaries. However, overstepping the limits would lead us to our moral and spiritual downfall. In addition, we will earn the wrath of Allāh and punishment in this life and in the Hereafter.

Do what you can: Many of us may have lofty dreams and ambitions in life. It is worthwhile to pursue our ambition. However, we should understand our limits. What we 'can do' versus what we 'want to do' are different. Our 'want' is endless. If we chase what we 'want' and fail to realize what we 'can', our life will be miserable. When we understand what we 'can', we realize our potential and create the atmosphere whereby we materialize our goal. Whereas if we chase our 'want', we may remain unhappy in life.

Choose to shape your destiny: There is a famous saying that 'destiny is not a matter of chance, it is a matter of choice.' Therefore, destiny is not something you wait for, it is something that you achieve. Your destiny in this life and in the Hereafter is shaped by what you believe and do.

In the matter of faith, you should always 'choose' to be a good Muslim. During Ramadan when you fast, you 'choose' not to eat. A part of a verse from Sūrah Al-Kahf states that:

وَقُلِ الْحَقُّ مِن رَّبِّكُمْ ۖ فَمَن شَاءَ فَلْيُؤْمِن
وَمَن شَاءَ فَلْيَكْفُرْ ۚ

And you say: "The Truth is from your Rabb; therefore whoever wishes then let him believe, and whoever wishes let him then disbelieve..." (18:29)

We should remember 'choice' is a gift of Allāh. The better you handle your ability to choose between alternatives, the better will be your life in this world and in the Hereafter. Ultimately you are responsible and accountable for what you do. How you choose to shape and direct your life is up to you. Choose to be righteous, choose to be happy, and choose to be successful.

homework**weekend 8**

1. Read verse 28:54. If you chose good and reject evil, how will you be rewarded?

....

2. Read verse 31:17. What did Luqmān teach his sons about making a choice between good and evil?

....

....

3. Allāh has given us two paths to choose from. What gifts did He give us to make the right choice? Read verses 90:8-10 (provided in the lesson) to identify these gifts.

....

....

4. People who chose to reject Allāh may feel that they are secure. But their security is similar to a flimsy house. Read 29:41, and then write who has a similar flimsy house.

....

5. Explain in a few sentences why choices made on emotional outburst are often bad choices.

....

....

6. Explain in a few sentences why it is important to make choices based on faith.

....

....

7. Explain what do you understand by staying within the limits.

....

....

8. Between 'can do' and 'want to do' approach in life, which is better? Explain.

....

....

9. Read verse 4:14. The verse speaks of crossing some limits. What will be the consequences of crossing these limits?

....

....

10. Read verse 65:1. In this verse Allāh mentioned certain limits for the Prophet (S), and through him to all of us. If we cross the limits what would happen to us?

....

....

classwork**weekend 9**

Dating in Islam

Objective of the Lesson:

Youths living in the West are increasingly exposed to the common and acceptable western social behavior called dating. As Muslims are we allowed to date? Can we date our would-be life partner? This lesson discusses some of the issues relating to dating and provides important tools to help students take the correct steps in life.

One of the dominant aspects of the "western" life is free mixing of men and women. Many men and women freely mix with each other, in intimate relationship, and for romantic reasons. The society does not see such relationship as a bad moral example, rather approves it and often encourages it. Words like boyfriend, girlfriend, and dating are not taboo.

'Dating' in English usage means to go out with someone usually for romantic reasons. Romance is an emotional loving attraction between two people who are not biologically related. A brother's love towards his sister is not romance, or a mother's love for her children is not romance. Simply stating, romance is when a man and a woman, who are not biologically related to each other, have loving relationship between them.

In the 8th grade we studied the issues of dating. In this lesson we are going to review what we learned. As Muslims we must understand what our religion says about free mixing of men and women.

Liking each other is divine plan: The attraction between man and woman is part of a divine plan for continuing the species. The species or the race can continue only when they reproduce. Without any physical attraction or emotional attachment between male and female members of a species, there will not be any urge among them to reproduce. Without the attraction or attachment, animals will not reproduce, and birds will not procreate. If there were no reproduction, entire living world will perish. The ecosystem will collapse and the food chain will break down. There will be a major chaos in nature. In order to prevent such disaster from happening, nature has devised the process of procreation and established a check and balance mechanism in the process so that every species may reproduce but no one species populates so much that they take up the entire world.

The Divine plan of men and women to like each other is given in the Qur'ān. Verse 21 of sūrah 30 discusses the attraction between man and woman as a sign of Allāh and wants us to ponder over it. Allāh has put love and mercy between man and woman. Because of these two desired qualities, man and woman get married, make a family, have children and continue the human race.

Liking each other is natural: We must first remember that Islam is the "natural" religion. By the word "natural" we mean normal, accepted, obvious, and time-honored religion. It is "natural" because it is the only religion acceptable to Allāh.[3:19,83]

Since Islam is the natural religion, the law of nature is also clearly noticeable in its principles. Just as the entire nature, universe, living and non-living things willingly and unwillingly submit to Allāh,[3:83; 13:15] so also human beings are required to submit and follow the laws of Allāh. One of the laws of nature is "survival of the race." This law applies for all plant, animals, micro-organism or any living being. In order for the race to survive, the living organisms must reproduce. The urge of reproduction is innate in all living organisms. In order for them to reproduce, nature devised a mechanism whereby opposite genders of each species attract each other. In lower organisms the attraction is purely physical in nature, but in most organisms the attraction also involves an emotional attachment.

Human beings are not like animals: In lesson 5 of this course, we have already studied human beings are the best of the creation. They have moral, ethical and spiritual instincts that no other animals have in them. Animals eat, sleep and mate instinctively. Since animals do not have moral, ethical and spiritual obligations, they will not be judged on the Day of Judgment. On the other hand, we, human beings, are obligated to follow moral, ethical and spiritual obligations because we will be judged based on our conduct. We cannot behave like animals; we have certain principles to follow, and certain codes of conduct to uphold.

If you look at yourself, only six to seven years earlier you did not know about human sexuality. The children in the lower grades do not know about human sexuality. As they grow, they will learn about the attraction between men and women. It will originate in them instinctively just as it originated in you. Nature is preparing you "naturally" so that you too can carry out what nature wants—to procreate the race.

Simplified dating not possible: When you are growing up—as teens, youths and young adults—you will be attracted towards the opposite gender. You may spend a great deal of your time thinking about the opposite sex. Such attraction may tempt you to defy all social order, family rules and religious instructions. You begin to reason that simple touching, hugging or kissing is not harmful. As many students in schools or colleges are involved in such behavior, you may begin to believe that these are acceptable. You begin to reason that life in the West is different—therefore certain degree of touching or hugging is a tolerable behavior.

Any argument in favor of simple touching, hugging or kissing cannot defeat the Qur'ānic instruction about appropriate behavior for men:

قُلْ لِّلْمُؤْمِنِيْنَ يَغُضُّوْا مِنْ اَبْصَارِهِمْ وَ يَحْفَظُوْا
فُرُوْجَهُمْ ؕ ذٰلِكَ اَزْكٰى لَهُمْ ؕ اِنَّ اللّٰهَ خَبِيْرٌۢ
بِمَا يَصْنَعُوْنَ ﴿٣٠﴾

Say to the believing men that they lower their eyes, and restrain their appetites. This is purer for them. Surely Allāh is Aware of what they do. (24:30)

For women too the message is similar: they also must control the gaze.[24:31]

The first step of attraction to opposite gender is the look. Holding of hands, hugging or kissing comes much later in the path of attraction. The Qur'ān puts the brake at the beginning of the process by asking us to lower our gaze in the presence of opposite sex. The Qur'ān also asks us to avoid meeting secretly unless we have something righteous to discuss.

It is reported that the Prophet (S) said: *whenever a man is alone with a woman, Shaitān is the third among them.* (Tirmidhī). Another hadīth reports that: *not one of you should meet a woman alone unless she is accompanied by a relative.* (Bukhārī and Muslim). The Qur'ān or Hadīth of the Prophet (S) did not give any permission to sexually touch a person unless that person is already married to the other.

Dating strongly discouraged: The Qur'ān uses strong words to condemn pre-marital or extra-marital sexual relations and admonishes those who knowingly violate chastity. The Qur'ān uses such words as sinner, transgressor, rejecter of faith, all your works will be in vain, you will be with the loser in the Hereafter.[23:7; 70:31]

Sexual contact outside marriage is considered a worst form of evil or *zulm* against yourself and the other person. Whoever commits this kind of *zulm*, will never prosper in the sight of Allāh. In the story of Yūsuf when the woman closed the door and invited Yūsuf, first he refused because it was a *zulm*. Then he gave the reason by saying:

إِنَّهُۥ لَا يُفْلِحُ ٱلظَّٰلِمُونَ ٢٣

...Surely the wrongdoers are never made to prosper. (12:23)

Developing good moral values: It seems that a young person who practices high moral values misses all fun of life. While many youths prefer fun, only a few understand that happiness is better than having fun. A person will be happy and blissful when he or she realizes that a large reward awaits in this world and in the Hereafter. The reward in the Hereafter is the entry to the paradise and living there permanently. In the Hereafter the time spent on earth will appear like a speck compared to the eternal life.[23:112-114] The rewards in this world for keeping a high moral standard are stable relationship between married couples, happy family, honor in the society and not having suspicion between the spouses.

The best way to resist the temptation is to use your faith, patience, commitment and trust. You have to believe and accept Allāh as your friend rather than taking Shaitān as your friend. Shaitān gives you false promise and tantalizes the earthly objectives as desirable and makes spiritual

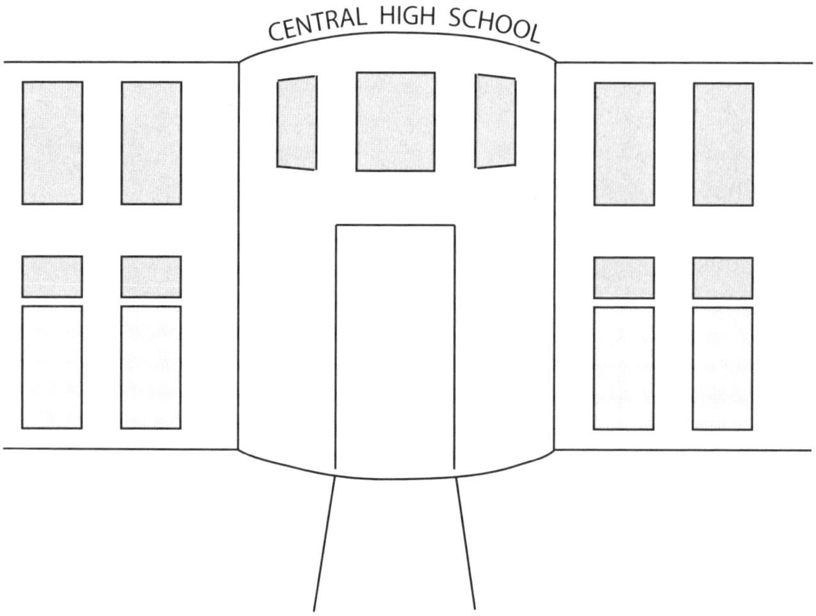

objectives as burdensome and disgusting. You should realize that feeling of passion is a test for you. You must do well in the test. This can be done by avoiding dating and controlling your passion. This is easy to say but difficult in real life. But all difficulties in life can be overcome through patience, hard work and trust upon Allāh.

If you follow the guidance of the Qur'ān, Allāh will make things easy for you. Initial passion may be difficult to control, but once you trust Allāh and work hard to overcome the urges, you will find that things are becoming easy for you. Just as serious disease requires strong medicine, so also intense desires will require great help from Allāh, strong will and solid devotion to Him. After all, Allāh created us, He can make things easy for us. In the Qur'ān Allāh say after hardship comes the ease.[94:6] This is Allāh's promise to us.

Marriage is an important decision: All of you insha-Allāh will get married one day. When you decide to get married, you are taking an important step in life. Therefore, the choice of who is going to be your marriage partner is very important. This choice cannot and should not be taken lightly, emotionally or hurriedly. It should be taken as seriously as you would take many other important decisions in life. You should consult your family, make careful investigations, seek guidance from Allāh and as far as possible let not your emotions or desires control your decision process. Parents should play an important role in the decision making process.

As a Muslim, you have to find out a way to avoid the temptation to date. Submit to Allāh wholeheartedly. Follow His guidance sincerely. Do not find excuses or faulty reasoning to allow dating. To avoid temptation, remember that Allāh is always watching us.

homework**weekend 9**

1. From a hadīth reported by Tirmidhī, it is narrated that whenever a man is alone with a woman, the third one among them is:

....

2. In Sūrah Ar-Rum, verse 21, Allāh says that He has put two emotional qualities between men and women. What are these two qualities?

....

3. Regarding attraction between opposite sexes, human beings should not act like animals. Based on the lesson write what three obligations that human beings must follow.

....

4. Read verse 2:221. In this verse the Qur'ān tells us who a Muslim should not marry. Who is said to be better for a Muslim to marry?

   a. Cannot marry: ....

   b. Can marry: ....

5. The Qur'ān strictly forbids sex outside of marriage. It says two things about sex outside of marriage in verse 17:32. Mention what are the two things.

   a. ....

   b. ....

6. In verse 23:1 the Qur'ān says success will come to those who follow certain things. Next few verses tell us some of the criteria to achieve success. One such criterion is in verse 5. Write the message below.

....

....

7. Explain how you can apply the message of 23:5 (that you read in response to Q. 6 above) in your life.

....

....

8. Read the message in verse 24:30 and answer the following questions:

a. What are the two things recommended for men to follow?

....

b. How does the message in the verse apply to dating?

....

c. Read verse 24:31 and answer what two things are applicable to women that are applicable to men as well. Compare verse 24:30 to find the answer.

....

9. Circle C if the statement is correct, circle W if the statement is wrong.

a.	Highest level of *Imān* is reached if a person never marries.	C	W
b.	Love and mercy between a man and a woman is a gift of Allāh.	C	W
c.	Sexual contact outside marriage is considered a worst form of evil.	C	W

Alcohol and Gambling

Objective of the Lesson:

Muslim youths growing up in the West are increasingly facing the challenges of social drinking during high school and college years. Even the adult Muslims are also facing similar challenge in many social events. The lesson discusses this important subject in the Islamic perspective.

Muslim youths living in the West face many challenges. Two of such challenges are drinking and gambling. Temptation to indulge in alcohol and gambling is everywhere. You may have heard about Muslim youths or adults quietly or openly trying out the prohibited. You may have even heard many strange arguments in support of limited drinking.

Understanding how and why Islam prohibited alcohol and gambling is important. In a few years from now, your lifestyle will change when you join a college or an university. You will make new friends, and you will have less supervision by your parents or guardians. Your parents will most likely not find out what you do during evenings, nights, or weekends. In the midst of life's excitement once in a while you will face the temptation to try alcohol. As a responsible young Muslim, you should understand why Islam prohibits alcohol and gambling.

Arabia before Islam: Before Islam came to Arabia, gambling and drinking were two common social habits of the people. The rich and the poor took part in gambling. People brewed alcohol at home. Drunk men and women were a problem in the society. Many of the tribal warfare and skirmishes began as a direct result of gambling and drinking. Many good hearted people knew drinking was bad, but the society did not have any standard guideline to follow. As a result nobody really objected at those who drank or gambled.

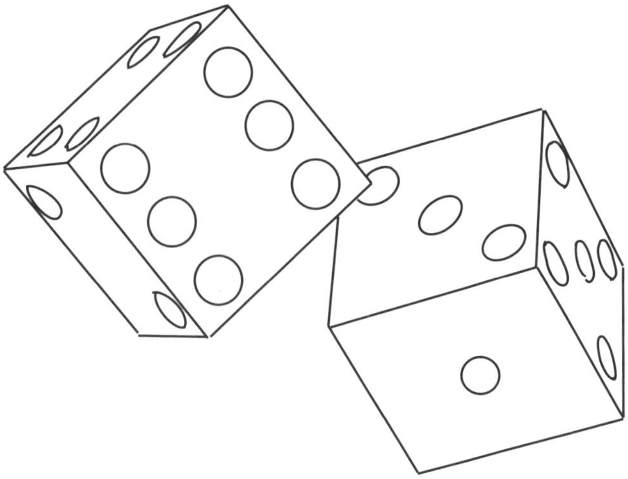

Islam changed the outlook: Islam recognized gambling and drinking as social evils and used strong words against these. However, the prohibition was not suddenly imposed in one verse. Several verses were revealed that criticized drinking and drew attention of the Muslims towards the evil of drinking. Finally, the following the verse clearly and effectively prohibited drinking and gambling.

يَاَيُّهَا الَّذِيْنَ اٰمَنُوْٓا اِنَّمَا الْخَمْرُ وَالْمَيْسِرُ
وَالْاَنْصَابُ وَالْاَزْلَامُ رِجْسٌ مِّنْ عَمَلِ
الشَّيْطٰنِ فَاجْتَنِبُوْهُ لَعَلَّكُمْ تُفْلِحُوْنَ ﴿٩٠﴾

O you who believe! Surely the intoxicants and gambling and setting up stones and divining by arrows are abomination and handiwork of Shaitān, therefore avoid these that you may attain success. (5:90)

In this verse four things are stated to be abomination (*rijsun*):

a. *Khamr*: Intoxicant,

b. *Maisiru*: Gambling, drawing lots,

c. *Ansāb*: An altar, a stone on which to sacrifice,

d. *Azlām*: Divining arrow, an arrow without a head for the purpose of divination.

The verse asks the believers to 'avoid' (*janaba*) these four to attain success. You may wonder why Allāh did not 'forbid' alcohol and gambling, but asked us to avoid these. In literal use, the word *janaba* is used to those acts that involve desire,

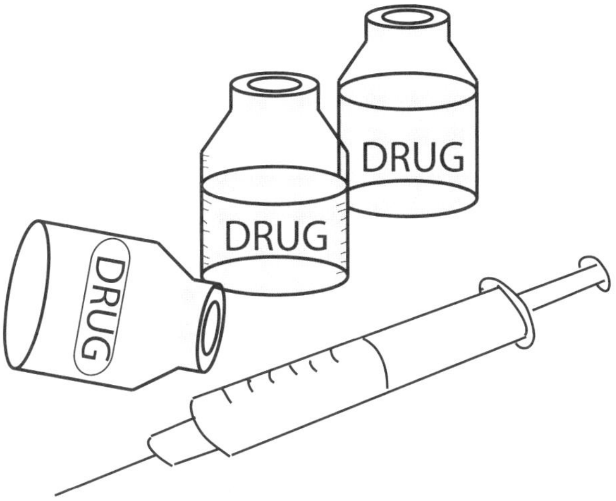

urge, attraction or intoxication. These acts are not similar to other prohibited acts, such as eating pork. Once habituated or addicted, drinking, drug use or gambling are not easy to give up. Avoidance requires conscious effort from within a person to stay away from the sin (see usage in 39:17; 42:37; 53:32). The Qur'ān, therefore, wisely used the word 'avoid' rather than 'forbid.' In the next verse, 5:91 Allāh asks us to 'abstain' from these abominations. Both avoidance and abstinence requires the person to take the initiative and efforts to shun these.

Abomination: Let us examine the word abomination and its derivatives in the Qur'ān. The root word of abomination is *rajisa*. It means any deed that is bad, filthy, that deserves punishment, that has no good in it, and suggested by Shaitān.

The following is an outline of the customs and practices that were considered to be abomination. All these verse used the root word *rijsun* to point out the offense involved in these.

- Hypocrisy is abomination (9:95)
- Idol worshipping is abomination. (22:30)
- Drinking and gambling is abomination (5:30)

Meaning of Khamr: The Arabic word for intoxicant is *khamr,* derived from the root word *khamara* which means to cover, to conceal, to hide. Any intoxicating drink or substance that clouds or obscures our intellect and good senses are *khamr.* This word is also used in verse 2:219 where wine or grape-wine is meant. The Arabic word for head scarf or *khumār* (plural) is also derived from the same root word, indicating that the scarf covers the head.[24:31] Although originally the word was used for fermented drink, specially from grapes, any intoxicant such as marijuana, heroin, cocaine, hashish, LSD and other drugs are included in the prohibition. Anything, whether liquid or not, that clouds or obscures our mind are covered under the definition of the word *khamr.*

Verse 4:43: The Qur'ān has four verses regarding the prohibition of intoxicants. The order in which they were revealed was 4:43, 2:219 and 5:90 and 5:91. The first revealed verse about intoxicant states:

O you who believe! Do not come near to salāt while you are befogged, until you know what you say, ... (4:43)

When verse 4:43 was revealed the people of Arabia, including some Muslims, used to drink as a social norm. Verse 4:43 prohibited the Muslims from coming near salāt when they were intoxicated without addressing whether or not drinking can be allowed. Some of the Muslims think that verse 4:43 permitted drinking. Whereas, instead the verse actually discouraged drinking in a subtle manner.

The prohibition in verse 4:43 is not limited to alcohol. The verse uses *sakr* to denote intoxicants. The word implies any agent that causes drowsiness. The word *sakr* also means intoxicated with sleep. It also means confusion of judgment. The criteria for this agent, whether chemical or not, is one that will cause the person not understand what he is saying.

Interestingly, Qur'ān has used the word *sakara* in places where it does not indicate any chemical use. In verse 50:19, *sakrat-ul maut* means disorientation due to impending death. In verse 15:72, the use is about intoxicated with lust. In verse 22:2, the Qur'ān uses the word *sakara* as intoxication without (chemical) intoxicant. Originally verse 4:43 prohibited (wine-consumed) drunk people from coming near salāt, the verse still remains valid for all kinds of distraction that befogs our senses away from our speeches. Such distraction could be any kind of worldly affairs such as sleep, lust, or being unmindful. It could also include any earthly affair such as thinking about business while paying no attention to what the tongue is reciting.

Great sin: The second revealed verse condemning alcohol and gambling branded these as great sin:

يَسْـَٔلُونَكَ عَنِ الْخَمْرِ وَالْمَيْسِرِ ۖ قُلْ فِيهِمَآ
إِثْمٌ كَبِيرٌ وَمَنَـٰفِعُ لِلنَّاسِ وَإِثْمُهُمَآ
أَكْبَرُ مِن نَّفْعِهِمَا ۗ

They ask you about the intoxicants and game of chances. Say, "in both these there is a great sin and benefit for people, but the sin of it is more serious than their benefits." ... (2:219)

Verse 2:219 is only a clarification of an issue raised by various groups of people including the Companions of the Prophet (S). The clarifications are given in response to what 'they ask you about'. A quick look at the next several verses like 2:215, 2:217, 2:220 or 2:222 indicates each of these verses was actually clarifying certain issues. The clarification regarding intoxicants given in 2:219 not only holds valid today but also substantiated by scientific evidences. Medical science has shown that drinking alcohol in moderation actually can lower blood cholesterol. However, this potential distant benefit is far smaller than the actual, imminent and real evil involved in drinking.

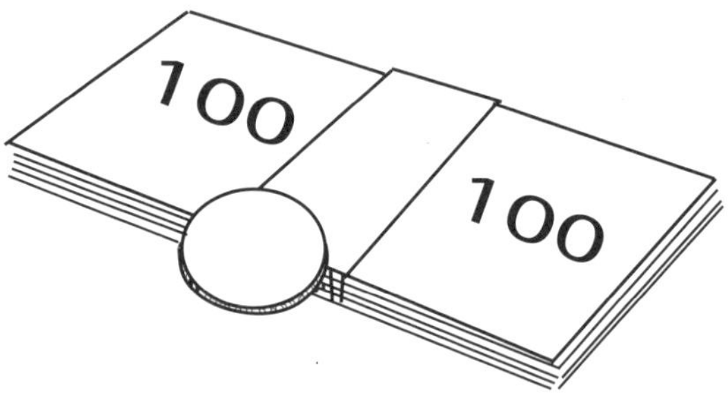

The game of chances, such as gambling and lottery, may have benefited a select few. The odd of winning a major lottery is about one in a million or more. Such huge odds of winning provides monetary gains to one or a few people, while thousands or millions become losers. Many lottery or gambling winners suffer as the easy gain is wasted in a few years.

Hadīth on prohibition of intoxicants: Several of the Prophet (S)'s sayings clearly point out the abomination of intoxicants.

Narrated by Abū Mūsā that when the Prophet (S) sent him and Mu'adh bin Jabal to Yemen, he said to them, "Make things easy for the people, and do not make things difficult for them, and give them glad tidings, and let them not have aversion and you both should work in cooperation and mutual understanding, obey each other." Abū Mūsā said, "O Allāh's Messenger! We are in a land in which a drink named Al Bit' is prepared from honey, and another drink named Al-Mizr is prepared from barley." On that, Allāh's Messenger (S) said, "All intoxicants are prohibited." (Bukhāri 8.145)

Narrated by ANās ibn Malik, Allāh's Messenger (S) cursed ten people in connection with wine: the wine-presser, the one who has it pressed, the one who drinks it, the one who conveys it, the one to whom it is conveyed, the one who serves it, the one who sells it, the one who benefits from the price paid for it, the one who buys it, and the one for whom it is bought. (Tirmidhī and Ibn Majah).

This hadīth is narrated by Jabir ibn Abdullah. A person came from Jayshan, a town of Yemen, and he asked Allāh's messenger (S) about the wine which was drunk in their land and which was prepared from millet and was called *Mizr*. Allāh's messenger (S) asked whether that was intoxicating. He said: Yes. Thereupon Allāh's messenger (S) said: Every intoxicant is forbidden. (Sahih Muslim)

Ibn Umar narrates that the Prophet (S) said: "Every intoxicant is *Khamr* and every intoxicant is *harām*." (Sahih Muslim, Sunan Abū Dawūd, Sunan Tirmidhī).

From the above discussion we can conclude that all intoxicants are unlawful. The intoxicants not only include fruit based wine, but also all such substances that clouds or obscures our intellect and good senses. Let us note the verse 5:91 where Allāh says: *Shaitān only desires to create enmity and hatred among you by means of intoxicants and gambling, and to divert you from the remembrance of Allāh and from salāt. Will you not then become abstained?*

Some Disturbing Facts

- According to National Institute on Alcohol Abuse and Alcoholism, use of alcohol among U.S. high school students is higher than use of cigarettes and marijuana combined.
- According to U.S. Department of Health and Human Services, about 5,000 people under age 21 die each year from alcohol related issues in the U.S.
- According to World Health Organization, alcohol is the cause of 20-30% worldwide of oesophageal cancer, liver cancer, cirrhosis of the liver, homicide, epilepsy, and motor vehicle accidents.
- According to World Health Organization, about 9% of all deaths worldwide are related to tobacco, and over 3% death are related to alcohol.
- According to National Council on Problem Gambling, about 2 million U.S. adults are pathologic or compulsive gamblers. Another 4-6 million adults are problem gamblers. Other than financial issues, these people suffer from psychological, physical, social or vocational problems.

homework**weekend 10**

1. To qualify as an intoxicant, what essential property should an element have? The element must:

   a. be available in a liquid form.
   b. be obtained from grapes.
   c. confuse the brain and thought process.
   d. have a pungent smell.
   e. be bought and sold in a controlled way.

2. What is the meaning of the root word *khamara*?

....

3. To qualify as gambling, what essential property should a game have? The game must:

   a. promise a hope of gain.
   b. use dice.
   c. be a board game.
   d. involve at least two players.
   e. be held in a casino.

4. In verse 2:219 what type of intoxicant is meant by the word *khamr*?

   a. Only grape wine.
   b. Only fermented drink.
   c. All possible forms of intoxicants.
   d. Chemical intoxicants.
   e. Artificially brewed intoxicants.

5. Which Qur'ānic verse says the sin in intoxicant and gambling are more than the benefits in them?

   a. 2:43
   b. 2:219
   c. 4:43
   d. 5:90
   e. 9:95

6. In verse 5:90 intoxicants and gambling are mentioned to be a type of *rijsa*. What is the meaning of the word *rijsa*?

....

7. Why do you think the Qur'ān did not specifically mention chemical intoxicants as prohibited items?

....

....

8. Read verse 5:91. According to the verse what does shaitān want to do by provoking us to drinking and gambling?

a. Induce pleasure in us.

b. Cause jealousy and anger in us.

c. Cause boredom and hangover in us.

d. Make us give up tawhid.

e. Cause enmity and hatred among us.

9. Explain how alcohol or gambling can have some benefit in them but the harm is much more than the benefit.

....

....

10. Explain what types of intoxicants are covered under the term *'sakr'*.

....

....

classwork**weekend 11**

Permitted and Prohibited Food

Objective of the Lesson:

The Qur'ān has clearly mentioned the permitted and prohibited food. However, with so many food choices available in the West, sometimes it becomes difficult to know which food is permitted and which are prohibited. At times permissible meat of an animal can turn out to be prohibited based on how and where it was slaughtered. At times prohibition is taken too casually and at other times prohibition is stretched too far. This lesson discusses the Qur'ānic injunction on this matter.

In this lesson we will take a critical look at permitted and prohibited food in Islam. Since the Qur'ān and Hadīth have clearly pointed out the permitted and prohibited food, there should not be any doubt about the types of food allowed and the types of food prohibited in Islam. However, with a wide variety of food items available in the market today, many Muslims are unsure about what is permitted and what is prohibited. This lesson will not list each and every food product or name the restaurants or supermarkets that serve or sell prohibited food. Instead it will try to explain the Qur'ānic rulings and some of the supporting Hadīth so that you can make an informed decision. We will exclude discussion on alcohol and intoxicants, as we discussed these last week.

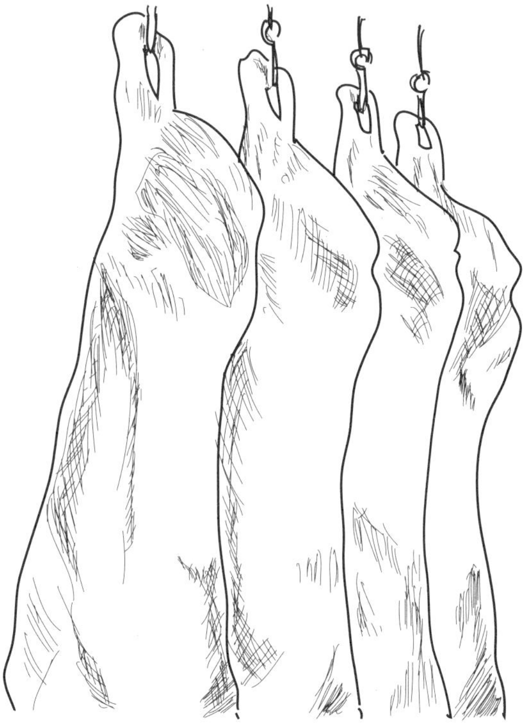

The Arabic word for food is *ta'ām*. Generally it covers all types of food including fish, meat, vegetable, grain, fruits, etc. However, the manner this word is applied in various verses dealing with dietary laws, it refers to *dhabiha* meat. The meaning of the word will be explained later in this chapter.

Dietary laws: Islamic dietary laws are those food laws that are divinely instituted and divinely inspired through the rulings given by the Prophet (S), as opposed to the laws governed by FDA or other government agencies. Before Islam was formulated, people in the past too had their own dietary laws. People of the Book received detailed dietary laws, some of which were stricter than the Islamic dietary laws. In the Bible, dietary laws are mentioned in Deuteronomy, Leviticus and Acts. In the Qur'ān dietary laws are specifically explained in four sūrahs—these are Baqarah, Mā'idah, An'ām and Nahl.

Broad standard for harām and halāl: Interestingly wherever the Qur'ān discusses dietary laws in detail, it strictly confines to discussion about animals, the manner it is slaughtered and its meat. No specific dietary laws are given about other food items, e.g. crops, vegetables, fruits etc., except a broad standard is specified about food that are harām and halāl, as illustrated in the following verses:

> *O you mankind! eat of what is on the earth, lawful, pure; and do not follow the footsteps of Shaitān. Surely he is to you an open enemy. (2:168)*
>
> *O you who believe! eat of the good things that We have provided you with; and give thanks to Allāh, if it is Him alone Whom you use to worship. (2:172)*
>
> *And do not say— because your tongues are given to telling lies: "This is lawful and that is unlawful,"— so that you forge a lie against Allāh. Surely those who forge a lie against Allāh do not prosper. (16:116)*

From these verses we see that the Qur'ān is asking people to eat not only the lawful food but also the good food. Furthermore, these verses remind us not to follow the footsteps of shaitān. They are also asking us to be grateful to Allāh for the food He provided. Equally important message from these verses is not to make lawful food unlawful. Based on these verses we can see that in order for a food to be halāl, it must be 'lawful' and 'good'. A harām food includes all food that are 'unlawful' and/or 'bad' food.

Are all good food halāl?: We learned that Allāh allowed us to eat lawful and good food. However, all 'good' or healthful food may not be always halāl. For example, cow or goat is perfectly lawful animal for Muslims to eat. Now, if someone serves us cooked meat of cow or goat, will it be permissible to eat? What is the Qur'ān's viewpoint in this matter?

Among the good and lawful food Allāh has allowed us to eat, it is further stated that we can only eat those meat of an animal over which Allāh's name is pronounced at the time of slaughtering. The process is called *dhabiha*. The Hadīth gave the clear instruction on the process of *dhabiha*. An animal becomes dhabiha when during slaughtering the throat of the animal is cut in such a way that its jugular vein, carotid arteries and trachea are cut off and Allāh's name is pronounced (Ibn 'Abbās, Mujāhid, 'Ikrimah—all quoted by Tabari, Ibn Kathīr).

The requirement to declare Allāh's name at the time of slaughtering is to acknowledge that all life belongs to Allāh alone and He alone has the right to give life and take away life. By declaring Allāh's name the believers acknowledge that the life of the animal is taken with His permission and not out of impiety or disobedience to His laws. This requirement also attempts to abolish the pagan custom of slaughtering animals to appease idols. Since the idols did not give life to these animals, they have no right to their take their life either.

فَكُلُوا مِمَّا ذُكِرَ اسْمُ اللَّهِ عَلَيْهِ إِن كُنتُم
بِآيَاتِهِ مُؤْمِنِينَ ﴿١١٨﴾

> *Then you eat of that on which the name of Allāh has been mentioned, if you are believers in His Messages. (6:118)*

Catch of a hunting animal: In the past hunting was one of the major method to catch animals to eat. Hunting was done by arrows, spears, booby traps, or by use of trained dogs, hawks, hounds, cheetahs or other such animals. If a trained animal is employed to catch a prey, the Qur'ān says its catch is allowed for human consumption, provided that Allāh's name is pronounced over it.[5:4] Under most circumstances the trained animal preys upon at a distance from its master. By the time the master locates the hunted animal or by the time the hunting animal drags or carries the prey back to its master, the prey could have died due to injuries.

Scholars gave the opinion that under such circumstance the animal should be slaughtered anyway in the name of Allāh, but Allāh's name should have been pronounced at the time of releasing the hunting animal. Similar principle also applies when releasing an arrow or gunshot to kill a lawful animal for consumption.

Harām (forbidden) food: The Qur'ān clearly states the types of food that are harām or forbidden. One such verse is from sūrah Baqarah:

> *He has forbidden you only what dies of itself, and the blood, and the flesh of swine, and that over which any other than Allāh on it. But whoever is constrained, without being disobedient nor exceeding the limit, no sin be upon him then. Allāh is certainly most Forgiving, most Rewarding. (2:173)*

Thus, four categories of food are stated as harām:

1. dead meat or carrion,
2. blood,
3. meat of swine or pork, and
4. meat of any animal on which names of anything, person or deity is invoked instead of name of Allāh (*ghayr Allāh*)

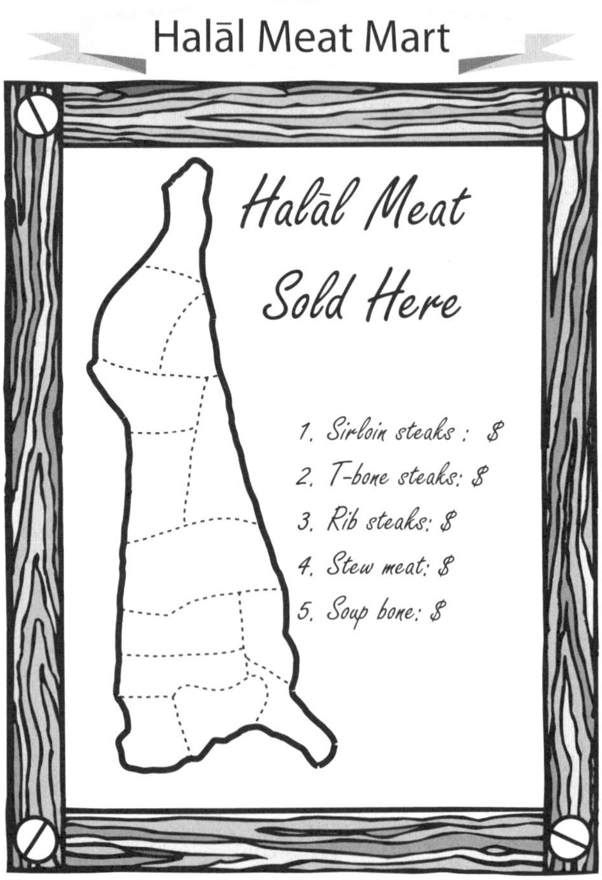

The same message is repeated at other places in the Qur'ān as well.

> *Say: "I do not find in what has been revealed to me anything forbidden to an eater to eat it except that it be dead by itself, or blood poured forth, or flesh of pig,—for that is impure indeed, or what is a disobedience— being slaughtered in other than that of Allāh on it; but whoever is compelled, without rebellion nor exceeding limits, then surely your Rabb is most Forgiving, most Rewarding. (6:145)*

> *He has forbidden you only what dies of itself, and the blood, and the flesh of swine, and what is slaughtered with other than Allāh upon it; but whoever is compelled by necessity, without being rebellious and not exceeding the limit, then Allāh is indeed most Forgiving, most Rewarding. (16:115)*

Forms of death that makes animal harām: The Qur'ān describes seven types of death of an animal that would make it harām.

> *Forbidden to you are— that died of itself, and the blood and the flesh of swine, and whatever has been slaughtered for other than Allāh on it; and the strangled, and stunned to death, and dead through falling, and killed by horns, and what wild-beasts have eaten, except what you have slaughtered; and what has been sacrificed on stones set up, and that you seek to divide by drawing arrows;— all that is transgression. (5:3)*

In summary, death of an animal by the following ways make the meat harām:

1. killing by strangling,
2. killing by violent blow,
3. death by a fall,
4. killing by stabbing or piercing to death,
5. killing by another animal that ate part of the meat,
6. killing by sacrificing on the altar as a part of idolatrous practice,
7. dividing meat by draw of lots, as done in the past with arrows, etc.

What if no name is pronounced: Difference of opinion arises among many Muslims when no name is pronounced at the time of slaughtering, as in an automated slaughterhouse in many Western countries including the United States. Muslim opinion differs whether such meat purchased from many supermarkets or meat products at many fast food restaurants can be consumed by pronouncing Allāh's name at the time of eating.

The difference of opinion can be settled if you follow the clear Qur'ānic instructions on this matter. Earlier we have seen in 6:118 the Qur'ān says to eat meat on which Allāh's name has been pronounced. Verse 6:121 clearly states not to eat any meat on which Allāh's name has not been pronounced.

وَلَا تَأْكُلُوا مِمَّا لَمْ يُذْكَرِ اسْمُ اللَّهِ عَلَيْهِ
وَإِنَّهُ لَفِسْقٌ ۗ وَإِنَّ الشَّيَاطِينَ لَيُوحُونَ إِلَىٰ
أَوْلِيَائِهِمْ لِيُجَادِلُوكُمْ ۖ وَإِنْ أَطَعْتُمُوهُمْ إِنَّكُمْ
لَمُشْرِكُونَ ﴿١٢١﴾

And do not eat of that on which Allāh's name has not been mentioned, for it is surely a disobedience. And certainly Shaitān will inspire their allies to dispute with you; and if you obey them, you will surely become polytheists. (6:121)

The instruction to declare Allāh's name in the verse and also in verse 6:118 is stated in past tense and in passive voice, which further confirms the requirement to declare Allāh's name arises well before the food is eaten. The passive voice indicates the name was to be pronounced by someone else, evidently by the slaughterer at the time of slaughtering. The Qur'ān does not put any kind of restriction on how a food is preserved, cooked or served. Therefore, pronouncement of Allāh's name by a cook or a server will not make it permissible, since the Qur'ānic injunctions are limited only to how an animal is killed.

It is important to realize that declaring Allāh's name at the time of cooking, serving or eating does not make unlawful food lawful. No Hadīth or Qur'ānic verse states Bismillah can render unlawful food as lawful. If it is unlawful, it remains unlawful.

In the next chapter we will investigate if Allāh's name is not uttered during slaughtering, whether the meat (*ta'ām*) prepared by the People of the Book can become permissible food (5:5).

homework**weekend 11**

1. Islam is the first and the only religion to promulgate dietary laws for its followers. True / False

All good and clean food are halāl. True / False

Beef is always halāl. True / False

Dhabiha is the correct Islamic process of slaughtering an animal. True / False

2. Which of the following choices is true about the dietary laws for the Jews?

   a. There were no dietary laws for the Jews.
   b. The dietary laws were very relaxed.
   c. The dietary laws were very strict.
   d. The dietary laws only covered crops and vegetables.

3. Which two chapters in the Bible specifically mentioned dietary laws?

   a. Mark and Matthew.
   b. Genesis and Psalms.
   c. Leviticus and Luke.
   d. Deuteronomy and Leviticus.
   e. Genesis and Exodus.

4. Which four chapters in the Qur'ān detailed the dietary laws for the Muslims?

....

5. How many different types of death are mentioned in verse 5:3 that would make an animal harām food?

....

6. Which of the following choices gives the reason why Allāh's name should be pronounced at the time of slaughtering?

   a. To acknowledge that Allāh gives life and He alone permits us to take life.
   b. To remember that we should kill an animal in least painful manner.
   c. So that a Muslim will always have a good selection of meat.
   d. So that Muslims can slaughter only lawful animals.
   e. So that Muslims can have available meat in the market.

7. A young Muslim boy scout was missing in the wilderness for three days. He had no food or water with him and had not eaten anything during these three days. On the third evening, at an abandoned campsite he found several cans of pork. He opened a can and ate the pork. Has he committed a sin? Briefly explain your answer. Mention a relevant verse # if applicable.

....

....

....

....

8. Some of the following choices state the forms of death that would make a meat harām. Mark ☑ if the statement is correct, and mark ☒ if it is wrong.

a.	Slaughtering an animal on a stone altar.	☐
b.	Killing by a violent blow.	☐
c.	Killing by strangling.	☐
d.	Death by a fall.	☐

9. Read verse 6:121 (given in the lesson). Who disputes with you to convince that it is not necessary to pronounce Allāh's name during slaughtering?

....

Food of the People of the Book

Objective of the Lesson:

The Qur'ān says food of the People of the Book is permissible for us to eat. How do we interpret this message? Is every food they prepare permissible, including the pork, or are there restrictions? This lesson discusses the types of their food that are permissible and the types of food that are not permissible.

Last week, we discussed several aspects of permitted and prohibited food in Islam. We have analyzed many Qur'ānic verses to understand the types of food allowed and the types of food prohibited in Islam. In this lesson we will analyze verse 5:5 and a related Hadīth by 'Ā'ishah (ra). We are discussing this verse and the Hadīth as a separate lesson since the interpretation of the verse made many Muslims confused about what is permitted and what is prohibited.

Review of halāl and harām: Let us briefly review the concept of halāl and harām. The Qur'ān instructs Muslims to eat not only the lawful food but also the good food. We have read that the Qur'ān asked us not to make lawful food unlawful. We have read that we can eat only those meat of an animal over which Allāh's name is pronounced at the time of slaughtering. We have also noted that the Qur'ān clearly states not to eat any meat on which Allāh's name has not been pronounced at the time of slaughtering the animal. We have also studied that four broad types of food are harām and seven different types of death of an animal would make the animal harām for human consumption.

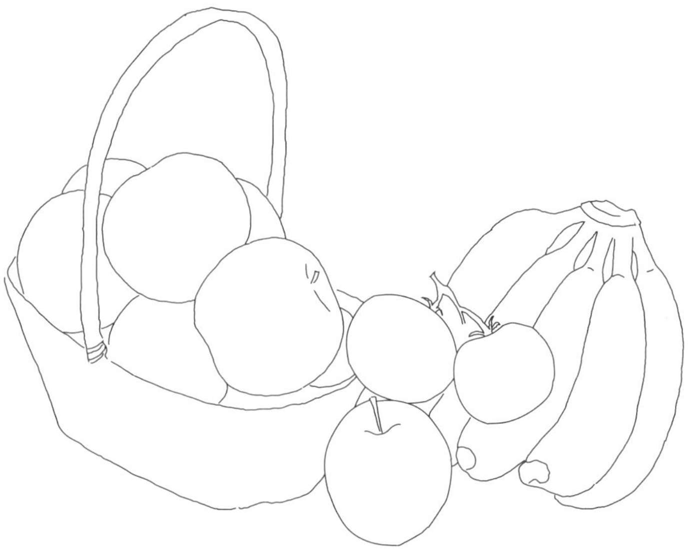

Food of the people of the book is lawful: Sūrah Mā'idah verse 5 gives a very interesting insight to the dietary laws in Islam. It states that the food of the People of the Book is lawful for Muslims and food of Muslims is also lawful for them. The term 'People of the Book' primarily means the Jews and the Christians. Let us read part of the verse 5:5:

اَلْيَوْمَ اُحِلَّ لَكُمُ الطَّيِّبٰتُ ؕ وَ طَعَامُ الَّذِيْنَ اُوْتُوا الْكِتٰبَ حِلٌّ لَّكُمْ ۪ وَ طَعَامُكُمْ حِلٌّ لَّهُمْ ۫

This day the good things have been made lawful for you. And the food of those who have been given the Book is lawful for you, and your food is lawful for them, ...(5:5)

When this verse is read without further analysis, it seems that the Qur'ān has allowed us to eat food of the People of the Book without any qualification. Based on reading the verse at a glance, many Muslims think every meat available in Western supermarkets and fast food restaurants are halāl for the Muslims since the meat may have been prepared by the People of the Book.

Is every food lawful: Let us try to understand if the verse 5:5 indicates every food of the People of the Book is lawful. Christians and many Jews consume pork and wine. If they offer us pork or wine, such food does not become permissible to us. Pork or wine is not lawful for us, therefore such food offered by the People of the Book still remains unlawful. If their food meets our Islamic standard, then it is lawful. If it does not meet our standard, then it remains unlawful.

In Jewish tradition, regular moderate alcohol consumption is allowed, and excessive consumption of alcohol is permitted on the holiday of Purim. Since consumption of alcohol in any amount is not permissible in Islam, any Jewish food containing alcohol remains off-limits to Muslims. Based on this thread of argument, we can eat the food of the People of the Book only if these food meet our standard.

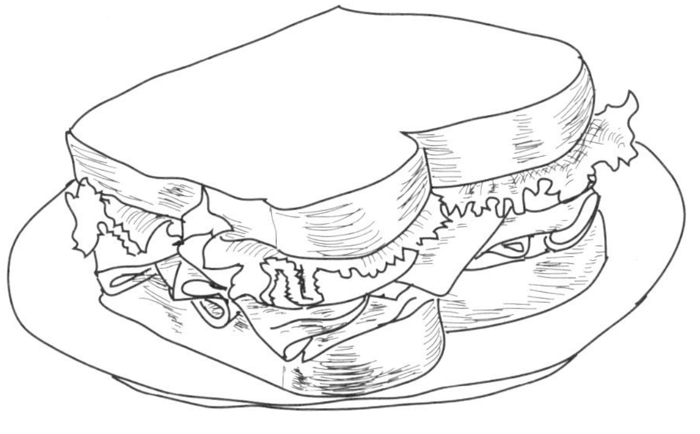

The standard of food of the People of the Book: Although our standard of food differs from the current standard of food by the People of the Book, many of their original standards were similar to ours. Some of their laws were more stringent than the dietary laws in Islam. Although the People of the Book changed many of the laws, the Old and New Testament still preserved many of the laws about proper food that are 'lawful' for them.

We will briefly study some of the laws in the Bible. Based the dietary laws in the Bible and Talmud, it becomes clear that meat sold in many Western supermarkets is forbidden even for the Jews and the Christians! If these meats are 'unlawful' to them, how can they be lawful for the Muslims?

Prohibited	Verses
Blood	Genesis 9:4; Leviticus 3:17; 19:26; Deuteronomy 12:16
Swine or pork	Leviticus 11:7; Deuteronomy 14:8
Animal that died by itself	Leviticus 11:39; Deuteronomy 14:21
Food offered to idols	1 Corinthian 8:1-13

Dietary laws in the Bible and Talmud: Since our objective here is to check what food is 'lawful' to the People of the Book, we will simply mention the laws and the sources in the Bible.

Methods of slaughter are given in detail in various Talmudic sources (see box in page 75).

Who slaughters the animals: In a predominantly Muslim majority country most of the slaughter houses are owned and operated by Muslims. To understand who slaughters animals in a Western supermarket, first we need to understand the demographics in the Western countries.

Over the past few decades the demographics in Europe and North America changed significantly due to migration of people. The societies in these courtiers are increasingly becoming multi-religious and multi-ethnic. People professing faith in Hinduism, Sikhism, Buddhism, Taoism, Confucianism, and many other tribal and polytheistic religions are migrating to western countries. At the same time, many exotic cults and alternative religious philosophies are emerging in America and Europe.

There is no guarantee that a person involved in the slaughterhouses in the West is indeed a Jew or a Christian. It is possible that the slaughterhouses will have at least one employee who is a follower of polytheistic religion or a cult member. It is also possible that some animals in these slaughterhouses are slaughtered by polytheists, or slaughtered without uttering any name, taking the name of an idol, or in some cases by uttering a curse or slur due to harshness involved in the business.

Does bismillah correct the lapse: We raised this question in the previous lesson, but we will raise the question again: does stating bismillah make a forbidden food lawful?

Clearly, uttering bismillah does not make a wine halāl to drink. The same rationale applies to meat also. If supermarket meat is not halāl, will saying bismillah make it halāl to eat? Let us take a look at the verse from sūrah An'am:

وَلَا تَأْكُلُوا مِمَّا لَمْ يُذْكَرِ اسْمُ اللَّهِ عَلَيْهِ
وَإِنَّهُ لَفِسْقٌ ۗ وَإِنَّ الشَّيَاطِينَ لَيُوحُونَ إِلَىٰ
أَوْلِيَائِهِمْ لِيُجَادِلُوكُمْ ۖ وَإِنْ أَطَعْتُمُوهُمْ إِنَّكُمْ
لَمُشْرِكُونَ ﴿١٢١﴾

And do not eat of that on which Allāh's name has not been mentioned, for it is surely a disobedience. And certainly the Shaitān will inspire their allies to dispute with you; and if you obey them, you will surely become polytheists. (6:121)

The instruction to declare Allāh's name in the verse and also in verse 6:118 is stated in past tense and in passive voice. This shows that the requirement to declare Allāh's name arises well before eating. The pronunciation of Allāh's name has to be made at the time of slaughtering—the time of taking the life away from the animal. Utmost care should be taken when taking away life, and utterance of Allāh's name help us to realize the seriousness of the process of killing an animal. We must remember that we cannot give life—only Allāh gives life, and He gave us permission to humanely kill an animal for food. Interestingly, the Qur'ān does put any kind of restriction on the dealing of the meat once the animal has been killed—grilling, baking, roasting, sizzling, frying or any other kind of cooking of the meat is allowed. The verse is not telling the Muslims that if Allāh's name was not pronounced at the time of slaughter, they can pronounce it at the time of eating. When the animal is already dead, how can we now make the killing process humane?

Hadīth of 'Ā'ishah (ra): What can we do when there is doubt if Allāh's name was pronounced at the time of slaughter?

A Hadīth of 'Ā'ishah is often quoted to settle the issue. Let us pay attention to the last sentence of the Hadīth:

A group of people said to the Prophet (S), "Some people brought us meat and we do not know whether they have mentioned Allāh's Name or not on slaughtering the animal." He said, "Mention Allāh's Name on it and eat." ***Those people had embraced Islam recently.*** (Narrated by Bukhāri, Abū Dawūd, Ibn Majah, Tirmidhī. Sahih Bukhāri, Volume 7, Book 67, Number 415)

This shows that these people were Muslims. As they embraced Islam recently, it was unclear whether they knew about the requirement to pronounce Allāh's name. Only on such a circumstance the Prophet (S) allowed them to eat meat by saying bismillah over it. This provision should not be generalized on meat purchased from supermarkets.

Fish, Fruits and vegetables: Food that do not contain meat are of a different category. All scholars agree that fish is halāl,[5:96] while some doubt that if a fish was dead before catching it is not halāl. Some scholars argue that a creature that live in and out of water, e.g., crabs and turtles, are harām. Some scholars consider a water-creature without scales, such as lobsters, shrimps, octopus, are doubtful or not encouraged as edible. Unless plant products are harmful or have not been offered to a deity, these are always permitted.

It is therefore safer for us to opt for fish dishes or salad when we are in a inter-religious group. However, many fish dishes in Western restaurants are cooked in wine. Some salad contain bacon bits. We have to be careful when we order our lunch or dinner. A quick check of the menu or a short question to the server can assure us of the content of the meal.

Saying Bismillah: We should always say bismillah before we eat anything. However, this does not turn a harām food to halāl. It helps us to acknowledge the blessings of Allāh in our lives.

Jewish regulation for slaughtering an animal:

Before slaughtering the slaughterer (shochet) must pronounce the blessing: Be praised our God, Ruler of the universe, who sanctifies us with commandments and commands us regarding the acts of slaughtering.

Slaughtering (shechitah) must be performed with a horizontal cut across the throat, severing the trachea and esophagus. The knife must be drawn quickly back and forth with no pausing. The slaughterer must spill the blood of the animal. The knife must be clean, smooth, without any dent and at least twice the length of the diameter of the animal's neck. Jewish tradition teaches them that the death of the animal should be as painless as possible. It prohibits cutting the throat in clumsy manner, or sawing it, or cutting or skinning them while the animal is still alive.

(See *A Guide to Jewish Religious Practice*, Jewish Theological Seminary, New York, 1979, pp. 307-312)

from**hadith**

Narrated Adi bin Hatim: I asked Allāh's Apostle. "We hunt with the help of these hounds." He said, "If you let loose your trained hounds after a game, and mention the name of Allāh, then you can eat what the hounds catch for you, even if they killed the game. But you should not eat of it if the hound has eaten of it, for then it is likely that the hound has caught the game for itself. And if other hounds join your hound in hunting the game, then do not eat of it." (Bukhāri).

Jundab b. Sufyan reported: I was with Allāh's Messenger (S) (on the occasion) of 'Id al-Adha. After he had completed the prayer with people, he found that the goats had been slaughtered, whereupon he said: He who slaughtered sacrificial animal before the prayer should slaughter a goat (again) instead and he who has not slaughtered he should slaughter it by reciting the name of Allāh. (Muslim).

Yahya related to me from Malik from Hisham ibn Urwa that his father said, "The Messenger of Allāh, may Allāh bless him and grant him peace, was asked, 'Messenger of Allāh! Some people from the desert bring us meat, and we do not know whether the name of Allāh has been mentioned over it or not.' The Messenger of Allāh, may Allāh bless him and grant him peace, said, 'Mention the name of Allāh over it and eat.' " Malik said, "That was in the beginning of Islam." (Muwatta of Malik).

homework**weekend 12**

1. Which sūrah has the verse that talks about food of the People of the Book is lawful?

....

2. Which of the following choices is correct when the Qur'ān says food of the People of the Book is lawful?

   a. All food offered by them are lawful.
   b. Only alcohol is unlawful but other food are lawful.
   c. Only lawful food offered by them are permitted.
   d. Saying Bismillah will make all of their food lawful.

3. Which of the following choices is correct about demographics in Europe and America?

   a. It is very homogenous with little diversity in religion and ethnicity.
   b. It is heterogeneous with diversity in religion and ethnicity.
   c. All immigrants are Muslims or People of the Book.
   d. Polytheists or cult members do not seek jobs in slaughterhouses.

4. Which two books in the Bible prohibit eating pork?

....

5. Which of the following choices is correct about the Hadīth of 'Ā'ishah narrated in the lesson?

   a. She asked the Prophet (S) whether the meat can be eaten.
   b. The Prophet said to eat the meat by pronouncing bismillah over it.
   c. She verified the religious faith of the Bedouin who brought the meat.
   d. She ate the meat but later asked the Prophet if it was forbidden.

6. Circle C for if the statement is correct, W if it is wrong.

Saying bismillah can turn a harām food into halāl.	C	W
Mentioning Allāh's name during slaughtering is mandatory.	C	W
To make a meat halāl, Allāh's name can be taken anytime during processing.	C	W
Only Allāh gives us permission to take away an animal's life.	C	W

7. Mark ☑ if the statement is correct, and mark ☒ if it is wrong.

a. A fish which was alive at the time of catch is halāl. ☐
b. Healthful plant products that have not been offered to a deity are halāl. ☐
c. A Jewish slaughterer is called a shochet. ☐
d. Muslims living in the West usually do not have a choice of food in a restaurant. ☐
e. Salad served in a Western restaurant may be halāl for Muslims. ☐
f. Some fish dishes served in a Western restaurant may contain wine. ☐

8. Read verse 6:121 (given in the lesson). Who argues with you to convince that it is OK to eat meat on which Allāh's name has not been mentioned.

....

9. List a few of the issues with Western slaughterhouses that may make a meat unlawful for consumption by the Muslims.

a. ....

b. ....

c. ....

10. From Islamic view point, circle the most important step in Jewish regulation of slaughtering an animal.

a. A blessing in God's name must be pronounced.
b. The cut across the throat must be horizontal.
c. The knife must be longer than the neck.
d. The knife must be drawn quickly.

classwork**weekend 13**

Khadījah (ra): *One of the Best Women Who Ever Lived*

Objective of the Lesson:

Khadījah (ra), the first wife of the Prophet (S), was an extraordinary woman. The purpose of the lesson is to describe the qualities of Khadījah that made her an ideal woman. The lesson will briefly describe the major incidents in her life that ultimately changed the way Islam was propagated.

In the 6th grade we studied about Khadījah (ra). In this lesson, we will analyze some of the traits that made Khadījah one of the greatest women to live on the earth. It is narrated that the Prophet (S) had said Khadījah, Fātimah, Maryam and Āsiyah, the wife of Pharaoh—were the four best women of the world. It is narrated in the Tradition of the Prophet (S) that Khadījah is one of the four women whom Allāh promised to grant Heaven.

Quick review of Khadījah: Khadījah bint Khuwaylid was the first wife of the Prophet (S). She was known as bint Khuwaylid or daughter of Khuwaylid of the clan of Asad. She was born in 555 C.E. She was fifteen years older than Muhammad (S). They were married in 595 C.E., fifteen years before the Prophet (S) received the first Divine revelation. They had six children born to them (some reports state that they had five children). She died in 619 C.E. shortly before the Prophet (S) 's migration to Madīnah.

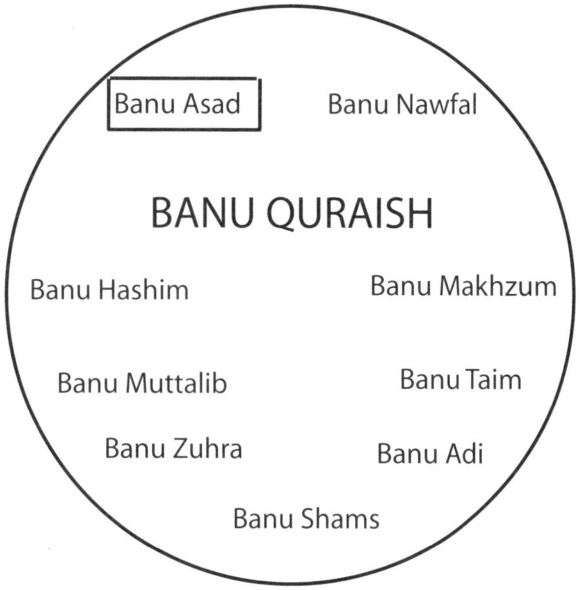

A prominent woman in Arabia: Khadījah's father was a trader, who had business in Yemen and Syria. After he died, Khadījah took over his business. At that time, women in Arabia hardly enjoyed any social or civil rights. Men would not honor them. Most women did not have any profession except to fulfill the roles of being a mother or a wife. In such a society, Khadījah stood as a solitary example of a woman who was respected by the males for being a successful business woman.

She was an example of righteousness, nobility and generosity all through her life, particularly during a period before the advent of Islam when women were

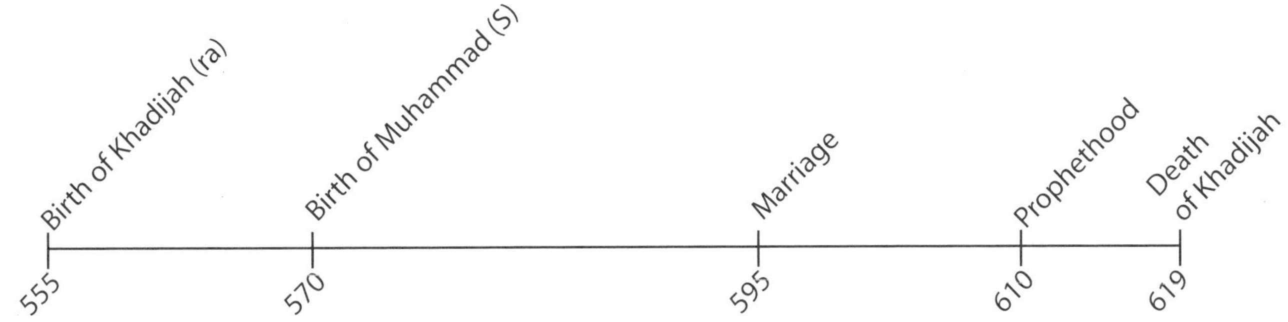

grossly abused or neglected. She was not only a successful businesswoman, but also a great humanitarian. During her married life with the Prophet (S), she emerged as an activist. An activist emphasizes or engages in vigorous action especially in support of or opposition of a cause. She supported the cause of Islam.

Woman of high moral: Her marriage with Muhammad (S) was unusual and unlike what the society was accustomed to see. When she proposed to Muhammad (S), she was forty years old, twice widowed and had a few children. At that time Muhammad (S) was a simple, young, unmarried man—without any wealth, societal position or authority. The society wondered why a noble, wealthy, aristocratic woman would ever want to marry such a person. Khadījah's decision to marry Muhammad (S) showed that she valued integrity, honesty and trustworthiness in a man. It was common at that time, as it is common today, to make marriage proposals based on wealth, physical appearance, social rank, etc., but the example of Khadījah showed some of the noble criteria for a successful marriage.

Marriage proposal: For one particular trade to Syria, Khadījah hired Muhammad (S) to manage the trade on her behalf. She knew the Quraish fondly named Muhammad (S) as ***al-āmīn***, or the trustworthy. Other than this qualification, Muhammad (S) did not have much experience in trade, but Khadījah knew that any lack of trade experience would be offset by his honesty.

Upon returning from Syria, Muhammad (S) handed over entire proceeds from the trade. He explained the trade and accounted for every dinar. Khadījah was impressed with his honesty and hardworking nature. Khadījah, twice widowed, had no desire to marry again. However, the qualities of Muhammad (S) impressed her much to consider a marriage. In selecting her husband, Khadījah exhibited astounding wisdom and sense of judgment. She left aside all earthly determinant of a person's worth and concentrated in the inner values in a person. As she always trusted these values, she remained a constant companion of Muhammad (S) during good times and difficult times. Their marriage prospered and became blissful due to mutual trust, respect, understanding and mercy. Their married life highlighted the ideals that all married couple should imitate. When couples lose one or all of these ideals from their marital life, their marriage suffers. The Qur'ān says:

> *And of His Signs is that He creates for you mates out of yourselves, so that you may find tranquility in them; and He has put love and mercy between you. Surely in this there are indeed Signs for a people who reflect. (30:21)*

Garment for each other: The Qur'ān says husband and wife are like garment for each other.[2:187] A garment provides comfort, honor and protection. The married life of Khadījah and Muhammad (S) is a perfect meaning of the verse.

When Muhammad (S) first received the revelation from Allāh, he retuned home with extreme fear and distress. At that time Khadījah comforted him and assured him that the experience was not satanic but Divine. She trusted him and supported him. Later when Muhammad (S) realized that he had been given the great responsibility of conveying the Divine message to the mankind, he found Khadījah was there with him during the challenging times.

She was truly a garment for Muhammad (S) as she covered him, literally with a cloak when he returned from **Cave Hira**, and later supported him morally and emotionally when entire Arabia refused to listen to the message. Just as a garment, Khadījah too shielded Muhammad (S) against physical, emotional and psychological hardship throughout their marriage.

Her dedication and trust in her husband is exemplified through various incidents. After Allāh ordered Muhammad (S) to publicly declare the call to Islam, the Prophet (S) first came to Khadījah, asking her to respond to the call. She immediately replied that she would be the first to believe in what he was saying and accept the call of Islam. It is important to note that the first person to embrace Islam was a woman.

Now, with her acceptance of Islam, her position among the Quraish deteriorated: instead of

receiving respect, she became a target of ridicule and intense hate. She knew she and her husband were in a mission against the authorities and established social system. She stood by her husband in every walk of his life as long as she lived. Her ability to support a revolution and stand against the established social system came from her earlier decision in her life. When she decided to marry the most unlikely candidate, she proved she had the ability to go against the established trend. Just as her decision to marry Muhammad (S) was full of wisdom, her decision to stand by her husband, when he became a Prophet (S), was full of wisdom.

Social boycott: The married life of Khadījah and Muhammad (S) had many difficulties. As Islam continued to make inroads in Makkah, the polytheists became increasingly hostile towards the Prophet (S), his family and the believers. The worst situation was in 615 C.E. when the polytheists economically and socially boycotted the Muslims. Most of the Muslims were forced to go outside of the city limits and live there as socially boycotted class of people. Being a woman of noble status, Khadījah never knew what it meant to be discarded or boycotted. Being a woman of wealth, she was rather a stranger to the life of poverty. However, she willingly abandoned her home and went to live with the Prophet (S) and the rest of the believers.

Her resilience, patience and steadfastness provided great lessons to those who faced adversity and difficulty in their lives. If she had not demonstrated these extraordinary qualities, the life of the Prophet (S) would have been even more difficult. Khadījah truly reflected the teachings of the Qur'ān, to seek help from Allāh with patience and perseverance.[10:109; 11:11,112,115; 13:22; 16:126-127] She found immense inner strength and tranquility of mind from having absolute faith in Allāh. The Qur'ān glorifies these types of character attributes when it says:

> *Surely as to those who say: "Our Rabb is Allāh", then stand straightforward, the angels descend upon them, saying: "Do not fear and do not grieve, rather be glad with the Garden that you were promised. (41:30)*
>
> *Surely as to those who say, 'Our Rabb is Allāh,and then remain firm(in their Faith) – then no fear upon them, nor shall they grieve. (46:13)*

Khadījah truly demonstrated these values with her entire life. During the years of boycott, she spent all her wealth to buy essentials like food and water for the Muslims. After the boycott was over and she returned to her house, her last bit of wealth was exhausted. When she died, there was not even enough money available in the house to buy a shroud for her funeral. Such was the level of philanthropy and the level of her commitment.

The bond between Khadījah and Muhammad (S) increased during good times and difficult times in their life. Their love and mercy did not wane due to hardship in life, instead strengthened them. Her death in the year 619 C.E. saddened the Prophet (S) so much that his biographers named that year as **The Year of Sorrow.** This was more so since his beloved uncle Abu Tālib, too, died in the same year.

After her death: Even after Khadījah passed away, the Prophet (S) continued to remember her with love, honor and compassion. It is narrated that if a gift was brought to him, he would immediately send it to a woman who used to be a friend of Khadījah. It is also narrated that at another time Khadījah's sister, **Halah**, came to the see the Prophet (S). When she called him out, his face suddenly changed color as Halah's voice reminded him of Khadījah. Whenever a goat was slaughtered in his household, the Prophet (S) would send some meat to Khadījah's friends saying, "I have great regard for her friends, as she has a special place in my heart." It is narrated the Prophet (S) had told, "she believed in me when nobody else did; she accepted Islam when people rejected me; she gave me children, and she helped me and comforted me through her person and wealth when there was no one else to lend me a helping hand."

Points to know:

- Khadījah was the Prophet's (S) wife for about 25 years until her death.
- Together Khadījah and Muhammad (S) had 6 (or 5) children born to them.
- Their first child was a boy, named Qasim. He died when he was only 2 years old.
- Ruqayyah and Umm Kulthum were married to two sons of Abū Lahab, the bitter enemy of the Prophet (S).
- Both the daughters were divorced/widowed. Uthman ibn 'Affān married Ruqayyah. After she died, Uthman married Umm Kulthum.
- Fātimah was married to 'Ali ibn Abū Tālib.
- All of the Prophet's (S) children died before his death, except Fātimah, who died six moths after the Prophet's death.

homework**weekend 13**

1. What was the complete name of the Prophet's (S) first wife?

   Khadījah bint ....

2. Khadījah was born in 555 C.E. According to Hijrah calendar, in which year was she born?

   .... B.H. / A.H.

3. Using Common Era calendar (C.E.) and Hijrah calendar (B.H. or A.H.) write the year in which Khadījah married the Prophet (S) and the year that she passed away.

   Marriage .... C.E. Death .... C.E.

   Marriage .... B.H. / A.H. Death .... B.H./ A.H.

4. Based on what you read in the chapter, Khadījah had various traits in her personality. In your own words, describe her patience and perseverance.

   ....

   ....

   ....

5. Some of the following choices correctly reflect Khadījah's decision to marry young Muhammad (S). Mark ☑ if the statement is correct, and mark ☒ if it is wrong. The decision was:

   a. to monopolize the business in Syria. ☐
   b. politically and financially motivated. ☐
   c. to help Muhammad (S) since he was an orphan. ☐
   d. out of respect towards an honest, upright and sincere person. ☐
   e. to become the wife of a person who was a prophet. ☐

6. As a rich and aristocrat woman in Arabia, Khadījah could have married any influential and rich man. Instead, Khadījah was encouraged to marry Muhammad (S) for several of his qualities. Write three of these qualities in the spaces below

   ....

7. One of the following incidents made Khadījah sick and due to the sickness she eventually passed away. What was that incident?

a. Three years of social boycott by the Quraish.
b. Injury suffered during migration to Madīnah.
c. Injury suffered in the battle of Badr.
d. Overall poverty and marital discord with her husband.
e. Trade in Syria.

8. Khadījah emphasized or engaged in direct vigorous action in support of Islam and opposed all un-Islamic activities. Therefore, according to the classwork material she could be called as a/an:

a. Reformer.
b. Preacher.
c. Activist.
d. Feminist.
e. Philanthropist.

9. What was/were unusual about Khadījah's desire to marry Muhammad (S)?

a. The marriage proposal was made by a woman rather than the other way round.
b. A wealthy woman wishing to marry a poor person who had no power or authority.
c. The age difference between Khadījah and Muhammad (S).
d. Twice divorced, mother of many children, wishing to marry an unmarried person.
e. All of the above.

10. During the social boycott of the Muslims, how did Khadījah help in the progress of Islam?

....

....

....

classwork**weekend 14**

Prophet (S)'s Multiple Marriages

Objective of the Lesson:

The Prophet (S) married thirteen women in his life. The significance of these marriages is sometimes misunderstood by everybody. In Western writing these marriages are, at times, discussed in poor taste. This lesson discusses why and under what circumstances the Prophet (S) married these women. This information will help students understand the issue in the right perspective.

Prophet Muhammad (S) was strict bachelor for his first twenty-five years of his life. Once married to Khadījah (ra), he led a monogamous life for next twenty-five years. At one particular phase in his life, Muhammad (S) had married several women. In this lesson we will try to understand the significance behind the Prophet (S)'s thirteen marriages.

We will find that Muhammad (S) was not a lustful man, rather he committed to these marriages for higher objectives.

Accepted custom in Arabia: At the time of Muhammad (S), it was acceptable custom to marry very young girls, or to marry two sisters at the same time. Some men would marry their step-mothers when their fathers died, to prevent others from inheriting the property. Marrying a widow was acceptable, but most men would not when unmarried women were available. Most men would marry women younger to them; hardly anyone would marry women who were older.

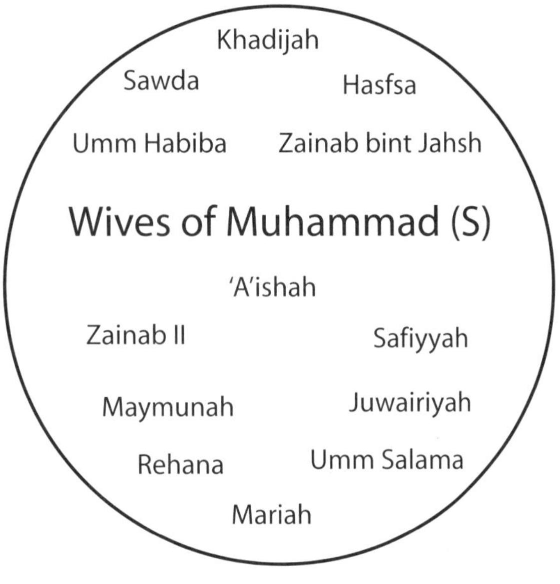

The prophet's marriages were "out of normal": In any society, marriage is an important event and helps in building the society. Therefore, Prophet (S) used his own life to show the acceptable variations of marriage. All the marriages in the Prophet (S)'s life were "out of ordinary" or "out of normal". By understanding the phrase "out of normal", the significance of the multiple marriages in the Prophet (S)'s life will become easy to understand.

In all the marriages we can see that the Prophet (S) did not follow the usual or the accepted standard of that time. When it was customary for a man to marry multiple women, during his prime youthful life the Prophet (S) was married to one wife Khadījah for long twenty-five years. When it was customary for men to marry younger, unmarried women, the Prophet (S) not only married a widow, but also a widow who was fifteen years older than him. A common Arab at the time of the Prophet (S) would not have married an older woman. Prophet (S) set an example, and his action was "out of normal". If he was a lustful person, he could have easily married a number of young women during his youthful life. Nobody would have frowned, since it was the accepted custom of that time.

Custom and practice changes: We often fail to notice many of the customs and practices in the same geographic area undergo significant change over a period of time. In a matter of few decades, many practices become unacceptable. In the United States about one hundred years ago most women stayed home, raised children and did not care for education. The thought of a woman taking a job was unusual, if not abnormal. Whereas today every woman cares for education and most would prefer to work outside the home. If we attempt to judge cultural tendencies in the past with the mind set of today, it is possible that we might end up with wrong conclusions.

The first two marriages: The first marriage of the Prophet (S) was with Khadījah, a forty years old widow. In today's context, a woman of forty years age is not old, but in the seventh century Arabia she would certainly be considered an old lady. At the same time, twenty-five year old Muhammad (S) was at peak of his youth.

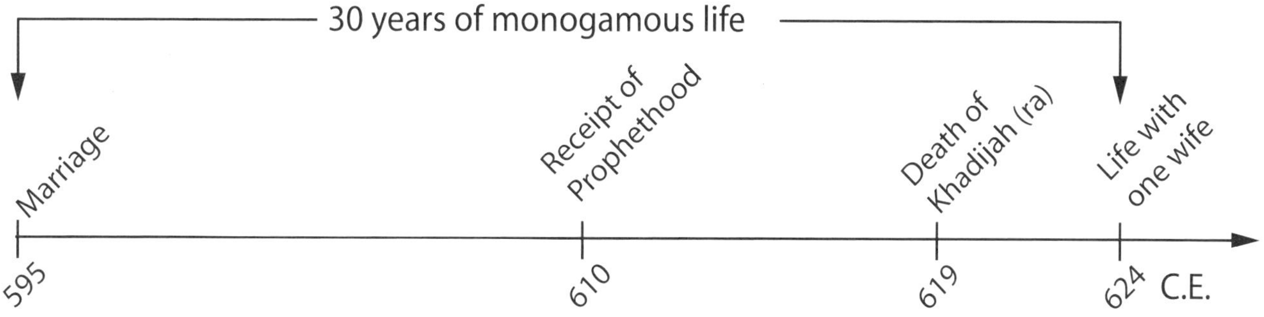

The Prophet (S) lived a happily married life with Khadījah for twenty-five long years and had six (or five) children born to them. During these twenty-five years of married life, if the Prophet (S) had wanted, he could have easily married other women. The fact that he did not marry other women during this period indicates the Prophet (S) was not a lustful person. When the Prophet (S) was fifty years old, his beloved wife Khadījah passed away. At that time Khadījah was sixty five years old.

After the death of Khadījah, the Prophet (S) felt a pressing need for a woman in his household to take care of his young children. If the Prophet (S) had any desire to marry a younger woman, he could have easily married one. He decided to marry Sawdah bint Zama'ah (ra), who happened to be a widow and a year older to him. He lived with Sawdah for five years in a monogamous married life. Thus, from the time of his first marriage with Khadījah until the end of the five years with Sawdah, the Prophet (S) was leading a monogamous life for thirty years.

Multiple marriages: Soon after Khadījah passed away, the Prophet (S) had to migrate to Madīnah. Thus, the first five years of married life with Sawdah was spent at Madīnah. Once the Prophet (S) was in Madīnah, his life was constantly embroiled in one battle after another. In these battles many of the companions were martyred. In Uhud alone, about seventy believers were martyred. Many of these believers were married men. Upon their martyrdom their wives became widows and the children became orphans. It was obligatory upon all Muslims to take care of the widows and the children financially and emotionally.

On the face of this unprecedented situation arising from the first two battles, the Prophet (S) felt an obligation to set an example to support the widows by volunteering to marry some of them and encouraging other believers to do the same. The Prophet (S) volunteered to marry wives of prominent companions, who were early converts and who contributed to the advancement of the religion. Thus, he set an example of solidarity and support to the destitute women.

a great show of courage and sacrifice for Umm Habiba to accept Islam when her family was strictly against Islam. She was one of the two women who migrated to Abyssinia to escape from persecution. Her husband was martyred in the battle of Uhud.

Hafsa bint 'Umar: She was the daughter of 'Umar ibn Al-Khattāb, one of the closest and prominent companions of the Prophet (S). When her husband was martyred in the battle of Badr, 'Umar (ra)

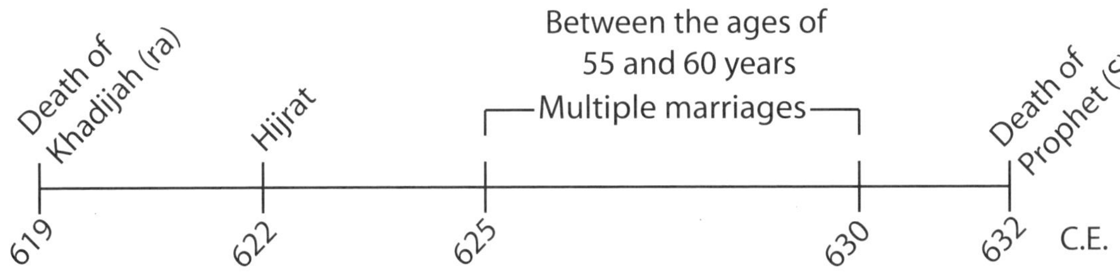

When the Prophet (S) was still married to Sawdah, he decided to marry Hafsa. This marriage took place when the Prophet (S) was 55 years old. Between 55 and 60 years of age, he married eleven women. However, his household never had these eleven noble women all at the same time. Many of them died due to illness or other natural causes. His household, according to most scholars, never had more than five wives at the same time. All these marriages can be broadly categorized under two headers: (a) honor marriages and (b) political marriages.

Honor marriages:

The honor marriages took place in order to honor the widows of the martyr-companions by taking them as wives in the honorable household of the Prophet (S). Most of these marriages can also be viewed as a social obligation on the Prophet (S).

The Qur'ān honors all the wives of the Prophet (S) by stating that they are symbolic "Mothers of all Believers" or *Ummul Muminum.*[33:6] It is truly a great honor for all the wives of the Prophet (S).

Umm Habiba (ra) : Umm Habiba was the daughter of Abū Sufyān, who was once one of the most prominent enemies of the Prophet (S). It was

first asked 'Uthmān and then Abū Bakr to marry her. Ultimately the Prophet (S) honored her by marrying her.

Zainab bint Jahsh (ra): She was a cousin of the Prophet (S). Her first marriage was with Zaid, who was once a slave of Khadījah and an adopted son of Muhammad (S). The Prophet (S) had arranged the marriage of Zainab with Zaid. This marriage was divinely ordained.[33:36] This marriage ended in a divorce. At that point, it was divinely ordered that the Prophet (S) marry Zainab. The wife of a former slave was now a wife of the Prophet (S)! This marriage also clarified one important issue that adopted sons are not equal to biological sons. If Zaid was the Prophet (S)'s biological son, he could not have married Zainab, since she would have been covered by prohibited marriage relations.[4:22-24] We will learn more about this marriage in the next lesson.

Umm Salamah (ra): In the battle of Uhud, Umm Salama's husband became a martyr. She was left with an infant daughter. The Prophet (S) married her to give shelter and honor her martyred husband.

Zainab bint Khuzaymah (ra): Because of her kind nature, she used to be known as *Umm al-Masākīn* (mother of the poor). When her husband became a martyr, she became helpless. The Prophet (S) married her and sheltered her against poverty and difficulty. She was weak and within a few months she passed away.

Rayhanah bint Zayd (ra): Rayhanah was the wife of the chief of the Jewish tribe Banu Qurayzah. In an uprising against the Muslims, many male members of Banu Qurayzah including the chief of their tribe were killed. She was taken as a captive during the encounter. When the Prophet (S) offered to marry her, she initially hesitated but later agreed. Her married life with the Prophet (S) was short lived as she passed away within a short time.

'Āishah Siddiqah (ra): She was the daughter of Abū Bakr. The Prophet (S) married her at the request of Abū Bakr, a good friend and one of the earliest Muslim.

Political marriages:

The Prophet (S) contracted four marriages for political reasons, to diffuse animosity and to establish friendly ties with hostile non-Muslim communities.

Juwairīyah bint Hārith (ra): She was the daughter of the chief of the Jewish tribe Banu Mustalaq. She was taken as a captive by the Muslims during one of the expeditions. She wanted freedom and asked the Prophet (S) to help her with ransom money. Prophet (S) helped with the ransom, and then raised her status even further by proposing to her. This marriage ended the enmity with the tribe. This action motivated the Muslims so much that they released about 600 captives.

Safiyyah bint Hayī (ra) : She was a widow of Kinānah, the Jewish chief of Banu Nadīr. Her husband was killed in the war of Khaibar. When she became a captive of a Muslim soldier, Muhammad (S) raised her status by marrying her. This marriage had a lasting effect in the relationship with the tribe. She was a learned lady, and used to help the needy.

Maimunah bint Hārith (ra): The Prophet's (S) marriage with her brought good relations with the Makkans. She was from the tribe of Hawazins against whom the Muslims fought a war. Her nephew was great warrior Khālid bin Walīd, who accepted Islam after Maimunah was married to the Prophet (S).

Mariah al-Qibtiyya (ra): She was sent as a gift by the Christian governor of Egypt. Marriage with Mariah paved the way for cordial ties with the Christian territories in Africa. Before marriage she believed in Coptic faith, a denomination of the Christians.

After the Treaty of Hudaibiyah in the 6th year of Hijri (628 C.E.), peace prevailed in entire Arabia. As the socio-political situation in Arabia stabilized, the need for the Prophet (S) to marry additional women also ended. Through a Qur'ānic revelation the Prophet (S) was told he could no more marry additional women.[33:52] When this revelation came, the Prophet (S) was 60 years old.

Many of the Prophet's (S) wives were very learned. Muslim women came to know about the Prophet's (S) private life through his wives—particularly about marital relationship, role of women in family, how to maintain honor and dignity of family, how to deal with relatives and neighbors, etc.

The Qur'ān recognizes that these women were extraordinary in many ways. Verse 33:32 states: *O wives of the Nabi! You are not like anyone of the (other) women.* They were embodiment of virtue, value, moral and pride for Muslim community at the time of the Prophet (S) and even today.

Interesting Facts

Before her marriage with Prophet Muhammad (S), Khadījah was twice married and widowed.

Other than Khadījah, Mariah was the only other wife to give birth to a child of the Prophet (S).

Umm Habiba was the daughter of Abū Sufyān.

'A'ishah was the only wife of the Prophet (S) who was never married before.

homework**weekend 14**

1. Although Muhammad (S) married several women, what characteristics of these marriages show that he was not a lustful man?

....

....

....

2. Explain why Muhammad (S)'s marriage to Khadījah was 'out of normal'?

....

....

....

3. After the Prophet (S)'s first wife died, he married an elderly lady. Who was she, and what was the reason for this marriage?

....

4. Of the wives of the Prophet (S), two wives were fortunate to see their fathers become khalīfas. Who are these two wives?

....

5. Read verse 66:5. List the six virtues of the wives of Muhammad (S)?

A. .... B. ....

C. .... D. ....

E. .... F. ....

6. Read Sūrah Al-Ahzāb, verse 28. If the wives wanted comfort and glitter of this world, how should Muhammad (S) deal with them?

....

7. Read Sūrah Al-Ahzāb, verse 29. If the wives wanted Allāh and His messenger, what does Allāh reserve for them?

....

8. Which of the following statement(s) is true about the accepted norm in Arabia at the time when the Qur'ān was being revealed? Mark ☑ if the statement is correct, and mark ☒ if it is wrong.

a. A man was allowed to marry young girls who were not married earlier. ☐

b. A man was allowed to marry two sisters at the same time. ☐

c. A man would marry his step mother when his father died. ☐

d. A man would marry any number of women as and when he liked. ☐

9. The Prophet (S) led a monogamous life for long .... years.

10. When Khadījah died, she was .... years old woman.

classwork**weekend 15**

Marriage with Zainab (ra)

Objective of the Lesson:

Zainab (ra) was the wife of the Prophet's (S) adopted son. When the son divorced her, the Prophet (S) married her, resulting in quite a bit of misunderstanding in the community. A revelation was sent to approve the marriage with the Prophet (S). This lesson discusses the issues relating to the marriage.

Of the multiple marriages of Muhammad (S), the marriage with Zainab bint Jahsh (ra) is often misunderstood and misinterpreted. Hostile critics of Islam cite this marriage to vilify the Prophet (S). The Prophet's (S) marriage with Zainab is significant since she was his 'daughter-in-law' at one time. How could a 'father-in-law' marry his 'daughter-in-law'? It seemed to puzzle many. We will analyze verses 36-38 of sūrah Al-Ahzāb to understand the background and purpose of this marriage.

Adopted son Zaid: Long before Muhammad (S) was selected to become a prophet, his first wife Khadījah (ra) brought a young slave by the name of Zaid ibn Hārith (r). Muhammad (S) had freed Zaid and adopted him as his son. Zaid was of African origin, and by adopting him Muhammad (S) set an example against racism. This action proved the great foresight of Muhammad (S) even before he became a prophet. We know from the life of Muhammad (S) that he had also honored another African person, Bilāl (r), who was the earliest muadhdhin. However, for some people the skin color of Zaid made him unsuitable to be a son of a Quraish.

Zainab's marriage with Zaid: When the Prophet (S) received the first revelation, Zaid was one of the earliest to believe in him and become a Muslim. Even though Zaid was a freedman, an adopted son of the Prophet (S) and a Muslim, there was a stigma about him that continued to haunt him. People would hesitate to socialize with a former slave and accept him as equal to them.

Zainab bint Jahsh, on the other hand, was unmarried beautiful young lady of noble descent. She was the Prophet's (S) cousin, a Quraish woman, and respected for her heritage. For such an eligible bride, the Prophet (S) selected a righteous person, Zaid. Again, by this action Muhammad (S) showed that race should not be a criterion in selecting a spouse. He valued character, faith and righteousness as the most important criteria for this marriage.

Verse 36 of sūrah Al-Ahzāb (Table 1) refers to this decision of the Prophet (S) by stating that it was a decision made by Allāh and His Prophet (S). When the marriage negotiations were being made, Zainab and her brothers wanted the Prophet (S) himself to marry her. However, the Prophet (S) was not aware of their wish. When the proposal for Zaid's marriage was finalized and presented to Zainab, she gave her consent thinking that it was a proposal to become the Prophet's (S) wife. Since the decision of the marriage was divinely planned, irrespective of any misinterpretation from any party, believing men and women are required to obey the divine plan. Analysis of the verse shows the point.

After Zainab understood the proposal was about marrying Zaid, she and her brothers were disappointed because their wish for the Prophet (S) to marry her would not be fulfilled. If Zainab and her brothers had rejected the proposal after agreeing to it, the Prophet (S) could not have compelled them to the agreement. At that point the above verse was revealed to clarify the situation and settle any misunderstanding.

Misunderstanding: The marriage that started with misunderstanding never turned into a loving relationship between the two. Historians mentioned that Zainab had disliking for Zaid for various reasons, mainly for his former status of being a slave. Both of them lived for a while as a married couple, but at one point Zaid decided to divorce Zainab.

What was being 'concealed': The true meaning of verse 37 appears confusing to many readers. Some early Arabic writings, likely to be generated by the enemies of Islam, indicate that the Prophet (S) had a secret desire in his heart towards Zainab, but he feared the society. This theory comes from the sentence mentioned in verse 37, where it says: *"and*

Table 1: Explanation of the meaning of verse 33:36

وَمَا كَانَ لِمُؤْمِنٍ وَّلَا مُؤْمِنَةٍ إِذَا قَضَى اللّٰهُ وَرَسُوْلُهٗٓ اَمْرًا اَنْ يَّكُوْنَ لَهُمُ الْخِيَرَةُ مِنْ
اَمْرِهِمْ ؕ وَمَنْ يَّعْصِ اللّٰهَ وَرَسُوْلَهٗ فَقَدْ ضَلَّ ضَلٰلًا مُّبِيْنًا ﴿٣٦﴾

And it is neither for a believing man nor for a believing woman, when Allāh and His Rasul have decided an affair, that they should have any choice in their affair. And whoever disobeys Allāh and His Rasul, then surely he has strayed off a clear error.

And it is neither (fit) for a:	
believing man	Zainab's brothers.
nor for a believing woman,	Zainab herself.
when Allāh and His Rasul have decided an affair	the marriage of Zainab with Zaid. This was clearly a decision of Allāh, abided by the Prophet (S).
that they should have any choice in their affair.	Zainab or her brothers should have any different choice in the matter of marriage, e.g. their wish that Prophet (S) should marry her instead.
And whoever disobeys Allāh and His Rasul, then surely he has strayed off a clear error.	disobeying the plan of Allāh and the Messenger would be a serious offence.

you were concealing in your mind that which Allāh was going to disclose, and you feared people, while Allāh has a greater right that you should fear Him."

Some early writers believed the pronoun "you" in the above sentence refers to the Prophet (S). If this thesis is accepted, then the meaning of the verse would be: the Prophet (S) was concealing in his mind that which Allāh was going to disclose, and the Prophet (S) feared people, while Allāh has a greater right that the Prophet (S) should fear Him. However this is a flawed interpretation as explained below:

Error in interpretation: First of all, the above interpretation indicates that the Prophet (S) was attracted to someone else's wife and developed a secret desire towards her. As if he wanted to have this woman as his own wife, but after thinking about the gravity of the situation, he was afraid of the people. Therefore, Allāh had to caution him by saying that Allāh has a greater right that he should fear Him rather than the people.

There are serious flaws in the above interpretation. Islam strictly condemns staring at other women. It is impossible that the Prophet (S) would demonstrate such a conduct. This sūrah was revealed in Madīnah, when Muhammad (S) was already a Prophet (S) for about 15 years. It is impossible that at this stage Allāh had to caution the Prophet (S) that he should fear Allāh rather than the people. In addition, the sentence is continuous with the previous text that Muhammad (S) is asking Zaid to keep his wife. In this sentence, Muhammad (S) continues his advice to Zaid that Zaid should not conceal the thought of divorce by fearing people.

Analysis of verse 37: Let us split the verse into individual parts (Table 2) and understand the implications of each part:

Zaid tried to hide the marital discord from everybody. He was unable to live in the family under the constant disliking expressed by Zainab, yet he was unable to let her go for fear of public reaction. He was afraid that people might criticize a marriage arranged and sponsored by the Prophet (S) turned out unsuccessful. He was afraid it would bring shame upon the Prophet (S) and also to his wife. As Zaid was fearful of public reaction, Allāh revealed that he should be fearful of Allāh rather than the people.

Prophet (S)'s marriage with Zainab: A divorced woman must wait for the mandatory period of three months, called *'iddat*, before she can remarry.[2:228; 65:4] If she is carrying a baby, the period of *'iddat* is until she delivers the baby.[2:228; 65:4] In case of Zainab, after three months of *'iddat* she became eligible to remarry. Just as her first marriage was divinely ordained, her next marriage was also divinely ordained. The Prophet (S) did not actively desire to marry her.

مَا كَانَ عَلَى النَّبِيِّ مِنْ حَرَجٍ فِيمَا فَرَضَ
اللَّهُ لَهُ ۖ سُنَّةَ اللَّهِ فِي الَّذِينَ خَلَوْا مِنْ
قَبْلُ ۚ وَكَانَ أَمْرُ اللَّهِ قَدَرًا مَّقْدُورًا ﴿٣٨﴾

There is no barrier upon the Nabi with what Allāh has ordained for him. The manner of Allāh regarding those who have preceded of old. For, the command of Allāh is a decree determined— (33:38)

Verse 38 says there is no barrier upon the Prophet (S) with what Allāh has ordained for him. The removal of barrier refers to the established custom in Arabia to consider the adopted son in equal footing with a biological son. In Islam adopted sons are not the same as biological sons.[33:4-6] In Islam adopted sons (or daughters) do not create 'blood' relations, therefore, marriage of such children does not create relationships as would result from biological parent-children relationships.[4:22-24] Through the divine intervention, Prophet (S)'s marriage with Zainab clarified the positions of adopted and biological children.

Table 2: Explanation of the meaning of verse 33:37

وَإِذْ تَقُولُ لِلَّذِيٓ أَنْعَمَ اللّٰهُ عَلَيْهِ وَأَنْعَمْتَ عَلَيْهِ أَمْسِكْ عَلَيْكَ زَوْجَكَ وَاتَّقِ اللّٰهَ وَ
تُخْفِي فِي نَفْسِكَ مَا اللّٰهُ مُبْدِيهِ وَتَخْشَى النَّاسَ ج وَاللّٰهُ أَحَقُّ أَنْ تَخْشٰهُ ط فَلَمَّا قَضٰى
زَيْدٌ مِّنْهَا وَطَرًا زَوَّجْنٰكَهَا لِكَيْ لَا يَكُونَ عَلَى الْمُؤْمِنِينَ حَرَجٌ فِيٓ أَزْوَاجِ أَدْعِيَآئِهِمْ
إِذَا قَضَوْا مِنْهُنَّ وَطَرًا ط وَكَانَ أَمْرُ اللّٰهِ مَفْعُولًا ﴿٣٧﴾

And remember, you did say to him whom Allāh had favored and whom you have favored: "Keep your wife with yourself, and revere Allāh; and you were concealing in your mind that which Allāh was going to disclose, and you were fearing people, while Allāh has a greater right that you should fear Him." But when Zaid decided on the marriage-tie from her, We married her with you, so that there might not be any barrier upon the Believers in the wives of their adopted sons, when they have decided on the marriage-tie from them. And Allāh's command is bound to be carried out.

And remember, you did say to him	The Prophet (S) said to Zaid.
whom Allāh had favored and whom you have favored:	Allāh had favored Zaid by giving the gift of Islam, and the Prophet (S) had favored by freeing him from slavery and adopting him as his son.
"Keep your wife with yourself, and revere Allāh;	The Prophet (S) told Zaid to keep his wife with him and fear Allāh as Zaid was contemplating divorce.
and you were concealing in your mind that which Allāh was going to disclose,	The addressee is Zaid who was concealing in his mind the thought of possible divorce. No matter how much he was trying to show there was no marital discord, Allāh would disclose it.
and you feared people, while Allāh has a greater right that you should fear Him."	Zaid, not the Prophet (S), feared people since he thought community would criticize that a marriage arranged by the Prophet (S) turned out unsuccessful.
But when Zaid decided on the marriage-tie from her, We married her with you,	After Zaid broke the marital ties and after the end of 'Iddat, Muhammad (S) married Zainab as an obligation (*fard*) mentioned in v. 38.
so that there might not be any barrier upon the Believers in the wives of their adopted sons, when they have decided on the marriage-tie from them.	The divine plan was to clarify from the life of the Prophet (S) that blood relations and adoptive relations are not held in the same footing in Islam.[33:4-6] Since adopted sons (or daughters) do not create 'blood' relations, marriage of such children does not create relationships as would result from biological parent-children relationships.[4:22-24]
And Allāh's command is bound to be carried out.	

homework**weekend 15**

1. As a groom for Zainab, what were the qualities of Zaid?

....

....

2. As a bride for Zaid, what were the qualities of Zainab?

....

....

3. Why were the brothers of Zainab not quite happy with the marriage of Zainab and Zaid?

....

....

4. Why did the marriage of Zaid and Zainab end up in divorce?

....

....

5. Based on the lesson, some of the following choices correctly describes the marital relationship between Zaid and Zainab. Mark ☑ if the statement is correct, and mark ☒ if it is wrong.

   a. Their married life was very happy. ☐
   b. Their married life was marred by Zaid's disliking of Zainab. ☐
   c. Their married life was blemished by Zainab's disliking of Zaid. ☐
   d. Their marriage was spoiled by the Prophet's (S) secret desire to marry Zainab. ☐

6. About Zainab's marriage, mark ☑ if the statement is correct, and mark ☒ if it is wrong.

   a. Only the marriage with Zaid was divinely ordained. ☐
   b. Only the marriage with the Prophet (S) was divinely ordained. ☐
   c. Marriages with Zaid and later with the Prophet (S) were divinely ordained. ☐

7. According to the lesson, who was concealing something that Allāh would disclose?

a. The Prophet (S).
b. Zaid.
c. People.
d. Zainab's brothers.
e. Zainab.

8. After Zainab was divorced by Zaid, why was the Prophet (S) obligated (*fard*) to marry her?

....

....

9. Write in one sentence the main social issue that was conclusively established from the marriage between the Prophet (S) and Zainab.

....

....

10. Prophet (S) had a secret desire towards Zainab. True / False

classwork**weekend 16**

The Prophet (S): *A Great General of Army*

Objective of the Lesson:

The military success of the early Muslims was largely due to the able leadership of the Prophet (S). He always fought from the position of disadvantage, yet he was very successful. This lesson discusses some of the military strategies of the Prophet (S) to show that he was also an excellent General of Army.

In a matter of a single decade, between 622 C.E. and 632 C.E., Prophet Muhammad (S) fought eight major battles, led about eighteen raids and planned another thirty-eight military operations in which he appointed his sahābas to command. He was wounded twice, nearly died once, and nearly suffered defeat twice. Although the role of Muhammad (S) as a prophet and a messenger is extensively studied, his accomplishment as a remarkable general of army is often overlooked. This is because his role as a prophet far outweighs his participation in the battles. He never wanted war. All the wars were thrust upon him by his enemies. As a leader of the emerging Muslim community, Muhammad (S) was responsible for success in the wars. Otherwise, the small community would have perished.

General of the Army is a relatively new term, used to denote the highest military rank of a nation's army. He is the commander of the army. The rank is equivalent to Marshal or Field Marshal. The Prophet (S) did not assign himself such a title, but his achievements show he was by all means a General of the Army.

No experience in warfare: The Prophet (S) started with no formal military experience. During his childhood nobody trained him in the basic warfare. He did not learn archery, sword fighting, wrestling or any other combat training that most Arab fathers provided their children. He did not participate in any tribal warfare either.

When the Prophet (S) was compelled to engage in raids or battles, he consulted experienced warriors and sought their advice. He always appointed his good warriors to lead small groups of army. He chose his military commanders on the basis of their experience and skill, and not on the basis of their closeness to him. He quickly grasped the strategic advantage in a battlefield and made the best use of it. He could see the bigger picture and work towards achieving the bigger objectives.

Negotiation for Madīnah: When Makkah became hostile, the Prophet (S) chose Madīnah as his base. He had to carefully negotiate and work out a methodology to ensure that Madīnah would be safe for Muslims. There were strategic advantages for selecting Madīnah. This city was sufficiently far from Makkah to freely propagate Islam, his main mission. Madīnah was close to the trade route that connected Makkah with Syria. This route was the lifeline for the Makkans for their economic prosperity. This route was also used by other Bedouins. Political alliance with the Bedouins and control of this route put an economic embargo on Makkah. These helped Muhammad (S) in his eventual success over the Makkans.

Constitution of Madīnah: Soon after migrating to Madīnah the Prophet (S) drafted an agreement between him and all the important tribes in and around Madīnah. The genius of the Prophet (S) clearly emerges from the concept, formulation and declaration of the constitution. The constitution provided the Muslims security, religious freedom, and stable society while it also established specific rights and duties for all citizens. By this constitution, Prophet (S) acquired the right platform to defend Muslims and citizens of Madīnah from any type of military aggression.

Need for war: The role of Muhammad (S) was to preach Islam and his life was to be an example for the mankind. From the beginning of civilization, people wondered if oppression should be tolerated, responded or prevented. Muslims in Makkah were persecuted and oppressed. Many of them migrated to Madīnah penniless. Makkans were further planning to hurt the Muslims in Madīnah. To recover the lost property and to prevent future aggression, a verse was revealed:

> *Permission to fight is given to those against whom war is made, because they have been oppressed. And surely Allāh is indeed capable of helping them: those who have been expelled from their homes without a just cause, but because they say: "Our Rabb is Allāh ." (22:39-40)*

Therefore, the oppressed Muslims launched a few raids (Arabic: *ghazu*) upon the Makkan caravans to recover some wealth. Such small scale unconventional guerrilla attack was the only experience Muslims acquired during the initial stage.

Intelligence service: All successful generals of army heavily require intelligence service. While the Prophet (S) was in Madīnah, he regularly received secret information about Makkan war preparations through his uncle Al-'Abbas. His alliance with Bedouins also helped him obtain secret information about the movement of enemies across the desert.

Tactical moves: The battle strategies of Prophet (S) were unheard of at that time in Arabia. During the battle of Badr, he strategically occupied the water-wells. Without steady supply of water, his enemies would become weak soon. He tried to divert the battles away from the heart of Madīnah. During the battle of Uhud, he foresaw the benefit of placing archers on the hillocks. When Salman

Farsi suggested him to dig a trench during the Battle of Khandaq, the Prophet (S) quickly realized its strategic effectiveness. As a battle strategy the trench was innovative and astounding operation for the contemporary Arabia. In many battles the Prophet (S) used non-military methods like building alliance, showing mercy, sending the enemies to exile and making religious appeal. During the Victory of Makkah, he wanted to avoid blood-shed. Therefore, he used a 'show of force' by surrounding the city from all sides. Makkans surrendered thinking that Muslim force was much larger.

Motivate an army: Soldiers are usually motivated in a war if they realize the justification of the war, and the greater benefit to the society from the war. Muslims soldiers knew the purpose of the wars, and knew that engaging in the war was important for their survival. Soldiers are also motivated when they realize that the leaders are also equally at risk in the war, and leaders are not using lives of the soldiers as cheap commodities. Rasulullah (S) himself and his closest sahābas participated in the wars, were injured, and many prominent sahābas were martyred. The motivation of the soldiers led to a steady growth of the army. In the Battle of Badr, there were hardly 313-men army. Within one year, in the Battle of Uhud the number increased to 1,000. When Makkah was conquered, the army numbered 10,000. In the Battle of Hunayn, the army numbered 12,000. During the expedition of Tabūk, the army was 30,000 strong.

Distribution of booty: As a farsighted General of Army, Muhammad (S) forever changed the way the booty from battles or raids were distributed. Usually the chief of the clan would take one-fourth of the booty. The Prophet (S) declared that he would take one-twenty-fifth of the booty.[8:41] It is generally understood that after dividing the entire booty in five equal parts one fifth was allocated to Allāh. Allāh's share was then divided into five equal parts and distributed among the Prophet (S), his relatives, the orphans, the poor and the wayfarer. Thus, the Prophet (S) being a leader of the Muslim community, got only one twenty-fifth of the booty. By distributing the booty among the poor, widows and orphans of the soldiers killed in battle, the Prophet (S) took care of the weaker section of the society.

Care of the war widows and orphans: The soldiers knew that their family would be well cared for even if they die in the war. The Qur'ān established strict rules about the properties of the orphans,[4:2,6] and allowed the surviving men to support the destitute women by marrying more than one.[4:3] Many war-widows found secure new homes, some even in the home of the Prophet (S). Muslims not only helped the widows of the Muslims, but also helped the widows of the enemies. These generosities by the Muslims helped in eliminating hostility by the enemies.

Prisoners of war: Only in the twentieth century, the Western world formulated laws about fair treatment of the prisoners of war, in the Hague and Geneva conventions. Muslims were asked to treat the captives fairly.[2:177, 76:8-9] Prisoners who would accept Islam were forgiven.[8:70] The prisoners who did not accept Islam were released after receiving ransom money or just out of kindness.[47:4] Muhammad (S), as instructed in the Qur'ān, prohibited continued war when the opponents would surrender.[2:190]

Military revolution: Along with bringing social, political and religious revolution in Arabia, the Prophet (S) also brought about military revolution in Arabia. Without having a formal defense budget, the Prophet (S) was able to bring together an army that was not only motivated, but also committed for the cause of Islam. He transformed the army from tribes raiding caravans to organized cadre capable of large-scale combat operations. Based on his methodologies, Muslim community was able to carry out conquest of other neighboring countries such as Byzantine and Persia.

In conclusion, in a single decade the Prophet (S) brilliantly transformed the Arab communities from small-scale warriors into a nation that would sustain the progress of Islam. No doubt, he was the all time brilliant General of Army.

homework**weekend 16**

1. What is true about the battle experience of the Prophet (S) before he became the messenger of Allāh?

    a. He participated in several tribal warfare.
    b. He learned archery and sword fighting from his uncle.
    c. He went to Syria to learn battle skills.
    d. He learned battle strategies from past history.
    e. He did not get any battle experience from any source.

2. Why the route by Madīnah was of strategic importance?

....

....

3. The genius of the Prophet (S) was reflected in the Battle of Uhud when he decided on a brilliant battle strategy. What was the strategy?

    a. Digging a trench around Madīnah.
    b. Forming an alliance with Abduallh Ibn Ubayy.
    c. Placing a group of archers on a hillock.
    d. Attacking the enemies by night.
    e. Setting up an ambush for the enemies.

4. What key battle strategy did the Prophet (S) always adopt before a battle that indicated to his genius as a great General of Army?

    a. He always hired skilled warriors.
    b. He always obtained large arms.
    c. He always obtained camels and horses for the warriors.
    d. He always obtained secret intelligence information about enemies.
    e. He always made a diagram of battle plans.

5. In many battles the Prophet (S) used non-military methods to win a battle. Name some of the non-military methods as mentioned in the lesson.

....

....

6. The Prophet (S) forever changed the way war booty was distributed. What was his share?

....

7. The genius of the Prophet (S) was reflected in the Battle of Khandaq when he decided on a brilliant battle strategy. What was the strategy?

a. Digging a trench around Madīnah.
b. Forming an alliance with Abduallh Ibn Ubayy.
c. Placing a group of archers on a hillock.
d. Attacking the enemies by night.
e. Setting up an ambush for the enemies.

8. One of Prophet (S)'s uncles sent secret information about the Makkan war preparations. Who was the uncle?

....

9. What was one of the main reasons the number of Muslim army increased from 313 men at the Battle of Badr to about 10,000 when Makkah was conquered?

a. The Prophet (S) was able to give good salary.
b. The Prophet (S) forced people to join the army.
c. Condition of becoming Muslim was tied with participation in the battle.
d. People were compelled to fight or face punishment.
e. The Prophet (S) was able to motivate people.

10. After the Prophet (S) migrated to Madīnah what important step did he take that showed his far-sight as a brilliant strategist?

a. He formed a volunteer army.
b. He drafted the Constitution of Madīnah.
c. He promoted Islam as a religion.
d. He obtained alliance from Persia.
e. He launched the expedition of Tabūk.

classwork**weekend 17**

God's Chosen People

Objective of the Lesson:

The Children of Israel claim they are the God's chosen people. The Qur'ān states Allāh favored them at one time. The lesson discusses what it means to be God's favored nation. We will investigate whether God's favor continues even if the favored nation rebels and rejects God? Are Muslims favored? If so, what to do to retain the favor?

Who is a better person? Whom does Allāh loves the most? Whom will Allāh chose for His rewards? We can find the answer in Sūrah Al-Hujurāt, as Allāh (swt) said: *"O you mankind! We have surely created you out of a male and a female, and We have made you into nations and tribes that you may recognize one another. Surely the noblest of you in the presence of Allāh is the most pious of you. Truly Allāh is all-Knowing, all-Aware."* (49:13) Muslims believe that a person can be better than other only by means of taqwa or piety. The word taqwa can roughly be translated as to love and fear Allāh, and to be aware of the omnipresence of Allāh.

Judeo-Christian idea about Favored Nation: People of some other faith, particularly the Jews, think that they are a better nation not because of their action, but by their birth. They believe that God has permanently chosen them over other people or nations. This belief primarily comes from a few verses in Genesis claiming that God made an unconditional covenant to Abraham: *"I will make of you a great nation, and I will bless you, and make your name great, so that you will be a blessing. I will bless those who bless you, and the one who curses you I will curse; and in you all the families of the earth shall be blessed."*(Gen. 12:2-3)

Although many Jews consider this is an unconditional commitment, the Old Testament clarifies that there were conditions: *"If you heed ordinances, by diligently observing them, the Lord your God will maintain with you the covenant loyalty that he swore to your ancestor."*(Deut 7:12) Their book further states that they lost the favor of God when they broke the rules: *"Remember and do not forget*

how you provoked the Lord your God to wrath in the wilderness; you have been rebellious against the Lord from the day you came out of the land of Egypt until you came to this place."[Deut 9:7] Because of their sin, *"But the Lord said to Moses, Whoever has sinned against me I will blot out of my book."*[Exod. 32:33] The Bible suggests that Moses had to argue with God in many ways to recover their lost status.

In spite of these stories in the Old Testament, many Jews strongly believe that the grant of a favored nation was permanent and unconditional. Interestingly, many Christians point out that the Jews are no more the chosen people, as they refused to accept a Jewish Prophet Jesus. Since Christians accepted Jesus, many of them believe they are now the rightful recipient of the favored nation status.

The concept of chosen people could have been a private issue to Jews or Christians, but many of them try to impose their understanding of their scriptures upon other religions. Interestingly, the Qur'ān also states that Allāh had favored the Children of Israel. Instead of going into the details of the Bible and trying to sort out the internal conflict of Jews and Christians, this lesson is aimed at understanding the Qur'ānic viewpoint on the concept of favored nation.

The Qur'ānic concept: The Qur'ān is clear that Allāh had favored the Children of Israel over others:

يَٰبَنِيٓ إِسۡرَٰٓءِيلَ ٱذۡكُرُواْ نِعۡمَتِيَ ٱلَّتِيٓ أَنۡعَمۡتُ
عَلَيۡكُمۡ وَأَنِّي فَضَّلۡتُكُمۡ عَلَى ٱلۡعَٰلَمِينَ ٤٧

O Children of Israel! remember My favor which I bestowed upon you, and that I distinguished you above the nations. (2:47, 122)

It is important to note that this favor to the Children of Israel was based on a covenant. Since Allāh never breaks His promise, He would fulfill His commitment only if the other party also upholds its commitment.

O Children of Israel! Remember My favors which I bestowed upon you, and fulfill covenant with Me, I shall fulfill covenant with you, and Me, Me alone, should you then fear. (2:40)

The covenant: The covenant to the Children of Israel are mentioned in 2:83 and 5:12:

1. worshipping none but Allāh,
2. kindness to parents, relatives, orphans and the needy,
3. to speak to people nicely,
4. to establish the salāt,
5. to pay the zakāt,
6. belief in the rasuls of Allāh and to support them, and
7. to lend a goodly loan to Allāh, i.e., spend in the path of Allāh.

Unfortunately, the Children of Israel continued to reject the rasuls by belying them, and trying to kill them.[5:70] The Old Testament projects Hārūn (A) as an idol worshipper and Dawud (A) as a man of loose character! A large segment of the children of Israel rejected 'Isa (A) and even tried to kill him on the cross. Most of them rejected Muhammad (S). Those who accepted 'Isa (A) became Christians, and those who accepted Muhammad (S) became Muslims. According to the Qur'ānic principles, the Children of Israel thus failed to fulfill their part of the covenant, at least on following the rasuls. They not only modified the Tawrāt, but also wrote Talmud, a man-made book of religious laws and by-laws, in order to offset the Tawrāt.

Why favor?: Allāh says that the favor granted to the Children of Israel was due to the extreme hardship that they faced under the rule of Pharaoh in Egypt.

And We desired to show favor upon those who were deemed weak in the land, and to make them leaders, and to make them inheritors; (28:5)

With this favor, the children of Israel were able to escape from the rule of the most powerful ruler of the earth at that time. The ruler, Pharaoh, died by drowning and Allāh saved his body as an example for the mankind.[10:92] The children of Israel also received favor by having a long chain of prophets who were raised from among them. The children of Israel could have continued to receive all the favor, but they wasted these favors themselves. The Qur'ān states:

This is so because Allāh never changes a favor which He has conferred upon any people, until they alter whatsoever by themselves. And because Allāh is all-Hearing, all-Knowing. (8:53)

There is not much substance in the claim of Jews and Christians that they will always be favored. History provides enough examples that they faced a good share of misfortune and difficulty:

And the Jews and the Christians say: "We are the sons of Allāh and His beloved ones." Say: "Why does He then punish you for your sins? In fact, you are but human beings among those He has created. He forgives whom He pleases and He chastises whom He pleases." And to Allāh belongs the Sovereignty of the heavens and the earth, and whatever is between the two, and towards Him is the return. (5:18)

Who can demand a favor? Suppose a ninth grader Adnan favors a classmate Jameel. However, Jameel decides to insult Adnan, back-bite him, and harm him in many ways. Surely, Adnan will not continue his favor to Jameel. It was the goodwill of Adnan to favor Jameel or someone else. Adnan keeps the right to favor someone else or to withdraw his favor. Nobody can demand favor. Allāh said bestowing favor is His wish:

Their rasuls said to them: "We are nothing but human beings like yourselves, but Allāh bestows favors upon whom He pleases of His bondsmen... (14:11)

Who can get a favor? While nobody can demand a favor, there are people who deserve favor. Since Allāh is Just, He gives His favor to the righteous. Obeying Allāh and His Rasul are important qualifications to receive the favor:

وَمَنْ يُطِعِ اللَّهَ وَالرَّسُولَ فَأُولَٰئِكَ مَعَ الَّذِينَ
أَنْعَمَ اللَّهُ عَلَيْهِمْ مِنَ النَّبِيِّينَ وَالصِّدِّيقِينَ وَ
الشُّهَدَاءِ وَالصَّالِحِينَ ۚ وَحَسُنَ أُولَٰئِكَ رَفِيقًا ﴿٦٩﴾

And whoever obeys Allāh and the Rasul, then they are with those upon whom Allāh has bestowed favors— from among the nabis, and the truthful, and the witnesses, and the righteous. And what a goodly friends are they! (4:69)

One of the best favor that we can get from Allāh is His guidance. Truly, the guidance of Islam is the best form of favor as it protects us from sinful acts, and ultimately allows us to enter the Garden. Allāh said:

They regard to have favored upon you because they have embraced Islam. You say: "Do not count your Islam a favor upon me; rather Allāh has favored upon you because He has guided you to the Faith, if you are truthful." (49:17)

Because Muslims are favored by the guidance, we should sincerely acknowledge it and thank Allāh for all the good things that we receive. Following is a du'a from the Qur'ān that we should memorize and invoke as often as possible:

رَبِّ أَوْزِعْنِي أَنْ أَشْكُرَ نِعْمَتَكَ الَّتِي أَنْعَمْتَ
عَلَيَّ وَعَلَىٰ وَالِدَيَّ وَأَنْ أَعْمَلَ صَالِحًا
تَرْضَاهُ وَأَصْلِحْ لِي فِي ذُرِّيَّتِي ۖ إِنِّي
تُبْتُ إِلَيْكَ وَإِنِّي مِنَ الْمُسْلِمِينَ ﴿١٥﴾

My Rabb! rouse me that I may give thanks for your favors with which you have favored upon me and upon my parents, and that I may do good— which may please you, and do good to me with regard to my offspring. Surely I turn to you, and I am indeed among the Muslims. (46:15)

Favor to whole mankind: Allāh's favor is not limited to Children of Israel or to Muslims only. Definitely we, the Muslims, have been favored the best by receiving the guidance through Prophet Muhammad (S). Allāh also favors the whole mankind, although many times mankind refutes those favors. The sūrah ar-Rahmān thus repeats the question:

فَبِأَيِّ ءَالَآءِ رَبِّكُمَا تُكَذِّبَانِ ﴿٣٦﴾

Which then of the favors of your Rabb will you two deny?

How to continue getting the favor? We can enjoy the favor of guidance only if we follow the Qur'ān. While the Children of Israel are a race, Muslims are not a particular race of people or a tribe. Any person from any background or nation can come inside the fold of Islam and receive the finest favor of Allāh. At the same time, we must remember that the favor comes with expectations and responsibilities on our side. If we do not fulfill our duties, we may not get the favor. Our duty is to follow the guidance in the Qur'ān, as shown by Muhammad (S).

from**hadith**

It is narrated that Messenger of Allāh, may Allāh bless him and grant him peace, said, "Every child is born on the fitra and it is his parents who make him a jew or a christian. Just as a camel is born whole - do you perceive any defect?" They said, "Messenger of Allāh, what happens to people who die when they are (very) young?" He said, "Allāh knows best what they used to do." (Muslim, Malik's Muwatta).

Narrated Abdullah ibn Mas'ud: The Prophet (S) said: He who swears an oath in which he tells a lie to take the property of a Muslim by unfair means, will meet Allāh while He is angry with him. Al-Ash'ath said: I swear by Allāh, he said this about me. There was some land between me and a Jew, but he denied it to me; so I presented him to the Prophet (S). The Prophet (S) asked me: Have you any evidence? I replied: No. He said to the Jew: Take an oath. I said: Apostle of Allāh, now he will take an oath and take my property. So Allāh, the Exalted, revealed the verse, "As for those who sell the faith they owe to Allāh and their own plighted word for a small price, they shall have no portion in the hereafter." (Bukhāri, Sunan Abū Dawūd)

homework**weekend 17**

1. According to Old Testament, (Deut 9:7, quoted in this lesson), the Children of Israel did something about their covenant with God when they came out of Egypt. Mark ☑ if the statement is correct, and mark ☒ if it is wrong.

   a. They remained faithful to God and the teachings of Moses. ☐
   b. They provoked God by their actions. ☐
   c. Their actions earned wrath of God. ☐
   d. They were rebellious against the Lord. ☐

2. When God chooses a person or a nation, He expects that person or the nation to do something. What is that?

   a. Change parts of the scripture.
   b. Enjoy the favor as long it lasts.
   c. Become more responsible towards divine commands.
   d. Become immune to accountability.

3. Which of the following statement is true about the Children of Israel being God's favored nation?

   a. They were favored for all period of time.
   b. They were favored as long as they remained loyal to God.
   c. They can bypass judgment.
   d. They obeyed Mūsā wholeheartedly.
   e. They followed the Torah and the Talmud.

4. Mark ☑ if the statement is correct, and mark ☒ if it is wrong.

   a. Allāh never said the Jews were a favored nation. ☐
   b. Allāh indicated that the favor upon the Children of Israel would be withdrawn. ☐
   c. The Children of Israel were favored due to their past suffering and bondage. ☐
   d. Even after the Children of Israel sinned, Allāh favored them by giving them respite. ☐
   e. Allāh favored them by sending many prophets among them. ☐

5. The Jews believe they are God's favored nation because Jesus was their prophet. True / False

6. The success of the present day Jews indicate Allāh favored them for all period of time. True / False

7. On the Day of Judgment most Jews will suffer punishment for only a few days. True / False

8. According to verse 14:11, favor of Allāh is a special blessing. Mark ☑ if the statement is correct, and mark ☒ if it is wrong.

a. A nation can demand favor of Allāh because of their heritage. ☐
b. A nation can get favor of Allāh only if Allāh so wishes. ☐
c. Once you get favor, you are guaranteed to have permanent favor. ☐
d. Human beings can force Allāh to continue granting favors. ☐

9. Mark ☑ if the statement is correct, and mark ☒ if it is wrong.

a. One of the best favors of Allāh is His guidance. ☐
b. To get favor of Allāh, we need to obey Allāh and His rasul. ☐
c. Allāh's favor is limited to Jews and Muslims only. ☐
d. The finest favor of Allāh is limited to a select race of humans. ☐

10. Read verse 45:16. Here the Children of Israel were given four things and they were made distinguished above other nations. What are these four things mentioned in the verse?

a. ....

b. ....

c. ....

d. ....

Mūsā (A)'s Personality

Objective of the Lesson:

Mūsā (A) was a prophet of Allāh, yet above all he was a human being. His handling of dramatic events in life reflects his personality. The purpose of the lesson is not to study the events, but analyze how Mūsā reacted as these events happened in his life. This analysis will help us understand the personality of Mūsā (A) based on major events in his life.

Several sūrahs in the Qur'ān are titled after the name of prophets, e.g., Nūh, Ibrāhīm, Hūd, Yūnus, Yūsuf, and Muhammad (S). Although there is not a single sūrah in the Qur'ān named after Mūsā, his name or his account is mentioned in twenty-seven different sūrahs in the Qur'ān. Mūsā's story is narrated from the time of his birth, his youth, his marriage, interaction with Pharaoh, and his dealings with the Israelites in Egypt and in Sinai Peninsula.

During ups and downs in his life, through trials and tribulations, through difficulties and successes, Mūsā demonstrated a highly dynamic personality. The objective of this lesson is to discuss some of the most prominent character attributes that readily stands out as we analyze his entire life.

In order to understand Mūsā's distinguished personality, we will divide his life into four broad phases.

Phase 1: This phase covers the part of Mūsā's life from the time of his birth, adoption in Pharaoh's palace, youth, until he ran away after accidentally killing an Egyptian.

Phase 2: After running away from Egypt, Mūsā arrived in Madyan—as a destitute. By Allāh's immense blessing, he found a family, married one of their daughters and found a secure shelter for about 8-10 years.

Phase 3: This phase started when Mūsā was appointed as a prophet of Allāh and was instructed to go to Egypt to accomplish two objectives: (a) rescue the Israelites, and (b) advise Pharaoh to surrender to Allāh.

Phase 4: After rescuing the Israelites Mūsā brought them to Madyan, gave them the Ten Commandments, wanted them to settle down in Canaan and inherit the Promised Land. At the end of this phase, amid some disappointment with the Israelites, he finally passed away.

Mūsā's dramatic life developed in him a distinguished personality and character. This lesson will discuss only a few important ones.

Knowledge and wisdom: Mūsā had a challenging life, a difficult ruler to interact with, and an unruly group of followers to deal with. He was able to tackle these difficult issues, as Allāh gave him the gift of knowledge and wisdom.

وَلَمَّا بَلَغَ أَشُدَّهُۥ وَٱسْتَوَىٰٓ ءَاتَيْنَٰهُ حُكْمًا وَعِلْمًا ۚ
وَكَذَٰلِكَ نَجْزِى ٱلْمُحْسِنِينَ ﴿١٤﴾

And when he attained his maturity, and stood firm, We granted him wisdom and knowledge. And likewise We reward the doers of good. (28:14)

As a child, Mūsā had two odd sources of knowledge—his own mother who acted as his nanny and exposure to the royal life of the palace. One gave him soft corner for the needy and destitute, and the other developed his analytical and leadership skills.

Some dramatic events in the life of Mūsā increased his wisdom. He once tried to intervene in a brawl between an Egyptian and an Israelite. During the brawl, Mūsā struck and killed the stronger and oppressive Egyptian. Mūsā became alarmed as Pharaoh conspired to put him in trial and to kill him. Mūsā was remorseful for the incident, gained wisdom and also prayed to Allāh for forgiveness.

The event turned dramatic. Spending days as a fugitive in the wilderness of the Sinai Peninsula, he finally found the company of an elderly wise man and his daughters in Madyan. He had helped the daughters at a water-well. In turn their father offered him to marry one of the daughters and settle down in Madyan for eight or ten years. Mūsā accepted the offer and decided to settle down. Life in this remote village was nothing compared to the royal palace in Egypt. In Madyan Mūsā gained first-hand experience of the life of common people.

During the later half of the life in Madyan, Allāh selected Mūsā as a prophet. Allāh instructed him to invite Pharaoh to accept Islam. When Mūsā went to the court, he knew that knowledge and wisdom were essential to convince the Pharaoh. Therefore, he prayed to Allāh to bless him:

رَبِّ ٱشْرَحْ لِى صَدْرِى ﴿٢٥﴾ وَيَسِّرْ لِىٓ أَمْرِى ﴿٢٦﴾
وَٱحْلُلْ عُقْدَةً مِّن لِّسَانِى ﴿٢٧﴾ يَفْقَهُوا۟ قَوْلِى ﴿٢٨﴾

My Rabb! expand for me my breast, and make my affair easy for me, and release the knot from my tongue, that they may understand my speech. (20:25-28)

Fight for justice: At least two incidents in Mūsā's life show that he always fought for the cause of justice or for law and order. The first incident was when he intervened in the brawl between the Egyptian and the Israelite. The second incident was when he helped the women in Madyan fetch water by chasing out the nomadic rogues from messing up the well. Although he was tired and exhausted from days of traveling in the Sinai desert, it did not deter him from helping those who were oppressed—the women in this case—and fight the oppressor. Later during his second phase of life in Egypt, Mūsā relentlessly fought for the civic rights of the Israelites—this time against the mighty oppressor Pharaoh.

Fear for uncertainty: No matter how strong and resourceful Mūsā was, even he was fearful of uncertainty just like any other human. After accidentally killing the Egyptian, Mūsā ran away as he was fearful of uncertainty. He was again fearful of uncertainty when he was asked by Allāh to go back to Egypt and preach to Pharaoh. This time he was fearful of getting arrested for the killing the Egyptian.

Fearless: Although Mūsā was at times fearful of uncertainty, he was not fearful when he intervened in the brawl between an Egyptian and an Israelite. He was fearless when he plunged into the wilderness of the Sinai desert and fled towards uncertainty—not knowing whether he would survive in the desert. He was fearless when he went to the valley of Tūa, the valley in Sinai where he received first revelation and talked to Allāh. He was fearless when he rescued the Israelites through the sea and when he assumed the role of spiritual leader of the unruly, disobedient people.

Determination: This character attribute was noted in Mūsā's personality when he was determined to face Pharaoh even when he ran the risk of getting arrested. He was determined to rescue the Israelites from their bondage in Egypt. He was determined to spiritually guide the Israelites even when they were not fully committed.

Farsighted: When Mūsā had received an offer to marry one of the women in Madyan, he accepted the offer knowing that the marriage would provide him with security and opportunity to settle down rather than continuing a nomadic life. The marriage provided him with emotional support and stability in life. This decision clearly indicates farsightedness in Mūsā's personality.

Inquisitive: Mūsā had been inquisitive, particularly when he wanted to see Allāh with his own eyes.

He was also inquisitive when he was traveling with the mysterious sage Khidir. Sūrah 18 narrates the events of the travel. Mūsā was not allowed to ask any question. However, each time Khidir acted strangely, Mūsā could not resist but asked a question.

Forgiving: A person who experienced forgiveness can in turn be forgiving to others. After killing the Egyptian Mūsā was very remorseful and sought forgiveness from Allāh. This forgiveness had a profound impact in his life and taught him the virtue of forgiveness.

Leadership: Mūsā could not have been a leader of the Israelites, unless he had leadership abilities. He could not have motivated thousands of Israelites unless he was compassionate and kind. Unless he was persuasive, he could have easily given up all his efforts in Egypt when Pharaoh and his companions rejected his mission. Unless he had strong faith in Allāh, he could not have assumed the role of prophethood and could not have been a spiritual leader of the Israelites.

Anger: There is one incident in the Qur'ān when Mūsā became furious. He returned from the Mountain after forty days of solitude and found the Israelites built a golden calf to worship. Mūsā was furious with his brother Hārūn thinking that he supported the golden calf.

These are just a few of the incidents from Mūsā's life that demonstrate his distinguished personality. He was truly a God-fearing man, a prophet who was wise, farsighted, determined, and upright.

homework**weekend 18**

1. After running away from Egypt, where did Mūsā find a shelter for 8-10 years?

....

2. Approximately in how many sūrahs in the Qur'ān are the event related to Mūsā related?

....

3. What are the two different sources of knowledge of Mūsā when he was a child?

....

4. List three incidents in the life of Mūsā's to show his desire for justice.

   a. ....

   b. ....

   c. ....

5. List three incidents in the life of Mūsā's to show that he was fearless.

   a. ....

   b. ....

   c. ....

6. List two incidents in the life of Mūsā's to show that he was inquisitive.

   a. ....

   b. ....

7. When Mūsā decided to accept the marriage proposal in Madyan, his decision showed a positive character. What is that positive character trait?

....

8. Which Sūrah in the Qur'ān narrates Mūsā's travel with Khidir?

a. Baqarah.
b. Tā Hā.
c. As-Shuarah.
d. Naml.
e. Al- Khaf.

9. In which of the following incident an angry outburst of Mūsā was noted?

a. When Pharaoh refused to accept Mūsā as a prophet.
b. When the Israelites refused to cross the sea.
c. When the Israelites refused to worship the golden calf.
d. When Mūsā noted that the Israelites built a golden calf.
e. When an Egyptian and an Israelites were involved in a brawl.

10. Other than the material discussed in the class, which of the following do you think is a positive character trait of Mūsā?

a. Thoughtful in his conduct.
b. Unmindful of law and order.
c. Desire for power.
d. Desire for affluence and comfort.
e. Ruthless towards Pharaoh and his followers.

classwork**weekend 19**

Prophecy of Muhammad (S) in the Bible

Objective of the Lesson:

The Qur'ān says 'Isa (A) foretold about the advent of Muhammad (S). If we study the Bible, we can find a few references about another prophet who would come after 'Isa. This lesson analyzes the prophecies in the Bible and connects them to the advent of Muhammad (S).

All the major ancient world religions were originally sent by Allāh. Over a time people changed the teachings of the religions. Some of the religions were changed so much that they lost their appeal, e.g., the religions of Sabeans and Magian as mentioned in the Qur'ān. Some other religions regained strength after people modified the original teachings, e.g. Christianity. Some other religion, e.g. Judaism continued to appeal a group of followers even after changes were made in their original teachings. All these religions, in one way or the other, made prophecy about the advent of a prophet. The exact identity of the prophet was not clear in some of these religions and even if it was clear, the interpretation of verses made the identity become confusing or misleading to their followers. The holy books of Christians, Hindus or Jews have profuse examples about the advent of a prophet, but the followers of these religions are disinterested about the prophecy. Due to limited time in this class, we will confine our study only to Christianity and the Bible. We will try to understand what Islam understands from the prophecy and what it means to the Muslims.

Prophecy about which Prophet: The religions that admit a prophecy about advent of a prophet are still waiting for the promised prophet. Hindus are waiting for a prophet to arrive later when humanity is about to be doomed. Christians are also waiting for a prophet to arrive sometime in the future. These religions do not try to see that the promised prophet had already arrived. They are fearful that they will lose their religion if they make the identification. If the promised prophet truly arrived as foretold in their religion, they would be duty bound to follow the prophet.

From Islamic perspective, the promised prophet is none but Muhammad (S). The following analysis show that with him the prophecies of the past scriptures has been fulfilled.

The Qur'ān about the prophecy: The Qur'ān cites about the prophecies contained in other scriptures. Such citations show that all these scriptures were originally revealed by Allāh, and that Islam is not a new religion. Islam is but a continuation of the same religion revealed in the past to various communities. Some citations in the Qur'ān are as follows:

وَإِذْ قَالَ عِيسَى ابْنُ مَرْيَمَ يَٰبَنِيٓ إِسْرَٰٓءِيلَ
إِنِّي رَسُولُ اللَّهِ إِلَيْكُم مُّصَدِّقًا لِّمَا بَيْنَ يَدَيَّ
مِنَ التَّوْرَىٰةِ وَمُبَشِّرًۢا بِرَسُولٍ يَأْتِي مِنۢ بَعْدِي
اسْمُهُۥٓ أَحْمَدُ ۖ فَلَمَّا جَآءَهُم بِالْبَيِّنَٰتِ قَالُوا هَٰذَا
سِحْرٌ مُّبِينٌ ﴿٦﴾

And behold! 'Isa, son of Maryam said: "O Children of Israel! surely I am the rasul of Allāh to you, confirming what is in my presence of the Tawrāt, and bring of glad tidings of a Rasul who will come after me, his name being Ahmad." Then when he came to them with clear proofs, they said: "This is an obvious enchantment." (61:6)

those who follow the Rasul— the Nabi, the Ummi whom they find described with them in the Tawrāt and the Injil; who instructs them doing good, and forbids them against evil; and who makes lawful for them the pure things, and makes unlawful for them the impure things, and who takes off from them their burdens, and the yokes that were upon them. Then as to those who believe in him, and honor him and help him, and follow the Light which has been sent down with him— these are themselves the successful ones." (7:157)

During the time of revelation of the Qur'ān, the Jews and the Christians in Madīnah clearly recognized that Muhammad (S) was the promised prophet. The advent of a promised prophet is mentioned in their holy books. However, they refused to believe he was the promised prophet. They pretended as if they were not sure about his authenticity. In response the Qur'ān states that recognizing him was as easy as recognizing one's own children.

الَّذِينَ آتَيْنَٰهُمُ الْكِتَٰبَ يَعْرِفُونَهُۥ كَمَا يَعْرِفُونَ
أَبْنَآءَهُمْ ۖ وَإِنَّ فَرِيقًا مِّنْهُمْ لَيَكْتُمُونَ الْحَقَّ
وَهُمْ يَعْلَمُونَ ﴿١٤٦﴾

Those to whom We have given the scripture recognize him as they recognize their children. But a group of them do surely conceal the truth, while they know. (2:146)

Verses from the Bible: Several verses in the Bible speak about the arrival of 'someone', after Jesus. Obviously from Christian perspective the meaning of the verses are different. However, when read with an Islamic perspective these verses seem to clearly indicate about the advent of a prophet after Jesus leaves the earth. Let us read some of these verses:

***John 14: [16] :** And I will pray the Father, and he shall give you another Comforter, that he may abide with you for ever;*

***John 15:[26]** But when the Comforter is come, whom I will send unto you from the Father, even the Spirit of truth, which proceedeth from the Father, he shall testify of me:*

***John 16:[7]** Nevertheless I tell you the truth; It is expedient for you that I go away: for if I go not away, the Comforter will not come unto you; but if I depart, I will send him unto you.*

These verses clearly indicate that a new prophet would come in future only after Jesus leaves the earth. Early Christians believed in the prophecy, but after Muhammad (S) came to fulfill the prophecy, they gradually disagreed about the meaning of the prophecy. They started interpreting the verse to say after Jesus would leave, Holy Ghost would come.

Holy ghost— why and why not: There is internal flaw in accepting Holy Ghost as the promised comforter. Holy Ghost is the Christian term for angel Gabriel or angel Jibril. He was specially recognized since he brought the revelations to Jesus. Before we discuss the issue let us read two other verses from the Bible. Notice in this verse the identity of the Comforter is stated to be Holy Ghost.

> ***John 14: [26]*** *But the Comforter, which is the Holy Ghost, whom the Father will send in my name, he shall teach you all things, and bring all things to your remembrance, whatsoever I have said unto you.*

Holy Ghost or Gabriel was constantly present at the time of Jesus. There was no need for him to come again after Jesus when he was already serving various missions at the time of Jesus. Therefore, to interpret Holy Ghost as the Comforter is nothing but a wrong interpretation of the verse.

Parakletos: When the original Aramaic Injil was being translated into Greek, the identity of the promised prophet was rendered with the word *parakletos*. The English translation of the Greek word *parakletos* or *periklytos* is "comforter" or "helper".

Often problem arises in translating a key word from one language to another. It is impossible to find the correct English word to cover all the meaning of parakletos. Depending upon which version of the Bible you are reading, the word parakletos is translated variously as *Comforter* in King James Version, *Helper* in New King James Version, *Counselor* in New International Version and Revised Standard Version.

The Qur'ān says 'Isā foretold about a new prophet would come after he is gone. The new prophet would be symbolically called Ahmad. The meaning of the word Ahmad is the most praising one. The name Muhammad or Ahmad is derived from the same root word hamada (lit. to praise). The reference of this prophecy is mentioned in the present version of Gospel of John (John 14:16,26; 15:26; 16:7). We have already read the Bible verses above.

In the Christian interpretations, the term Parakletos refers to the Holy Spirit. We have already seen why Holy Spirit cannot be the Comforter. Regardless of whatever meaning of Parakletos is adopted, after Jesus was gone, there was none other than Muhammad (S), who came as '*the Comforter*' comforting the entire mankind against suffering, loss, moral and spiritual ailment, worries about future, and as '*the Helper*' helping mankind overcome the spiritual dishonesty and attaining peace and happiness in this world and in the Hereafter; and as '*the Spirit of Truth*' testifying Jesus, conveying glory to him, accepting his prophethood against the denial of the Jews. Without doubt the Israelites and the Christians believed the prophecy and waited for the advent of the Parakletos. When the promised Comforter in the form of Muhammad (S) arrived about 600 years after 'Isā, the contemporary Israelites recognized him as clearly as they would recognize their own children[2:146; 6:20], however they refused to believe in him.

Songs of Solomon: An interesting read is in the book Songs of Solomon, which is a part of the Old Testament. Although many Christians dismiss this section as a poetry of love, the verse 15:6 of Songs of Solomon is as follows:

> *hikwō mamėťaqqîm wėķullwō* ***mahămadîm*** *zeh dwōdî wėzeh rē'î bėnwōť yėrûšālāim:*
>
> *His mouth is most sweet: yes, he is altogether lovely. This is my beloved, and this is my friend, O daughters of Jerusalem.*

The word ***mahămad*** literally translates to beloved, desire, goodly, lovely, pleasant. It is possible that this word refers to Muhammad (S).

It is up to the people of other faith to recognize the promised prophet and obtain the guidance that they are looking for.

homework**weekend 19**

1. All the previous religions were modified by their followers, and the results were not the same. Mark ☑ if the statement is correct, and mark ☒ if it is wrong.

   a. Sabean and Magian faiths are widely practiced. ☐
   b. By modifying the original teachigns, Christianity revived . ☐
   c. Judaism appeals to a small group of people even after the changes. ☐

2. Some of the following statements are correct about the advent of a prophet mentioned in ancient scriptures. Mark ☑ if the statement is correct, and mark ☒ if it is wrong.

   a. All scriptures contain several prophecies about the advent of a prophet. ☐
   b. Interpretation of the verses containing a prophecy is usually vague or secretive. ☐
   c. The verses containing a prophecy are usually deleted from the scriptures. ☐

3. In verse 61:6 in the Qur'ān, the prophecy about the advent of Muhammad (S) was foretold by Jesus. What name did Jesus use for Muhammad (S)?

   a. Holy Ghost.
   b. Holy Angel.
   c. Ahmad.
   d. Parakletos.
   e. Comforter.

4. Give two reasons why Holy Ghost cannot be the promised prophet to come as prophesized by Jesus.

   a. ....

   b. ....

5. Some of the following choices are correct about the prophecies of Muhammad (S) contained in past scriptures. Mark ☑ if the statement is correct, and mark ☒ if it is wrong.

   a. All past scriptures containing a prophecy were originally revealed by Allāh. ☐
   b. The prophecies indicate that Islam is a continuation of past religions. ☐
   c. The prophecies indicate a grand plan Allāh about sending the final guidance. ☐
   d. Only Muslims believe in these prophecies, but people from other faith do not. ☐

6. The Greek word "Parakletos" means: ....

7. The Qur'ān says that the Jews in Madīnah recognized the promised prophet mentioned in their scripture was Muhammad (S) as clearly as they would recognize their particular relation. What relation was used to emphasize the point?

   a. Father.
   b. Children.
   c. Uncle.
   d. Rabbi.
   e. Wife.

8. Which book in the Bible contains many verses that indicate about the advent of a new prophet?

   a. Mark.
   b. Matthew.
   c. Luke.
   d. John.
   e. Psalms.

9. What is the meaning of the word ***mahămad*** as mentioned in Songs of Solomon?

....

classwork**weekend 20**

Shī'ah Muslims

Objective of the Lesson:

Who are the Shī'ahs and what do they believe? This lesson provides a brief understanding of the major belief and practices of the Shī'ah Muslims. The purpose is to show that there are differences in the matter of interpretation, but they are Muslim by all means.

In the previous year we studied about the origin and early history of Shī'ah Muslims. This year we are going to study Shī'ah Muslims to cover some of the areas that we did not discuss earlier. In the world today there are about 180 million people who are Shī'ah Muslims, representing roughly 15% of the Muslim population. It is worthwhile to know about Shī'ah Muslims, who are our close brethren in Islam. Unfortunately religious tension and animosity between the Sunni and Shī'ah Muslims in various parts of the world have damaged the spirit of Islam. It is true Sunnis and Shī'ites are dissimilar in the manner they interpret and practice the religion, yet the similarities between them are connected to the Qur'ān and belief in Allāh.

The tension between Sunnis and Shī'ites calls for taking a fresh look at intra-faith tolerance and finding out if there is any way we, and the future generation Muslims, can alleviate the tension. Often the cause of tension is due to lack of knowledge and belief in self-righteousness.

The singular or adjective form of Shī'ah refer to an individual who follows Prophet Muhammad (S) and 'Ali Ibn Abi Tālib as an Imam. They follow the Qur'ān, the teachings of the Prophet (S) and religious guidance of the Prophet's family, whom they refer to as ***Ahl-al Bayt*** or the "people of the [Prophet's] house." The word Shī'ah is a short form of the original term ***Shī'at 'Ali***, which means "the followers of 'Ali." The term was coined during the early years of Islam, soon after Prophet Muhammad (S). A group of companions wanted 'Ali to become the successor or Khalīfa of the Muslim community. He did become a Khalīfa, but after Abu Bakr, 'Umar and 'Uthmān served the community for many years. The people who did not like the appointment of Abu Bakr as the Khalīfa began identifying themselves as Shī'at 'Ali. After 'Ali was appointed Khalīfa of Muslim community, the rift between the Sunnis and Shī'ites became prominent and continued ever since.

First three Khalīfa: At the time of the Prophet's (S) death, Abu Bakr was the senior-most companion, well respected and admired by all. He was one of the closest companions of Muhammad (S) and a partner with him during many turbulent periods. Immediately after the Prophet (S)'s death, when the companions wanted to formally appoint a successor, the key people involved in the decision making unanimously agreed to appoint Abu Bakr as the Khalīfa. He was 59 years old at that time, compared to 'Ali, who was 32 years old. 'Ali was not present at the time of decision making. The decision was not made by a process of "election", but by a process called *ijmā'* or consensus of a group of key people.

Within two years of the appointment, Abu Bakr passed away in the year 634 C.E. While lying in the death bed, Abu Bakr nominated 'Umar to become the next Khalīfa, who eventually was assassinated by a Persian Christian slave in 644 C.E. 'Umar did not find opportunity to nominate the next Khalīfa. After he passed away an advisory council deliberated as to who should be the next Khalīfa. The decision fell upon 'Uthmān. When 'Uthmān was assassinated, the choice of next Khalīfa fell upon 'Ali. Since the time of appointment of 'Ali, a rift occurred among Muslims that persists even today in the form of Sunni and Shī'ah.

Mu'awiyah's disappointment: Long before 'Ali was nominated to become Khalīfa, Mu'awiyah was appointed as the governor of Syria by 'Umar. He was the son of Abū Sufyān, and a prominent member of the Umayya clan. He believed assassination of 'Uthmān, also an Umayya member, could have been prevented had 'Ali responded in a more careful manner. He believed 'Ali would not take the necessary steps to punish the culprits since his own members were involved in the conspiracy. As a result Mu'awiah refused to recognize 'Ali as the Khalīfa. This tension between 'Ali and Mu'awiyah escalated into a battle, known as ***Battle of Siffin***, that was fought in the year 657 C.E. near Euphrates river in Iraq. 'Ali did not want to shed the blood of fellow Muslims, so he agreed to submit all disagreements to a process of settlement. The committee overseeing the settlement decided against 'Ali and chose Mu'awiyah as the next Khalīfa.

Opinion of 'Ali's camp: The supporters of 'Ali not only rejected the decision, but also believed that he should have been the Khalīfa immediately after Prophet Muhammad (S) passed away. These supporters were truly the companions of the Prophet (S). It is therefore not surprising to see some of the most notable companions like Bilal, Salman Farsi, Abdullah Ibn Abbas, Abu Dharr and many others were Shī'at 'Ali or Followers of 'Ali.

They believed 'Ali was unfairly ignored as the rightful khalīfa in each of the three previous occasion. They believed, the Khalīfate, which they called Imamate, was non-elective, i.e. the position was not subject to election. The imamate means institution of Imam. According to them, the head of Muslim state must be descendants of Prophet Muhammad (S). 'Ali was not a descendent of the Prophet (S), but his first cousin and son-in-law. 'Ali married Fātimah, the Prophet's (S) daughter.

According to Shī'at 'Ali, offsprings from 'Ali and Fātimah were the only legal heirs to Imamate. They do not recognize the first three khalīfas. They also do not believe in the caliphate, instead believe in the imamate. According to the Shī'ah, 'Ali Ibn Abu Tālib was the first Imam. Most Shī'ahs believe in twelve Imams, thus they are also called the Twelvers. The list of the twelve imams are as follows:

1. 'Ali Ibn Abu Tālib (600-661), also known as 'Ali, Amir al-Mo'mineen (commander of the faithful),
2. Hasan Ibn 'Ali (625-669)
3. Husayn Ibn 'Ali (626-680)
4. 'Ali Ibn Husayn (658-713), also known as Ali Zainul Abideen
5. Muhammad ibn 'Ali (676-743)
6. Jafar ibn Muhammad (703-765), also known as Jafar as-Sadiq
7. Mūsā ibn Jafar (745-799)
8. 'Ali Ibn Mūsā (765-818)
9. Muhammad ibn 'Ali (810-835), also known as Taki
10. 'Ali ibn Muhammad (827-868), also known as Naki'
11. Hasan Ibn 'Ali (846-874)
12. Muhammad Ibn Hasan (868 - ?), also known as Al-Mahdi

Denominations among Shī'ites: Over a time several denominations or groups emerged from the original Shī'ah. Some of the groups had to do with who was their Imam and how many Imams were recognized, others had to do with the principle and ideologies. Some of the denominations are Ismaili Shī'ah, Naziri Ismaili, Dawoodi Bohras, Seveners, Zaidis. The Seveners believe there were only seven Imams. They do not recognize any further of the Twelvers' Imams beyond Jafar.

Differences among Shī'ites and Sunnis: Both Shī'ites and Sunnis follow the Qur'ān and believe Muhammad (S) was the last prophet. They both pray five daily prayers and fast and pay zakāt. However, they both disagree on the matter of interpretation of law. Many of the Islamic laws are based on Hadīth. The Shī'ites reject some of the Sunni Hadīth and the Sunnis reject most of the Shī'ah Hadīth. The Shī'ahs particularly reject the Hadīth that were not narrated by Alh-al Bayt. Both of the groups celebrate Eid ul Fitr and Eid ul-Adha and go for pilgrimage.

The Shī'ahs also believe the place of burial of Imam 'Ali is sacred and visit the place. They celebrate the ***Festival of Muharram*** and ***'Ashūrā*** to commemorate martyrdom of Husayn. The Sunnis have no problem with the 'Ashūrā, but give less importance to its celebration. Other lesser events of commemorations are **Arab'een**, which occurs 40 days after 'Ashūrā to commemorate the sufferings of women and children of Husayn's household. ***Eid Al-Ghadeer*** is celebrated to commemorate the Prophet's announcement of Imamate of 'Ali. ***Milad un-Nabi*** is celebrated to commemorate the birth of the Prophet (S). The Shī'ahs do not have high regards for 'Ā'ishah for two reasons: her perceived 'shameful' conduct after losing necklace during the expedition of Banu Mustaliq. The Prophet (S) investigated and determined 'Ā'ishah was not guilty of any misconduct and any slur on her was the handiwork of the hypocrites. The second reason is her participation in the ***Battle of Camel*** against 'Ali.

What should our position be: The split between Shī'ahs and Sunnis began soon after the Prophet (S) passed away. In the long history of Islam, Shī'ahs and Sunnis expressed hate and anger against each other. In many countries Shī'ahs and Sunnis killed each other due to intolerance. Islam teaches us to tolerate and respect every religion and the people of other faiths. Shī'ahs and Sunnis are not following different religions—they are all Muslims. Even though there are some differences between Shī'ahs and Sunnis, we should learn to respect everybody despite the differences among each other. These differences are in the matter of interpretation. We should remember that Allāh will ultimately judge a person's faith and reward or punish them accordingly. We human being should not declare another person non-Muslim when that person has declared faith in the oneness of Allāh and believed in the Prophet (S).

homework**weekend 20**

1. According to the history, when was the term of Shī'at 'Ali coined?

   a. After Imam Husayn was murdered.
   b. Soon after Muhammad (S) passed away.
   c. Soon after the Shī'ahs settled down in Iran.
   d. Long before the birth of the Prophet (S).
   e. When the Umayyad dyNāsty was formed.

2. According to Shī'ah belief who were the second and third Imams respectively?

   a. 'Ali and Mu'awiyah.
   b. 'Ali and Husayn.
   c. Hasan and Husayn.
   d. Jaffar and Zainul Abedin.

3. Which of the following statement is true about the majority of the Shī'ahs in the world?

   a. Majority are the Twelvers.
   b. Majority are the Seveners.
   c. Majority are the Bohras.
   d. Majority are the Fatimids.
   e. Majority are the Ismailis.

4. Which of the following statement is correct about how Shī'ahs view about the Khalīfas?

   a. They do not believe in Abu Bakr but they accept 'Uthmān.
   b. They do not believe in any of the three Khalīfas.
   c. They do not believe in the institution of Khalīfas.

5. Mark ☑ if the statement is correct, and mark ☒ if it is wrong.

   a. Both Sunnis and Shī'ahs believe in One Allāh. ☐
   b. Both Sunnis and Shī'ahs believe in Muhammad (S) as the Last Prophet. ☐
   c. Both Sunnis and Shī'ahs offer salāt, observe fasting, and pay zakāt. ☐

6. According to Shī'ah belief, who has the right to be appointed as an Imam?

....

7. According to Shī'ah belief, which of the following is correct about the appointment of an Imam?

a. Appointment of Imam is non elective.
b. An Imam can be appointed through election.
c. An Imam can be appointed only through the process of ijmā'.
d. An Imam can be appointed only by Allāh.
e. An Imam can be appointed by a king.

8. Which of the following choices is correct about the Battle of Siffin? It was fought

a. between 'Ali and 'Ā'ishah.
b. between 'Ali and Mu'awiah.
c. between Mu'awiah and Yazid.
d. between 'Umar and Mu'awiah.
e. soon after the battle of Uhud in 627 C.E.

9. According to Shī'ah belief which of the following statement is correct about the appointment of Khalīfas?

a. 'Ali was offered to be the 1st Khalīfa, but he declined.
b. 'Ali was made the 1st Khalīfa, but Abu Bakr intervened.
c. 'Ali's camp wholeheartedly accepted all three Khalīfas.
d. 'Ali's case was overlooked during each of the first three appointments of Khalīfas.
e. 'Ali never wanted to be a Khalīfa but he was forced to become one.

10. What is the meaning of the term Shī'at 'Ali?

a. The Sword of 'Ali.
b. The Ruling of 'Ali.
c. The Followers of 'Ali.
d. Rejection of 'Ali.
e. The Family of 'Ali.

Early Muslims in North America

Objective of the Lesson:

Arrival of Muslims in the North America appears to be recent phenomena. However, long back they were routinely coming to the continent. Some reports even suggest they arrived before Columbus discovered America. This lesson analyzes the early history of Muslims in the North America.

The history of Muslims in America appears to be recent. It is true that Islam in North America flourished recently and is still flourishing. However, the presence of Muslims in the New World goes back several centuries. New World is a general term for all land outside of Africa, Europe and Asia, and includes America and Australia. The first official discovery of the New World is credited to Christopher Columbus. In 1492, he sailed from Spain and reached several islands in the Caribbean, the present day Bahamas and Cuba. During the subsequent voyages Columbus discovered the islands in the Gulf of Mexico and Central America.

Our question is when did Islam come to the New World, particularly America? Did it come around the time Columbus discovered America or did it come later? To find this answer we will have to search the seven centuries of American history—from 1300 C.E. to 2000 C.E.

You will be surprised to know that Islam came to the land long before Columbus officially discovered the land. People dispute this claim, however, there are growing number of records and other supporting documents that indicate people from the Muslim world came and lived here. Records of the earliest arrival of people other than Columbus and the contemporary Europeans are sketchy. Nevertheless when Columbus and his subsequent explorers arrived here, they were surprised to notice many lands and places in the new country had Arabic names. One or two names could be coincident, but names of large number of places had clear Arabic connection. How could it have happened unless people from Arabian region

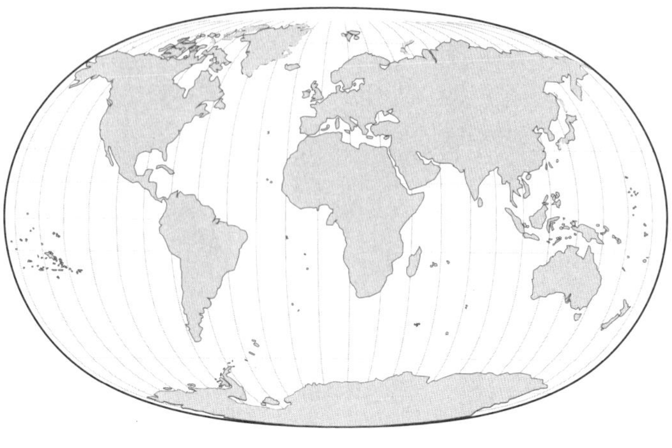

already arrived here and inhabited the place? Wherever they lived, they named the un-named territories with words of their language.

Earliest records: In 1312, about 180 years before Christopher Columbus, African Muslims arrived in Gulf of Mexico for exploration of the New World. They traveled along the Mississippi River. Most of them came from Mali and other parts of West Africa. It is reported that a Muslim king of Mali, known as **Abu Bakri** sent several sea voyages to the New World. These African Muslims were known as **Mandinga**. Once a trade route was established, the West African people conducted several explorations over the years. These people did not record their travel in detail, as did the later European explorers. Most of these African explorers voyages ended in the Gulf of Mexico. They used the Mississippi River as their access route to the interiors of the New World.

Earliest immigrants: During his famous voyage, Columbus brought with him copies of travel documents written by Portuguese Muslims who had sailed to the New World in the 12th century. Particularly notable is the work of 13th century Arab scholar, **Al-Idrissi**, who was an adviser to King Roger of Sicily. Al-Idrissi narrated discovery of a new land by eighty Muslim explorers. His work was known as '**The Sea of Tears**', a title aptly reflects the perilous journey. The narration mentions visits to fourteen islands. Later about half of these islands were traced to be the Canary

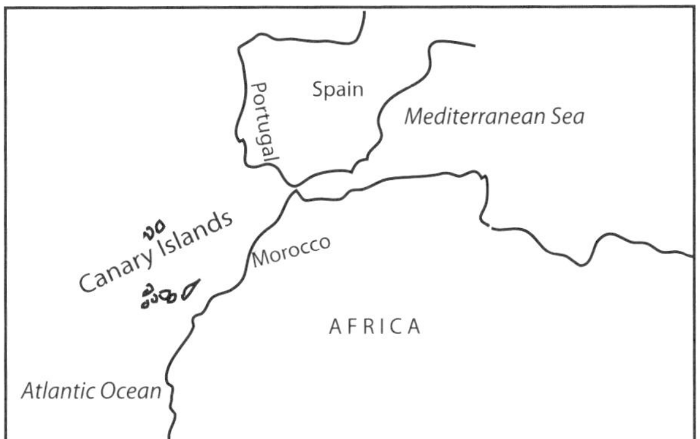

Interesting Facts

A small city in Ohio, south of Cleveland, is named Medina. It was originally known as Mecca, but another Ohio town had this name, so the name was changed to Medina.

Each of the states CA, TX, OH, ND, TN, NY and MN has a town named Medina.

Each of the states VA, GA, AR and PA has a town named Damascus.

A village near Champaign, IL is known as Mahomet.

A town in Indiana is known as Mecca. Another small town outskirts of Los Angeles is known as Mecca.

In Alabama a small town is named Arab. Few miles from Arab another city is known as Egypt.

Indiana has a small town named Morocco.

Islands. These islands are south of Spain and west of Morocco. Columbus brought with him copies of Al-Idrissi's work that helped him during his voyage.

Other than this, there were several other travel documents indicating people from West African region, particularly from the present day Morocco arrived in the New World hundreds of years before Columbus. Most of them came to the present day Mexico and the islands in the Caribbean.

Muslims encouraged to travel: The ancient Arabs were predominantly tribal nation that preferred to live in close connection with members of same ethnic origin and background. Yet they traveled to far off places. The Qur'ān was revealed to the Arab nations who lived in deserts. However, the Qur'ān repeatedly speaks of ships sailing in the sea and hazards of the sea. Here are some of the verses:

> *...and in the ships that sail in the sea that profits mankind...there are sure signs for people who apply sense. (2:164)*
>
> *Don't you see that the ships sail in the sea with the favor of Allāh, that He may show you some of His signs. (31:31)*
>
> *And a Sign to them is that We carry their offspring in the loaded ships. (36:41)*
>
> *And of His Signs are the ships in the sea like mountains. (42:32)*

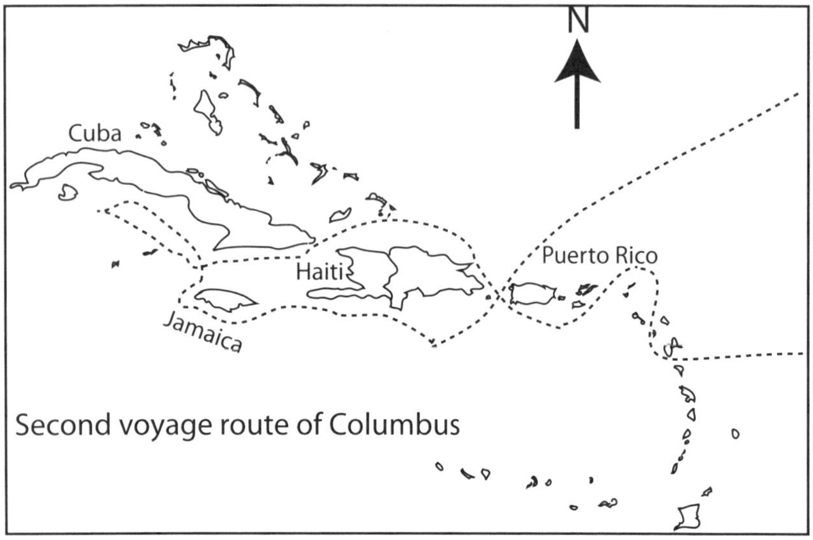

Second voyage route of Columbus

The earliest audiences of the Qur'ān were the Quraish and the Arabs. Unless they knew about ships and sea voyages, speaking to them about these would not make sense. This clearly indicates they knew very well about ships and sea travels. The travels may have taken place in the Arabian Sea, Red Sea, Mediterranean Sea or Indian Ocean. After the advent of Islam, Muslims increasingly felt the need to carry the message to far off places. Although unknown, it is possible that some of the earliest Muslims in the seventh of eighth century voyaged all the way to America. The Qur'ān encouraged them to undertake *Hijrat* and spread the message of Islam around the globe.

Immigration at the time of Columbus: Documented arrival of Muslims in the continent dates back to the time of Columbus who arrived in the year 1492. Among his crew were several Muslim navigators, who had already aided Spanish and Portuguese sailors visit the continent. It is important to note that during the period of Columbus, Islam in Spain and Europe suffered great setbacks at the hand of rising power of Christianity. Many of the Muslims abandoned their religion and many outwardly pretended to be Christians. Those who pretended to be Christians were called ***Mariscos*** i.e. Spanish Muslims who pretend to be Christians. By sixteenth century, thousands of Mariscos arrived with the Spanish and Portuguese colonial armies.

What happened to the immigrants: The Mariscos in North America felt that they were free to profess their religion without any reservations. Most of the Christian immigrants felt the same way about professing their religion free from obligations and sanctions from Church. However, once the Mariscos disclosed their identity and faith, they were persecuted. The fearful ones continued to outwardly profess Christianity. Within a generation or two these Mariscos lost their Islamic undertone and fully assimilated in the mainstream Christianity.

African Immigrants: Although earliest Muslims in America came from the north-western corners of Africa, large groups of Muslims came as part of the slave trade, starting from the seventeenth century. They were sold in various east coast cities. Many of these African Muslims rose to eminence even as slaves. Some of them were able to earn their freedom and become independent workers.

Famous among such African Muslims were **Sulaiman Ibn Diallo** who was a practicing Muslim. He was well versed in Arabic, wrote several letters in Arabic, translated coin inscriptions and drew map of West Africa. Other important names are

Interesting Facts

In 1730 Ayuba Soleiman Dijallo, a well educated Muslim merchant, was enslaved and brought to Maryland.

In 1767 Kunta Kinte from Gambia was captured, enslaved and brought to Maryland. Alex Haley based his best seller 'Roots' on the struggle and survival of Kunta Kinte.

In 1788 Ibrāhīm Abdul Rahmān was brought as slave from Guinea. He was known as 'Prince of Slaves' because of his noble heritage.

In 1803 Sālih Bilali was enslaved. He served as plantation manager and Muslim leader of African people.

In 1807 Yarrow Marmood was freed from slavery. He was well known Muslim leader in Washington DC area.

In 1893 Alexander Russell Webb was the first known white American to accept Islam.

Sālih Bilali, Yarrow Marmood, Lamine Jay, Omar Ibn Sayyid, Abrahim Abdul Rahmān, Nicholas Said.

1700's: Majority, if not all, of the Muslims in North America in this century were slaves at least once in their life time. Several state historical societies have records of Muslim names. Portraits of some of these Muslims are also available in museums. Many of the slaves of this period escaped and earned freedom. Some slaves became successful in different fields of trades. The relationship of United States started to develop with Muslim countries. Morocco was the first country in the world to recognize the United States of America in 1777. This recognition allowed easy traffic for American ships. Sultan Mohammed III of Morocco and President George Washington had established diplomatic communications.

Alex Haley's Roots: In 1976 Alex Haley published a historical novel titled *Roots: The Saga of An American Family*. In this novel Haley depicted a story of Kunta Kinte, who was kidnapped from Gambia in 1767 and shipped to Annapolis, Maryland to work as a slave. Kunta Kinte was a Muslim, from the village of Juffure, Gambia. Kunta Kinte fought hard to maintain his Muslim heritage. He learned many small sūrah from the Qur'ān when he was in Gambia. As a slave he tried to remember the sūrahs as he used to scratch the verses on the sand. The novel Roots was translated into 37 languages and made into a popular TV miniseries.

1800's: The contributions of Muslims to the United States in this century are well documented. Although most were still slaves, many were free. Some of them participated in the Civil War. As Suez Canal opened, many Muslims from Yemen, Lebanon, Syria and other Arab regions arrived in North America. Mohammed Alexander Russell Webb was the first known white American revert to Islam. He accepted Islam in 1888. He was a diplomat by profession and was active in spreading the message of Islam.

In the 1800's, several townships were named with Arabic words, such as Medina, Mecca and Mahomet.

Current trends: In twentieth century Muslim population continued to increase. A major section of Muslims are new immigrants who arrived voluntarily from Europe, Africa and Asia. They realized the importance of building mosques and continuing the Islamic teachings. Some of these Muslims lost their Islamic identity as they failed to pass on the Islamic values to their children and grandchildren. A large section of the Muslims in North America are revert from other religions. Another section of the Muslims are born in the Americas, to immigrant or revert Muslim parents. The history of Muslims during the nineteenth and twentieth centuries is vast and rich. Muslims have positively and negatively affected the fabric of North American society. Insha-Allāh we will cover this vast history in another lesson.

Optional Readings

The following are some books in alphabetic order that discuss about Muslims in North America:

1. A Muslim in Victorian America: The Life of Alexander Russell Webb. Umar F. Abd-Allāh. Oxford University Press. 2006
2. African Muslims in Antebellum America: Transatlantic Stories and Spiritual Struggles. Allan D. Austin. Routledge. 1997
3. Islam in America. Jane I. Smith. Columbia University Press. 2000
4. Islam in the United States of America. Sulayman Nyang. Kazi Publications. 1999
5. Muslims in America: Seven Centuries of History. Amir Nāshid Ali Muhammad. Amana Publications. 2003
6. Muslims in American History: A Forgotten Legacy. Jerard F. Dirks. Amana Publications. 2006
7. Prince among Slaves. Terry Alford. Oxford University Press. 2007
8. Servants of Allāh: African Muslims Enslaved in the Americas. Sylviane Diouf. NYU Press, 1998
9. Yankee Muslim: The Asian Travels of Mohammed Alexander Russell Webb. Mohammed Alexander Russell Webb and Brent D. Singleton. Wildside Press. 2007

homework**weekend 21**

1. According to the history, when did Muslims first arrive in North America?

   a. They traveled with Christopher Columbus.
   b. They were brought by force as slaves in 17th century.
   c. They came about 180 years before Christopher Columbus.
   d. They came at the time of Abu Bakr, the first khalīfa.
   e. When the Umayyad dyNāsty was formed.

2. Which river route did the early Muslims use in North America?

   a. Hudson river.
   b. Mississippi river.
   c. Missouri river.
   d. Rio Grande river.
   e. Amazon river.

3. Columbus had used some travel documents created by a Muslim scholar. Who was this scholar?

....

4. How many states in the U.S.A. have a town named Medina?

....

5. Read Sūrah Al- 'Ankabut, verse 20. What is command in this verse that Muslims should follow to see how Allāh originated the creation?

....

6. Who were the Mariscos?

   a. Portuguese navigators and sailors.
   b. Spanish rulers who persecuted the Muslims.
   c. Spanish Muslims who used to hide their identity.
   d. African slaves in the cotton fields of the South.
   e. Traders who bought and sold slaves.

7. The Mariscos assimilated with the mainstream society due to persecution. True / False

8. Which is the first country to recognize the United States of America?

a. Great Britain.
b. France.
c. Yemen.
d. Morocco.
e. Mexico.

9. Mark ☑ if the statement is correct, and mark ☒ if it is wrong.

a. Sultan Mohammed III and President George Bush had diplomatic communications. ☐
b. Alex Haley was the first white American Muslim. ☐
c. Several African slaves were well versed in Arabic and Qur'ān. ☐
d. The Panama Canal allowed easy travel for many Arabs to America. ☐

10. What are the current three major sections of Muslim population in North America?

....

....

classwork**weekend 22**

Life Cycle of Truth

Objective of the Lesson:

Truth passes through several stages before people can readily accept it. The truth passed through a 'life cycle' each time past prophets preached their message. It passes through the cycle even today. This lesson discusses the 'life cycle' of truth with evidences from history of the prophets.

The term 'life cycle' typically means a series of stages through which an organism passes, starting from embryonic origin, birth, development, maturity to death. Apart from living organisms, non-living and abstract objects may go through their own life cycle. A star in the universe has its own life cycle. A river or a pond has its own life cycle. A manufactured product has its own life cycle. Even our culture and nation have their own life cycles.

The stages of life cycle for organisms and abstract things are different. All living organisms and plants go through similar life cycle of birth, growth, maturity and death. However, the life cycle of abstract things follow somewhat different stages. Truth is an abstract thing and it passes through its own life cycle. The life cycle of some truth becomes evident in a short period of time and some takes long period of time. Eventually all truth becomes evident.

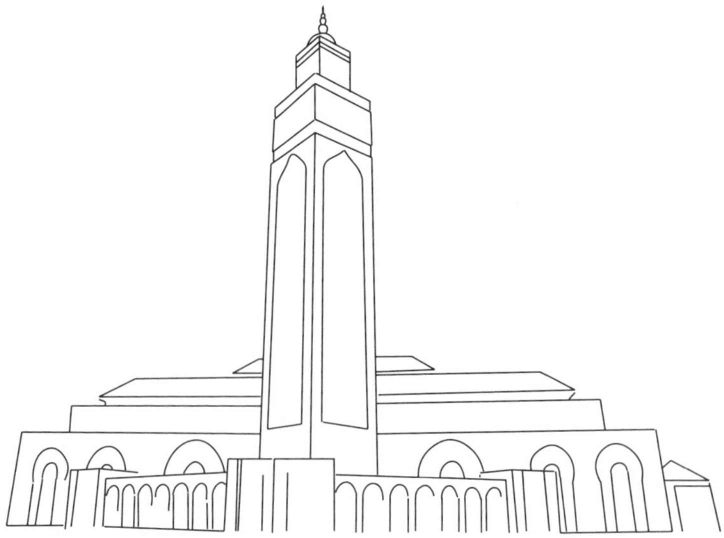

Truth and falsehood: Before discussing about the life cycle of truth, let us understand the origin of truth and falsehood. There is a fundamental difference about how truth and falsehood appear. Truth is always present; truth does not require to be invented. We may have to 'discover' truth; and once discovered, it cannot be denied. Sometimes truth surfaces or appears without any effort.

In contrast, falsehood has to be invented. Falsehood cannot surface on its own, because it cannot exist unless someone fabricates it.

Truth is never afraid of any amount of scrutiny. The more one investigates the truth, the more it is affirmed and established. In contrast, falsehood always fears scrutiny. The more one examines falsehood, the more it shatters.

Truth is important: Allāh created the heavens and the earth with Truth. He requires people to base their lives on truth, to speak the truth, to act with truth and to believe in nothing but the truth. If we are truthful in life, we will receive great benefit on the Day of Judgment. Allāh says that the successful people would be those who are truthful. For them, Allāh has reserved the Paradise, and Allāh will be happy with them.[4:119]

Life cycle of truth: As truth goes through various forms of investigations, it passes through different stages of life cycle. These series or stages of life cycle are as follows:

1. In the first stage truth is ridiculed,
2. In the second stage it is rejected,
3. In the third stage it is violently opposed,
4. Ultimately truth triumphs.

The Qur'ān about truth: Many verses in the Qur'ān points at the life cycle of truth without mentioning about the cycle. However, as you read the verses, you can see the stages through which truth must pass until it is firmly established.

> *This then is Allāh,— your true Lord; what is there then after the Truth but error? Then why do you turn away? (10:32)*
>
> *In order that He may prove the Truth is right and prove the Falsehood as false, even though the guilty may dislike. (8:8)*
>
> *And you say: "The Truth has come, and falsehood has vanished. Surely the falsehood is bound to vanish away." (17:81)*
>
> *In fact, We hurl the Truth against the falsehood, and it knocks out its brains, and it disappears. And woe be to you on account of what you assert. (21:18)*
>
> *Say: "The Truth has come, and falsehood cannot originate, nor can it reproduce." (34:49)*
>
> *...But Allāh wipes out the falsehood and establishes the Truth with His words. He is indeed Knower of what is in the hearts. (42:24)*

Examples from the Prophet (S)'s life: The examples from the life and activities of the Prophet (S) clearly show the life cycle of truth.

During the first few years of prophethood, Muhammad (S) was a target of ridicule. People could not believe that an ordinary person like Muhammad (S) was a prophet. They thought he did not deserve to be a prophet. Most of the noble and aristocrat people in Makkah thought Muhammad (S) became crazy.

People ridiculed him by saying he was a poet, magician, and a fraud. We will read about these accusations against the Prophet (S) in a separate chapter. People charged that if indeed the Qur'ān was true, it should have been revealed to an important person in Ta'if or Makkah.[43:31] They refused to accept that Allāh would revive the dead people who were now dust. They would not leave aside the idols, and they saw no benefit in worshipping one Allāh. They did not understand many things that Muhammad (S) told them. This initial stage of ridicule lasted for several years.

In the second stage, people began to reject the truth. They charged that the Muhammad (S) was lying about his claim of prophethood. Their rejection was not only verbal, but also they created pressure upon others not to believe in the message of Muhammad (S).

In the third stage, people began to oppose Islam violently. This was the most difficult stage for the Prophet (S). People boycotted his family and close companions for three years. Muslims were forced to live outside of Makkah and nobody was allowed to keep any social terms with them. During this phase, many Muslims sought temporary asylum in Abyssinia. The life of Muhammad (S) was then at risk. The clan members decided to kill him in order to stop him from preaching Islam.

During this stage the Prophet (S) migrated to Madīnah to save himself from the atrocities. Even in Madīnah his mission was not without problem.

Prophet (S) was forced to engage in several battles against the Makkan Quraish. The opposition was determined to stop the progress of truth at any cost. Battle after battle the Makkan Quraish suffered defeat, yet they continued to attack the Muslims.

When the Prophet (S) wanted to perform an *'umrah*, he was forced to return before entering Makkah. The polytheists forced him to sign a humiliating peace treaty. However, Allāh indicated that this treaty will pave the way for the fourth stage of the life cycle of truth. The Qur'ān identifies the treaty as *Fath Mubin* or a Grand Victory.

In their opposition to the truth, the polytheists soon violated the treaty. As it was the time for full exposure of the truth, Muhammad (S) and about 10,000 Muslims reached Makkah. Truth did not require any force, its appearance shattered falsehood. The leaders of Makkah surrendered their falsehood and Makkah was conquered without any bloodshed. Everybody in Makkah accepted Islam and truth was finally established.

Perception of truth: Despite truth being so important, it often undergoes rigorous investigation as we have seen from the life of Muhammad (S). Truth about God particularly takes most serious ridicule, rejection and violence. Falsehood, such as worshipping multiple deities or idols, do not undergo similar testing. Therefore, it is easy to fall prey to falsehood.

Examples from prophets: Examples from the lives and activities of other prophets show they too witnessed the life cycle of truth.

With Nūh (A), the leaders of the community ridiculed and rejected Nūh as he was only a human being. They called him a liar.[11:27] They thought he was possessed by devil.[23:25] They laughed at him when he was constructing a boat on dryland.[11:38]

And he was building the Ark; and every time the chiefs of his people passed by him, they laughed at him. He said: "If you laugh at us, then surely we will laugh at you just as you are laughing. (11:38)

The people of Hūd (A) ridiculed him when he was preaching the truth.[7:76] They did not accept that Allāh would send a human being as prophet. Much later when prophet Sālih (A) preached to a different community, they too ridiculed his teachings. These people later became vicious to him and wanted to destroy the propagation of truth. Similar was the treatment against 'Isa (A), who was rejected violently by most of his community.

The Qur'ān says all the prophets were ridiculed.[6:10; 13:32; 15:11; 18:106] It is beyond any doubt that the truths brought by each of the past prophets were ultimately established.

Message for us: In our daily life we come across challenges to understand and accept truth. Sometimes we are propagating truth, sometimes others are telling us about truth that we did not know. To deal with truth is difficult. Sometimes truth brings hardship. We should remember, if we seek the truth and we are truthful, Allāh will help us. Truth will always prevail. The examples of the prophets show us that truth always prevails.

homework**weekend 22**

1. What are the four stages through which all truth must pass until it is fully established?

....

2. Based on your knowledge about the life of Muhammad (S), mention four incidences from each of the four stages of life cycle of truth.

   a. ....

   b. ....

   c. ....

   d. ....

3. Read verse 34:49. When truth comes what two things cannot happen to falsehood?

....

4. During which stage(s) of life cycle of truth, the Prophet (S) migrated to Madīnah?

   a. During the first stage.
   b. During the second stage.
   c. During the third stage.
   d. During the fourth stage.
   e. During the first and second stages.

5. During which stage(s) of life cycle of truth, the Muslims suffered social boycott in Makkah and lived outside of Makkah for three years?

   a. During the first stage.
   b. During the second stage.
   c. During the third stage.
   d. During the fourth stage.
   e. During the first and second stages.

6. Based on the life of Muhammad (S), how long do you think it took for truth to be fully established?

   a. First five years of prophethood.
   b. Thirteen years during the Makkan period.
   c. Ten years during the Madīnah period.
   d. Last fifteen years of prophethood.
   e. Full twenty three years of prophethood.

7. The lesson refers to a peace treaty signed by the Prophet (S) with the Makkan Quraish during his plan to do ‘umrah. By what name the peace treaty became famous?

....

8. Read verse 11:38. How did the people react as they passed by the prophet?

....

Ramadan Can Bring the Best in Us

Objective of the Lesson:

Purpose of the month of Ramadan will be understated if we it is only about fasting. The objective of the word sawm is much more than skipping food during daytime. The month of Ramadan can bring the best in us only if we choose to make an effort. If not, we might simply be fasting and torturing our body without getting any benefit. This lesson discusses how the month can bring the best is us.

Faith of any person, whether Muslim or non-Muslim, increases or decreases under different circumstances and challenges in life. Sometimes a person of strong faith vacillates towards the wrong, and a person of weak faith emerges stronger in faith. Such changes happen as faith is not a fixed object that remains firm in a person's life. We cannot guarantee that our faith will never suffer from occasional erosion. The faith occasionally erodes for two reasons: human character is weak and prone to mistake,[4:28] and every human being is under constant attack from our open enemy Shaitān.[17:53; 35:6]

Our faith has two basic parts: (i) faith in Oneness of Allāh, (ii) willingness and commitment to submit to One Allāh and follow His commands. Usually, Muslims are the last to compromise their faith in Oneness of Allāh; however, many Muslims willingly or unwillingly compromise their commitment to follow the commands of same Allāh they believe so ardently. For this reason, we often hear the distressing question: *why are there so many Muslim in the world yet so few believers*?

This lesson will discuss how Ramadan can consolidate our faith and elevate us to a higher level spiritual uprightness.

Annual cleansing: Ramadan provides us with once a year opportunity to purify ourselves. We might argue, a good Muslim purifies him or her through performance of salāt, as the Qur'ān says surely the salāt restrains from indecency and evil.[29:45] Through salāt we establish direct link with Allāh. It helps us attain righteousness and nearness to our Creator. Since everyday we show devotion to Allāh through salāt, why do we need of this annual purification through performance of sawm?

Before analyzing this issue, let us take an example of a fast moving stream. We will find some rocks have green moss or algae on them. The rapid water cannot cleanse all the rocks and cannot prevent growth of moss or algae. If we swab inside of the drain pipe of a kitchen sink, we will invariably find accumulation of grime. Despite the volume of soapy water flowing through the sink, over time grime develops.

Similarly, despite daily remembrance of Allāh, there is possibility that over time our soul accumulates grime that need cleansing. Fasting provides us the opportunity to scrub away the accumulated scum in our soul and elevate ourselves to a higher moral and spiritual standard.

Fasting is a gift: Truly, prescription of fasting is a divine gift to mankind. Allāh prescribed fasting to all the people in all period of time.[2:183]

يَٰٓأَيُّهَا ٱلَّذِينَ ءَامَنُوا۟ كُتِبَ عَلَيْكُمُ ٱلصِّيَامُ كَمَا كُتِبَ عَلَى ٱلَّذِينَ مِن قَبْلِكُمْ لَعَلَّكُمْ تَتَّقُونَ ﴿١٨٣﴾

O you who believe! Sawm is prescribed for you, as it was prescribed to those who preceded you, so that you may practice taqwa. (2:183)

A hadīth narrates that the Prophet (S) said, whosoever fasts in the month of Ramadan, with faith and anticipation, whatever sins he has committed will be forgiven (Bukhāri, Muslim). Another Hadīth mentions that the Prophet (S) said, when the month of Ramadan begins, the doors of Paradise are opened and the doors of Fire are closed, the devils are chained (Bukhāri). When we reflect on the verse of the Qur'ān and the ahadīth, we will realize fasting is indeed a gift from Allāh.

Why fast in Ramadan: The four sacred months in Islamic calendar[9:36] are Muharram, Rajab, Dhul Qadah and Dhul Hijja. Ramadan is not one of them. Why did Allāh prescribe fasting in the month of Ramadan but not in the sacred months or other months? One reason is the Qur'ān was first revealed in the month of Ramadan.[2:185] The word Ramadan comes from the Arabic root word *ramada* which means to burn or to make burning hot. While fasting in the month of Ramadan, we symbolically burn all the bad natures, habits and emotions in our mind and body and improve ourselves as the best of Allāh's creation. Fasting calls for staying away from sins, big or small. Even the permissible and necessary acts to sustain life and propagate human race is given up.

Preparing for Ramadan: In a hadīth it is reported that the Prophet (S) said: how many there are that fast but attain nothing from it except hunger and thirst (Ibn Majah, Nāsa'i). In another hadīth it is reported: fasting is for me (i.e. Allāh) and I alone shall reward it (Bukhāri). The gravity of both these ahadīth calls for thorough preparation for Ramadan.

Prepare to abstain: During the period of sawm we give up acts that are normally permissible and necessary for our survival, such as eating, drinking and physical relationship between spouses. Now imagine if we can give up eating and drinking for a certain period of time, we should be able to give up other things that are not necessary for our survival. For example, jealousy, hatred, anger, backbiting, lying and many other emotional feelings are not necessary for our daily living. Thus, fasting is a form of spiritual training. We get this training once a year, every year.

Increase Taqwā: The main purpose of fasting is to increase our *taqwā*.[2:183] A simple meaning of the word *taqwā* is to increase awareness of Allāh—fear Him, submit to Him, and obey Him. We go through the pains of hunger as we know Allāh is constantly watching us. A month-long drilling of the realization that Allāh watches us all the time should carry us through the remaining eleven months of the year. If we utilize the month of Ramadan to increase our *taqwā*, obviously we would give ourselves the finest gift.

Recognize our sins: In the month of Ramadan let us recognize our sins—small and big. Think of the sins you committed knowingly and many other committed unknowingly. Mere recognition of sin prompts us to express repentance and seek forgiveness. It helps us realize our dependence upon our Creator and prepares us to submit to Him like never before.

Promote discipline: Fasting requires taking pre-dawn meal, staying without food or water all day long and eating at a specific time after sunset. It is a systematic process of disciplining ourselves. Let this process help us organize our lives and bring a set discipline that we would follow the rest of the year. Let fasting be a formal training for our body and mind. No matter how hot the day is, no matter how hungry or thirsty we are, no matter how tired we are, we cannot give up fasting. Fasting not only increases will power, but also develop commitment to our faith. We are to carry the lessons learned during Ramadan through the rest of the year.

Strengthen belief: Fasting requires our time, commitment and ability to withstand the difficulties of not eating or drinking all day. We cannot do this for long thirty days unless your faith is strong. Fasting, therefore, increases our faith. Let this increased level of faith remain with us the rest of the year.

Invest for Hereafter: It is mentioned in a Hadīth collected by Imam Bukhārī, Ibn Majah and Ahmad that the Prophet (S) said "every work of a child of Adam is counted for him except fasting. It is for Allāh and He rewards for it." Therefore, fasting is one of the finest investments we can make for our Hereafter. It is also reported by Imam Bukhārī and Muslim that the Prophet (S) said those who fast during Ramadan by devoting to Allāh, his or her sins will be forgiven and he or she will turn to be as pure as a new born.

Earn blessings: The month of Ramadan is full of blessings. The revelation of the Qur'ān started on a blessed night called ***lailatul qadr*** in Ramadan. How can we expect to get the blessings unless we fast? Therefore, fasting with sincere mind is the key to earn blessings. These blessings are multiplied throughout the month, particularly during the last ten days of the month. Additionally, it is multiplied many times on the night of *lailatul qadr*.

Fasting for errors: Although every able grown-up Muslim must fast during the month of Ramadan, fasting is also required for other kinds of errors or sins. The failure to complete the rituals of Hajj is made up by sacrifice and/or fasting.[2:196] If someone kills an animal while in *ihram*, then one way of making it up is by fasting.[5:95] If a Muslim kills another Muslim by mistake, and cannot pay blood-money or free a slave, he must fast for two full months.[4:92] Failure to keep an oath has to be made up with feeding the needy, clothing them or freeing a slave. If someone cannot make up with these, then he must fast for three days for breaking an oath.[5:89]

Clearly fasting is one of the finest ways to achieve *tawqā*. Let us approach the month of Ramadan with this objective in mind—to achieve *taqwā*. The process is a rigorous exercise. Our objective should be to perform our best. If we can do this for entire month, there is no reason why we cannot bring the best in us.

homework**weekend 23**

1. What are the two basic parts of our faith?

   a. ....

   b. ....

2. Based on the verse 2:183, what is the purpose of fasting?

   ....

3. What are the four sacred months in Islamic calendar?

   ....

   ....

4. Briefly explain the meaning of the root word *ramada*.

   ....

   ....

5. What permissible actions Muslims give up during fasting?

   ....

   ....

6. Mark ☑ if the statement is correct, and mark ☒ if it is wrong.

   a. When we have taqwa, we remember that Allāh is watching us. ☐
   b. Fasting of Ramadan is all about going hungry and thirsty. ☐
   c. Salāt restrains us from indecency and evil. ☐
   d. Teachings of Ramadan should be carried for rest of the year. ☐

7. Who is chained during the month of Ramadan ?

   ....

8. Briefly explain how Ramadan promotes discipline in us.

....

....

9. If someone fails to keep an oath, what are the action one can undertake to erase this sin? Also mention the appropriate verse number.

....

....

10. If someone cannot pay blood money for a mistaken murder, what is the Qur'ānic injunctions on the killer? Also mention the appropriate verse number.

....

....

classwork**weekend 24**

Indecency

Objective of the Lesson:

The Qur'ān strongly prohibits us from all forms indecency. However, what is indecency is open to wide range of discussion. This lesson discusses why indecency is prohibited and what constitutes indecency.

The simple meaning of the term indecency is something inappropriate, unsuitable, crude, unacceptable or improper. Antonym of indecency is decency. The word decency means something consistent and in agreement with socio-cultural standards of conduct and speech. Just as standards of decency vary widely from culture to culture, nation to nation, so also the interpretations of indecency vary across the board. Most societies relate indecency to certain sexual suggestions and activities in public. As such they attempt to regulate such human behavior.

Let us try to apply this simple meaning of indecency and decency to understand the position of Islam on the subject. Islam provides clear guidelines about proper codes of conduct and speech. These standards are defined by the Qur'ān and Sunnah. Interestingly, many of the Qur'ānic instructions are specific while some are left for interpretation. The Qur'ān leaves some instructions open for interpretation as its teachings are not restricted to a certain nation, geographic location, or period in time. The message is valid for every nation, every period in time. In the Qur'ān, the issues related to indecency is related to both sexual and non-sexual matters.

Indecency about sexual matter cannot be compromised at any cost. Therefore, the Qur'ān is very precise about this issue. However, about non-sexual matters, sometimes the Qur'ān clearly mentioned a particular human behavior as indecent, and at other times it left the meaning of indecency open for different interpretation, as we will see later in the lesson.

Fāhishah: The Qur'ān uses a word, *fāhishah*, to denote various forms of indecency. The origin of the word is from *fahusha*, which means to be shameful or infamous. The word *fāhishah* means an act of indecency, a manifest improper conduct, a shameful or dishonorable conduct, a conduct falling short of highest standard of faith. The word also means filthiness, uncleanness, an abominable crime, adultery or fornication. In over twenty instances in the Qur'ān we can find one or the other derivatives of the root word *fahusha*.

Shaitān commands indecency: The identity and role of Shaitān is known to us. He is our open enemy.[17:53; 36:60] He raises vain desires in our heart, gives false promise and deceive us in the end.[4:120] One of his major roles is to encourage us to indecency.

> *Surely Shaitān bids you to evil and **indecency** so that you may speak against Allāh what you do not know. (2:169)*
>
> *Shaitān threatens you with poverty, and bids you to **indecency**... (2:268)*
>
> *O you who believe! do not follow the footsteps of Shaitān; because whoever follows the footsteps of Shaitān, he then indeed commands **indecency** and evil.... (24:21)*

What is indecency: In the three verse mentioned above, Allāh has not mentioned what actions would constitute indecency. He cautions us to watch for the prompting of Shaitān who bids us to indecency. Therefore, all forms of misdeeds and improper conducts are included under the definition of indecency. We should also realize some of the socio-cultural standards of conduct and speech are bound to change over time. Therefore, without listing the activities that constituted indecency, the Qur'ān instructed us to avoid all forms of indecency. However, since not all socio-cultural changes are necessarily morally and ethically good, therefore, the Qur'ān promulgated clear restrictions about some social and behavioral activities that are indecent, regardless of advancement of civilization.

Open and hidden indecency: The Qur'ān prohibits both open and hidden indecency.[6:151,7:33] The Qur'ān says:

قُلْ إِنَّمَا حَرَّمَ رَبِّيَ الْفَوَاحِشَ مَا ظَهَرَ مِنْهَا
وَمَا بَطَنَ وَالْإِثْمَ وَالْبَغْيَ بِغَيْرِ الْحَقِّ وَأَنْ
تُشْرِكُوا بِاللَّهِ مَا لَمْ يُنَزِّلْ بِهِ سُلْطَانًا وَأَنْ
تَقُولُوا عَلَى اللَّهِ مَا لَا تَعْلَمُونَ ﴿٣٣﴾

> *Say: "My Rabb has forbidden only the indecencies— which of them are open and which are hidden, and the sin and rebellion without just cause, and that you associate with Allāh that for which He has not sent down an authority, and that you say against Allāh what you do not know." (7:33)*

The open indecencies are those that are committed in the public. At least two parties are involved in this kind of indecency, one who commits the indecency and the other who views it to enjoy. The hidden indecencies are those committed away from public view, such as in a private life. This kind of indecency can involve two parties, if there is physical relationship or activity. The private indecency can involve only one party, e.g. if the person is indulged in viewing or reading pornographic materials.

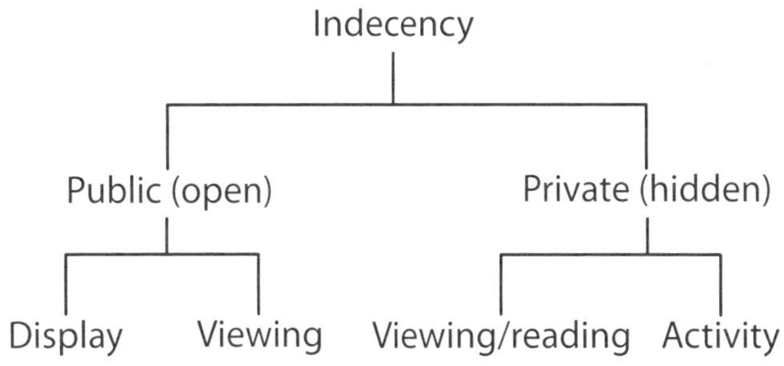

The Qur'ān instructs both men and women to lower their gazes,[24:30-31] to control themselves even if the other party is not indecent.

Indecency of women: Most societies and nations relate indecency to certain sexual suggestions and activities in public. The Qur'ān recognizes the problem of women themselves becoming indecent or becoming target of indecency. In sūrah an-Nisā' the issue of indecency is raised:

And whoever of your womenfolk commit an indecency, then call to witness against them four from among you, then if they bear witness, then confine them inside the houses until death overtakes them or Allāh makes for them a way. (4:15)

Here again, the definition of what actions of the women would constitute indecent (*fāhishah*) are not specified. Some of the scholars interpreted the meaning of *fāhishah* as adultery or fornication. It is just one shade of meaning, but not the complete meaning. The punishment for fornication, as mentioned in verse 24:2, is flogging the culprits one hundred stripes without showing any mercy. In the current verse the punishment for indecency is confining them inside their houses. Thus, intended meaning of the term *fāhishah* is grossly immodest act conducted openly. Such act must be so wanton, that at least four witnesses can testify. For such indecency, her punishment is to curtail her liberties. Unless she redeems her honor by repenting and amending,[4:16] curtailment of her liberties would continue indefinitely, implied by the phrase until death overtakes them or Allāh makes for them a way for them to their liberty through their sincere repentance.

Urge to display: The feminine urge to display women's beauty is another form of indecency. Wearing revealing outfit or clothes that exaggerate the shape of the body may appear the norm of the day; however, Islam discourages such conduct. All beautification and make-up aimed at attracting other men is nothing but sheer ignorance. Women should be careful not to beautify themselves to attract other men. If the hidden desire of beautification is to attract other men, then the divine command is to remain in the house so as not to display their sensual beauty as the women used to do during the time of *jāhilliyyah*.[33:33]

The divine command to draw down the head covering over the bosom of women comes from the same urgency to preserve decency and nobility of women.[24:31] The divine command for women not to walk with provocative gait also comes from the same spirit of decency.[24:31]

Voice and indecency: The voice of a person can lead to indecency for both men and women. Even normal conversation between a man and woman can be indecent if there is a hidden desire in the heart. Both men and women should be cautious about it. Women are advised not to speak in such soft voice lest men with perverted mind cherish false desires towards them.[33:32] Under all circumstance men and women should speak nothing but good speech. During conversation, the proper Islamic manner is to speak in a gentle, low voice. The Qur'ān compares speaking loudly with the braying of a donkey.[31:19]

Homosexuality is indecency: Islam does not give any rights to have sexual attraction between people of same sexes. Such attraction is clearly viewed as gross indecency (*fāhishah*). The Western world seems to tone down their voice against such forms of indecency to the extent that society is ready to allow certain civic rights to the same sex couple. Prophet Lūt (A) pronounced such forms of indecency as abomination.[21:74] It is a sin and the punishment for such sin is severe.

Behold! Lūt said to his people: "Certainly you commit an indecency which has not been practiced before you by any of the nations. (29:28)

Violation of civil manners: Violation of many of the civil manners also constitutes indecency. Some of the manners are clearly mentioned in the Qur'ān. Backbiting is a social evil—a gross form of indecency that the Qur'ān discourages by comparing it to eating flesh of dead brother.[49:12] Similarly defamation of other people constitutes indecency, therefore hateful in the sight of Allāh.[4:148; 24:23] Trespassing in other's houses without taking their permission is certainly improper, therefore indecent behavior.[24:27-28] The Qur'ān also states that name calling, spying upon others, arrogant behavior, mocking of others religion, belittling others are improper acts, therefore indecent conduct.

Salāt restrains indecency: The best way to restrain ourselves from all forms of indecent behavior is to remember Allāh and perform salāt. The Qur'ān says:

You recite what has been revealed to you of the Scripture, and establish the salāt. Surely the salāt restrains from indecency and evil. And the remembrance of Allāh is indeed the greatest. For Allāh knows what you perform. (29:45)

We should remember decency and modesty in dress and behavior are qualities of good Muslim. We should not violate the sense of decency. Islam encourages preserving modesty (*hayā*). If we learn to protect our *hayā*, we will be able to refrain from indecencies. Let not shaitān control us to become indecent in our conduct and let not indecency be part of our personality.

homework**weekend 24**

1. What is the basic definition of indecency?

....

....

2. About Shaitān inviting people to indecency, mark ☑ if the statement is correct, and mark ☒ if it is wrong.

   a. Shaitān wants us to speak against Allāh. ☐
   b. Shaitān ask us to indulge in indecency to avoid poverty. ☐
   c. Shaitān asks us to indulge in indecency by following his footsteps. ☐
   d. Shaitān 's plan is limited to indulging in sexual indecency. ☐

3. About the two types indecency, mark ☑ if the statement is correct, and mark ☒ if it is wrong.

   a. Indecency can be open or hidden. ☐
   b. Public indecency can involve two or more parties. ☐
   c. Private indecency can involve two or more parties. ☐
   d. Private indecency may not be known to others except Allāh. ☐

4. How many witnesses are needed to confine a woman for conducting gross indecency or *fāhishah*?

....

5. What steps a woman can take to avoid the confinement due to gross indecency or *fāhishah*? Find the answer in verse 4:16.

....

....

6. In verse 33:33, an act is considered the practice of *jāhilliyyah* or time of ignorance. What is this act?

....

7. Based on verses 24:30-31, how should a man or a woman deal with their gazes ?

....

8. In verse 33:32, the wives of the Prophet (S) were told something about their speech. As the wives of the Prophet (S) are honorable *Mothers of the Believers*, what do Muslims women learn from this instruction?

....

....

9. To what does the Qur'ān compare the indecency of backbiting?

....

10. Mark ☑ if the act is indecency, and mark ☒ if it is not.

a. Defamation of others. ☐
b. Trespassing. ☐
c. Spying. ☐
d. Homosexuality. ☐

Allegations Against the Prophet (S)

Objective of the Lesson:

Contemporary people hurled many types of allegations against the Prophet (S)—crazy, soothsayer, liar, poet, forger to name a few. This lesson analyzes the significance behind these allegations. The analysis shows that the allegations were very sinister not only for the Prophet (S) but also for Islam.

During the early phases of the Rasulullah's (S) life, the contemporary audience accused him in many different ways using many different derogatory words. These accusations were serious in nature and the Qur'ān did not overlook them or leave them unanswered.

In the early Makkan revelations, the Qur'ān repeatedly quoted many such accusations and refuted these in the strongest terms. In most of the cases the Qur'ān strongly rejected the allegations, and at other times it challenged the accusers. Sometimes it counter-accused the accusers in a way to expose their wicked mentality, and at other times it simply condemned the accusers. By refuting or challenging the allegations, the contemporary misgivings were settled, and provided answers for all such allegations that would arise in future after the Prophet (S) passed away.

These accusations provide an interesting insight into the socio-cultural environment at the time of the Prophet (S). These charges give us an idea of how difficult and challenging the Prophet's (S) job was and how much criticism he had to withstand.

Common accusations: The allegations against the Prophet (S) were mostly raised by the disbelievers. There were also many hypocrites who outwardly confessed faith but did not truly believe. They too raised various accusations to undermine the spirit of Islam and to create confusion in the minds of the believers. Some of the most common allegations against the Prophet (S) were: he was i) a liar (*kadhdhāb*), ii) a soothsayer *(kahin)*, iii) a poet *(shā'ir)*, iv) a forger, v) an enchanter *(sāhir)*, or vi) an insane person *(majnūn)*.

Accusation of being a liar : The most common way to discredit a statement of a person is to tell the person that he is lying. To accuse him as a "liar" will take the allegation little further. The word "liar" indicates the person habitually lies and cannot be trusted. A liar does not speak one lie, but always lies about everything.

In short, a liar is one who falsifies the truth. He may cover it up, deny it, or make up a new statements or change a prior statement. When a person accuses another person as a liar, the first person implies some of the following things:

1. He implies that he knows the matter correctly, and tells the truth,
2. He implies that the other person may know the matter, but is misleading,
3. He implies that the other person cannot be trusted,
4. He implies that he is more reliable,
5. He implies that the other person changes his words,
6. He implies that the other person falsifies truth.

The Prophet (S) was accused of being a liar since people claimed his words were untrue, he was falsifying, and he was making up stories. These people wanted to convince others that he was not reliable. They implied that he was not only lying about one thing, but also lying about many other things. For example, not only Awakening was a lie, but also his claim of prophethood was a lie. Since these false allegations were raised many times, the Qur'ān addressed the issue in many verses, e.g. 6:33-34; 25:4; 34:43; 38:4. Below are quotes of two such verses:

But those who disbelieve say: "This is nothing but a lie which he has forged, and other people have helped him on it." So indeed they have brought forth an injustice and a falsehood. (25:4)

For, when Our clear Messages are recited to them, they say: "He is nothing but a man who wishes to keep you back from what your forefathers used to worship." And they say: "This is nothing but a lie forged." And those who disbelieve say regarding the Truth when it comes to them: "This is nothing but an obvious enchantment!" (34:43)

Accusation of being a soothsayer: In contemporary Arabia a *Kahin* used to earn great attention and awe from the audience. A *kahin* was a title given to a person who showed strong aptitude at reciting couplets. They also made predictions about future. Most of the predictions were derived from Shaitān or from the sources of jinns. The *kahins* were often reported to go into spells induced by some devilish spirits.

When the disbelievers accused the Prophet (S) of being a *kahin*, they implied he was no different from other *kahins* in Arabia—influenced by devil, recited couplets and made predictions about the future. They cleverly related the prophecy made by Muhammad (S) with the predictions made by the soothsayers. These were outwardly similar—but the prophecy originated from Allāh, whereas soothsaying originated from the Shaitān . Ordinary people could not tell which one was from Allāh and which one was a trick from Shaitān . Needless to say, such allegations prevented many people from accepting Islam or recognizing Muhammad (S) as messenger of Allāh. Verses dealing with the issue of *Kahin* also speak about the allegation made about the Prophet (S) being a poet, e.g. 21:5; 36:69; 37:36; 52:29-30; 69:40-43.

"In fact", they say: "medleys of dreams! of course, he has forged it! rather he is a poet. Then let him bring us a Sign as the former were sent with." (21:5)

Accusation of being a poet: If someone says you are a poet, probably it is a compliment. For a person, the title of 'poet' or 'novelist' or 'story-teller' would not mean anything derogatory. Therefore, it may appear that calling Muhammad (S) a poet is not very alarming. However, the implication of the allegation was as vicious as any other accusations.

Most of the poets in Arabia used poetry as a social past-time and to please the audience. The themes of many of the poems were eulogies of the ancestors, nature, women, or these were just word play without any serious meaning. Most importantly, none of the famous poets at that time claimed to be Allāh's messenger. None of them claimed the verses they composed were divine.

Thus, by equating Muhammad (S) to the poets, the opponents wanted to refute his claim of being a *nabi*. The implied argument was if none of the poets were prophets, Muhammad (S) could not be a prophet. The opponents wanted the Arabs to take his messages as mere word play. If the leaders could establish the concept of Muhammad (S) being a poet, then people would not worry about morality and Awakening so often emphasized in the early revelations.

They had a reason behind raising these allegations. Most of the early revelations had strong rhymes and assonance in the verse. Assonance means resemblance of sound in words or syllables. When read out loud, the audience noticed the rhyme and assonance in many sūrahs. These features in the early Makkan revelation attracted the audience. The disbelievers wanted to twist these features to write off the Prophet (S) as an ordinary poet. The Qur'ān says:

> *And We have not taught him poetry, nor is it proper for him. This is nothing but a Reminder and a perspicuous Qur'ān, (36:69)*
>
> *and they said: "Shall we indeed give up our deities for the sake of an insane poet?" (37:36)*

Accusation of being a forger: The question of forgery is addressed in 21:5; 25:4; 32:3; 34:8; 38:7; 52:33; 69:44-47. You will notice many of these verses also speak of several allegations, such as verse 21:5 speaks of forgery as well as being a poet, verse 37:36 speaks of being insane and a poet.

> *Or do they say that he has forged it? No, it is the Truth from your Rabb in order that you may warn a people to whom no warner has come before you, that perhaps they may follow guidance. (32:3)*

The disbelievers raised allegation of forgery after they listened to the Prophet (S) recite some of the most spellbinding sūrahs. They argued if it was not for forgery, how can an unlettered person, without any eloquence or skill in literary composition, all of a sudden began saying phrases rich in literary styles, resonance and assonance, unparalleled in the history.

Frequent mention of past events in the Qur'ān also led the skeptics argue that Muhammad (S) forged the information. The Makkans vaguely knew about some of the past events through legends and through the books of Christians and Jews. Muhammad (S) provided details about these events, and many times differing from the Bible. The people thought unless these were plagiarized, he could not have known the details. They argued that he must have heard these events from other sources during his early life or at that time from some unknown foreigner.[16:103] The Jews of Madīnah knew about Biblical descriptions, and they argued that Muhammad(S)'s version distorted what they knew.

Accusation of being an enchanter: The Prophet (S) was often accused of being an enchanter. The term *sihr* primarily denotes sorcery or magic. In an act of magic the magician creates an illusion of changing one thing into another by subtle maneuvers that beat ordinary observation. All magic are for entertainment but no magic expects to make a lasting effect. For example, a magician 'cuts' a person inside a box into two pieces, and a few moments later the person jumps out of the box to the surprise of the audience. In other words, no lasting effect or permanent damage was done to the person in the magic show. The fools take the magic for real, while other people know the magic is a trick.

The Prophet's (S) mission and preaching appeared to challenge the contemporary social philosophy and ideology to such an extent that most skeptics thought it was not achievable, therefore illusory in nature.[10:2; 21:3; 25:8; 38:4; 74:18-25] Once the magical spell would be over, things would return to the normal. Maybe the fools were taking the message for real.

....The Unbelievers say: "Certainly this is obviously an enchanter." (10:2)

Now they wonder because a warner from among themselves has come to them; and the Unbelievers say: "This is an enchanter a great liar. (38:4)

Interestingly not only the disbelievers of that time brought such allegations towards the Prophet (S), but earlier people also similarly blamed their prophets.[51:52]

Accusation of being insane: A mad or insane person is one who is unsound in mind and body. Either he has a dysfunctional brain or a retarded brain. Sometimes a person can be fully discredited if the word he says does not make any sense to the hearer. The influential contemporary leaders ridiculed the Prophet (S) as an insane person to let fellow naïve people believe his sayings were worthless. If the general audience were made to believe the Prophet (S) was unsound in mind, his words would not warrant second attention. The leaders thought people might write off his words as senseless and would not follow his religion. The allegations of the Prophet (S) being a madman is addressed in 7:184; 15:6; 34:8,46; 37:36; 52:29; 68:2,6,51; 81:22.

And they say: "O you upon whom the Reminder has been revealed! you are certainly mad indeed. (15:6)

and they said: "Shall we indeed give up our deities for the sake of a mad poet?" (37:36)

Have they not reflected? Their Companion has no madness. He is none but a perspicuous warner. (7:184)

Accusations by hypocrites: The hypocrites did not have full faith in the religion. They might have accepted Islam, but their commitment towards Islam was weak. As such many of them accused the Prophet (S) for not becoming forthright with them. During the battle of Uhud, Khandaq and expedition of Tabūk, as well as at many other occasions, some of the half hearted believers and hypocrites accused the Prophet (S) for being deceptive. Obviously their purpose was to weaken the Muslim spirit since they themselves were not fully committed towards Islam.

Medieval and recent accusations: Starting from medieval European period until today, critics of Islam have charged Muhammad (S) as a war-monger and a lustful man. Interestingly, the opponents who lived at the time of Muhammad (S) did not bring such charges. In another lesson (weekend 16) of this course, we saw that Muhammad (S) tried his best to avoid bloodshed. Battles were thrust upon him. He was not a coward; he fought the battles bravely to secure the lives and properties of Muslims. Whenever possible, he opted for peace instead of war.

In two other lessons (weekends 14 and 15), we learned about the family life of Muhammad (S). Again, we saw that he was not a lustful man. Most of his wives were widows whom he had married to provide an honorable life.

homework**weekend 25**

1. The contemporary Arabs raised the accusations for several reasons. List a few of the main reasons.

   a. ....

   b. ....

   c. ....

2. When the people accused Muhammad (S) as a poet, what did they want to achieve?

   a. ....

   b. ....

   c. ....

3. What were the three major themes of the poems composed during the time of the Prophet (S)?

   a. ....

   b. ....

   c. ....

4. Read verse 25:4. What accusation did the Qur'ān refute in the verse?

   ....

   ....

   ....

5. What are the accusations raised in the verse 38:4?

....

6. What were the foundation of the charges against the Prophet (S) being a forger?

a. ....

b. ....

c. ....

7. In Arabia a *kahin* used to be a person who specialized in certain activity. Which of the following choice correctly identifies the key activity of a *kahin*?

a. Plagiarist of past scriptures.
b. Quack physician.
c. Worshipper of devil.
d. Recites couplets and foretells about future.
e. Hypocrite.

8. Allegation of forgery did not arise as much in Makkah as in Madīnah. Write the main reason this allegation flourished in Madīnah?

....

9. Read the verse 16:103. In connection with the allegation of forgery, who is said to have taught the Prophet (S) about past scriptures?

....

10. Write a short section to refute the current charge that Muhammad (S) was a war monger.

....

....

....

Family Values

Objective of the Lesson:

Who we are and what we do is determined by the type of family values we advocate and promote. In Islam family values play important role in shaping our personality and future. This lesson discusses some of the family values that all of us should espouse and encourage others to follow.

The simplest meaning of the word 'family' is a group of individuals living under one roof and usually under one head. A family is the basic unit of a society and is made up of parents and children. Each family may have its own moral and social values, which are termed the family values. For Muslims, many moral and social values are common. These are the Muslim family values. A Muslim family may have some other values based on culture or education. However, this lesson will restrict to family values originating from the Qur'ān and the sunnah of the Prophet (S).

Before discussing about family values in Islam, let us first understand how Islam portrays the concept of family. In Islam, a family starts only when a man marries a woman. If a man and woman are not married to each other, they cannot form a family. For this reason, students living in a dorm are not a family. They may live under the same roof of the dorm, have good feelings for each other, they may eat and play together, but they are not a family. In a family, if the father dies and the mother lives with her children, it still remains a family since the mother and the father were married together and they had started a family. A man and a woman, if they are not related and are not married, cannot be a family. Similarly two men or two women living together do not constitute a family.

Closely knit family: One of the important characteristics of a good Muslim family is their unity and bond of togetherness. The finest example of a family comes from the life of Muhammad (S). The Prophet (S) and Khadījah (ra) supported and nourished each other and also other members of the family. They were close to each other during ups and down of life. Due to such bonding, their family created a safe, loving, positive and supportive environment for all members in the family. Following the examples of this finest family, if one person in a Muslim family suffers, others in the family also feel it. They do many things together. Doing things together creates an atmosphere of love, mercy, understanding and sacrifice. They are able to utilize and distribute resources together and create a healthy environment under one roof.

The head of household: An adult member in a Muslim family is the head of the household. Typically the father is the head of the household. He serves as the role model for the family. He provides direction, support, commitment and goal of the family.

Although a mother usually does not serve as the head of the household, her role is extremely important. We know that Khadījah was wealthy, and she was Muhammad's (S) employer before their marriage. After the marriage, her role changed. It does not mean that a woman becomes inferior to a man after marriage. The Qur'ān has ordained the man a stage higher (*daraja*) than the woman.[2:228] This higher stage for man increases the responsibilities to his wife. The man needs to support and provide for the woman.[4:34]

From the example of Khadījah, we see that it is perfectly valid for a Muslim woman to have her own income. However, many times in the life, such as during pregnancy and raising a child, a woman may not be able to earn livelihood. Therefore, the father takes up the responsibility to maintain and provide for the family. Both the father and the mother work together to solve problems and they pass the values, morals, teachings and skills on to the next generation.

In many large families the grandfather is the head of the household. As Muhammad (S) was born after the death of his father, during his childhood his guardian was his grandfather. When Muhammad (S) himself had grandchildren, he was the head of the greater household.

Sources of the values: The core values of a Muslim family come from the teachings of the Qur'ān and the Sunnah of the Prophet (S). A Muslim family will not do things that are prohibited in Islam. If we see a member of the family is violating the values of Islam, it is our responsibility to remind each other about it. This is important because the Qur'ān says:

كُنتُمْ خَيْرَ أُمَّةٍ أُخْرِجَتْ لِلنَّاسِ تَأْمُرُونَ
بِالْمَعْرُوفِ وَتَنْهَوْنَ عَنِ الْمُنكَرِ وَتُؤْمِنُونَ بِاللَّهِ ۗ

You are the best community raised up for mankind, you bid doing right and forbid from doing wrong, and you believe in Allāh... (3:110)

Before we go out to encourage others to do the right and forbid others to do the wrong, we should start it from home. Once we exercise good moral teachings at home then whatever we do outside of home will automatically reflect these values. Teaching the values of morals to our own families is very important as mentioned in the following verse:

O you who believe! save yourselves and your families from a Fire whose fuel is men and stones... (66:6)

We do not want our families to become the fuel of fire—the Fire of Hell—where sinners and all objects of worship, particularly the idols will be thrown into.

Bond and attachment: When baby Mūsā (A) was left on a basket in the river, his sister ran by the river bank to keep an eye on the basket. She ran the distance because she had developed a deep bond for her brother.

A good Muslim family demonstrates a great bond and attachment. The family bonding builds the sense of closeness with other members of the family. It is true that each person in a family is different and each person develops his or her individuality, yet collectively we support each other and demonstrate the sense of love.

At one point in the Prophet's (S) life in Madīnah, he had several wives in his family. While each wife had her individual personality and mode of action, they were tied together with good degree of attachment.

In our family we can show Islamic values by committing ourselves to develop bonding. We can do this by spending time together, developing sense of love, respecting other members and establishing sense of belonging.

Communication: Inside a good Muslim family you will find members always communicate with each other. If we want to create a healthy family environment, we should keep the door of communication open. Lack of communication can bring serious problems in a family and destroy them. As a youth we often have the tendency to shut off the channel of communication with the seniors in the family. We do this due to fear and lack of trust upon them. Whereas if we open up and express our thoughts, concerns, problems, tensions and questions with others in the family, it will only increase security and trust. When Ibrāhīm (A) had a dream about sacrificing his beloved son Ismā'īl (A), he asked the son to express his opinion about the dream.[37:102] The father did not impose his understanding of the dream, but opened up a path of communication.

Respect and kindness: As we communicate, we also learn how to respect each other. Members in a good Muslim family always respect each other. Respect is not a fear of the other person. Respect means appreciating, honoring and understanding the person. All brothers and sisters are different, and they may have different likings. In a family we respect the likings and disliking of everyone. We do not hate each other.

Yūsuf (A) had stepbrothers who once wanted to physically harm or even kill him. Many years later, when Yūsuf had his chance, he won over them by showing kindness.[12:92] He gave his stepbrothers an opportunity to realize their sins, but left any decision of their fate upon Allāh.

Sharing and caring: A good Muslim family loves to share with each other. When people learn to share, they learn to care for each other. We see an excellent example of sharing and caring between two brothers, Mūsā (A) and Hārūn (A). Mūsā had a limitation with his speech. When he had an important encounter in the Pharaoh's court, he solicited the help of brother Hārūn.[20:29-30] Hārūn not only helped his brother in this visit to the court, but also continued to help him in their common mission. Hārūn was different: he was made weak by the Israelites when they started worshipping a calf. They even wanted to kill him.[7:150] Mūsā was much stronger—he forcefully rebuked the Israelites for their sins. In the midst of this chaos of calf worshipping and the rebuke, Mūsā cared for his brother and prayed to Allāh for mercy upon both of them.[7:151] When we live in a family, we learn how to live with people who are similar yet different.

Self sacrifice: The sense of sharing also teaches us sense of self sacrifice. We learn to live for other, not live for the self. We do not want to satisfy our needs at the cost of others in the family. A little giving, a little sacrifice, and a little adjustment not only create a cordial environment in the family, but also create a sense of belonging. When Muhammad (S) slipped out of his house for *hijrat*, we see a grand example of sacrifice from 'Ali (r). Without worrying about his own life, 'Ali had decided to sleep on the bed of Muhammad (S). He knew that assassins were planning to strike at the person on the bed. He could have easily been assassinated that night.

Flexibility: A good Muslim family should demonstrate great deal of flexibility in the family roles. Rigidity in thoughts and strictness of conduct often blocks the path of progression. If there is a problem in the family, we can approach it from many different angles. Sometimes, two or three novel approaches can be better than a traditional approach. However, we should remember in the matter of some principles, such as religious duties, there cannot be compromise.

Upholding ties of kinship: A good Muslim family always preserves the ties of kinship. A kin is a near relative. Islam emphasizes importance of keeping the ties of kinship. We can do this by being kind and considerate with our relatives by treating them well and by giving them financial help if they need.

And give to the near of kin his due, and to the needy and the wayfarer, and do not squander wastefully. (17:26)

They ask you as to what they should spend. Say: "Whatever good things you spend, it is then for the parents and the kindred, and the orphans and the needy, and the wayfarer."... (2:215)

Surely Allāh commands the doing of justice, and doing good, and giving to the kindred; and He forbids indecencies, and evil, and rebellion. He exhorts you that you may mind. (16:90)

Education: A time will come when you will have your own family. Upholding the Islamic family values is important for all of us. One of the values of a Muslim family is to educate the children about Islam. From the life of Luqmān (A), we learn a father's caring teaching towards his children.

We should love our children, as they are gift to us from Allāh.[25:74] As children, we should also pray to Allāh to be kind to our parents.[46:15] If we can uphold the Islamic family values, we will not become losers.

...The losers are indeed those who have caused loss to themselves and to their families on the day of the Awakening. Is it not that the unjust will be in a lasting chastisement? (42:45)

homework**weekend 26**

1. List a few types of relationship that do not make a family.

    a. ....

    b. ....

    c. ....

2. As a man has a higher stage *(daraja)* over his wife, what should his responsibilities be?

    a. ....

    b. ....

    c. ....

3. How does upholding good family values help us to bid doing right and forbid doing wrong?

    a. ....

    b. ....

    c. ....

4. Read verse 37:102. What did Ibrāhīm (A) tell his son Ismā'īl (A)?

    ....

5. A good Muslim should always obey his or her parents, except in one situation. Read sūrah al-'Ankabut, verse 8, and then write the only situation when we should disobey our parents.

    ....

    ....

6. Mark ☑ if the statement is correct, and mark ☒ if it is wrong.

a. Yūsuf (A) harbored his grudge against the step brothers to take a revenge. ☐
b. Hārūn (A) helped Mūsā (A) in their common mission. ☐
c. Mūsā (A) had prayed to Allāh to grant mercy him and his brother. ☐
d. Ibrāhīm (A) had imposed his opinion about the dream on his son. ☐
e. Abu Bakr (r) had slept on the bed of Muhammad (S) to foil the assassination plan. ☐

7. Based on the verse 2:215, given in this lesson, on whom should we spend our wealth?

....

....

8. Based on the verse 42:45, given in this lesson, who are the losers?

....

....

classwork**weekend 27**

Sharī'ah

Objective of the Lesson:

Sharī'ah is Islamic law. Sharī'ah deals not only with the English concept of "law" but also spiritual and moral dimension of human activity. This lessons discusses the goals and roles of sharī'ah in Islam. The classification and historical development of sharī'ah are discussed.

Sharī'ah is a complex subject to fully understand at this level in school, but nonetheless in this lesson we will get an overview of sharī'ah in Islam. Briefly speaking sharī'ah is Islamic Law. This law broadly regulates both public and private life of a person regardless of where the person lives. It is different from the law of a country or a state since such law is applicable to the country or state where a person lives. Sharī'ah is beyond the boundaries of city, county, state or country because it regulates a Muslim's public and private life.

The literal meaning of sharī'ah is a path leading to the water, or a path that leads a person to the source of life. The word sharī'ah is derived from the verb *shara'a* which means a system of divine law allowing certain practice and belief and prohibiting certain other. The Qur'ān says in sūrah al-Jāthiya:

> *After that We have placed you upon a sacred law concerning the Affair; therefore you follow it, and do not follow the whims of those who do not know. (45:18)*

Components of sharī'ah: The topic of sharī'ah is intricate. Some scholars separate the Islamic laws into three distinct categories: sharī'ah, *fiqh* and *fatwā*. To them, sharī'ah is divine or divinely inspired. Sharī'ah is thus based on only the Qur'ān, which is divine, and the sunnah, as all the actions of Muhammad (S) was divinely inspired. The *fiqh* is based on the clear directives from the Qur'ān and the sunnah, and

Classification 1.

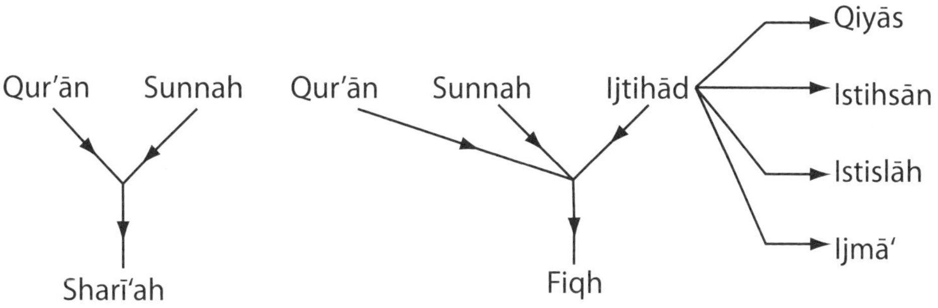

Classification 2.

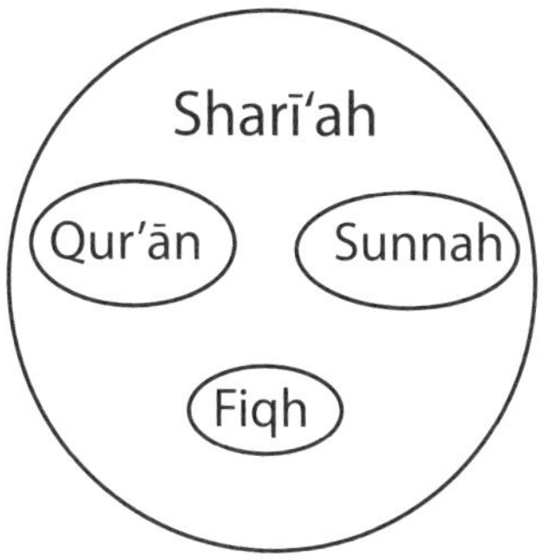

reasoning (*Ijtihād*) of the scholars. The *Ijtihād* or juristic reasoning is based on *qiyās* (analogical reasoning), *istihsān* (preference of the jurists), *istislāh* (public interest) and *ijmā'* (consensus). To other scholars, sharī'ah is a combination of the Qur'ān, sunnah and *fiqh*.

Simply speaking *fiqh* is jurisprudence, which means it is the science or philosophy of law or the system of law. The study of law, particularly Islamic law is called *Fiqh*. People who specialize in Islamic law are called *fuquah* or jurist. *Qiyās* is application of various forms of reasoning and analogy in deriving a conclusion. *Ijmā'* is consensus of group of experts who agree upon a particular decision. Usually these experts are proficient in the matter of law.

Ijtihād is not the same as *fatwā*. *Ijtihād* is a result of extensive study on a topic and is supported by thorough evidences. A *fatwā* is usually a brief opinion on a topic, which may or may not require equally exhaustive evidence. It is agreed that *ijtihād* should be limited to highly qualified legal scholars *(mujtahid)*, while *fatwā* can be issued by a scholar who may not be highly qualified. While the rulings of the Qur'ān and sunnah are binding on every Muslim, the rulings of *ijtihād* or *fatwā* may not have similar strict binding.

About 350 verses of the Qur'ān are legal verses *(ayat al-ahkam)*. The sunnah does not contradict these verses, but may add explanation to some other verses and clarify the general rulings. Sunnah also provides ruling on concepts not thoroughly discussed in the Qur'ān.

The law based on the Qur'ān and the Sunnah is absolute and these laws cannot be changed over time. However, laws based on *fiqh, ijmā'* and *qiyās* are said to be ever-evolving because the need and circumstances in each period changes. This may require re-interpreting a particular law over a period of time.

Roles of sharī'ah: Before we proceed any further let us try to understand how "law", as we understand in English usage, is different from sharī'ah. In English usage "law" refers to commands and prohibitions. For example law tells that you drive (on most interstate) at 65 miles per hour. Law requires that you pay taxes on your annual income.

Unlike federal and state laws which deal with civil and criminal issues, the scope of sharī'ah also include spiritual issues. The spiritual aspect of sharī'ah deal with *'ibadat*: e.g. specifying how salāt is to be performed or what penalty to give in case of a missed ritual of hajj. The civil laws of sharī'ah include rules on exchange of wealth or property, inheritance, matrimonial laws, litigation, etc. Criminal laws and administrative rulings are also part of sharī'ah.

Sharī'ah covers five additional categories of actions that English concept of "law" does not cover. These are: (a) the required, (b) the recommended, (c) the indifferent, (d) the discouraged and (d) the forbidden.

Examples of human activity: We understand what is "required" but let us look at what is "recommended" under sharī'ah. It is required that we perform *fard* part of the five daily salāt. But it is recommended that we also do several other types of salāt, i.e. sunnah and *nawafil* part of the salāt. All the five daily salāt have several recommended parts to it. Similarly, it is required that we fast during the month of Ramadan, but it is recommended that we fast on certain other parts of the year.

Many things are discouraged under sharī'ah. For example, divorce is fully permissible in Islam, however it is discouraged. Use of water for wudu is fully recommended, but excessive waste of water is discouraged. Eating a good meal is permissible, but excessive eating is discouraged. Similarly prescribed movements in salāt are allowed, but unnecessary movement, such as scratching is discouraged.

Goals of Sharī'ah: The purpose or *maqasid* of the Sharī'ah is threefold: 1) to increase the wisdom of people, 2) to bring justice, and 3) to benefit people.

It is expected that with the rulings of shari'ah, people will come out of ignorance, establish a community based on wisdom and thus honor and value its members. The sharī'ah, therefore, tries to eliminate *jāhilliyyah* that creeps into society in various forms.

Justice or *'adl* is a basic objective of Islam. When justice is served, goodness (*ihsān*) comes to the society. Sharī'ah thus continually tries to abolish injustice when the concept of justice and injustice evolves. The rulings of the Qur'ān and guidance from sunnah are permanent. However, based on the principles of divine rulings, the jurists reform the *fiqh* to counter injustice.

The third goal of sharī'ah is to bring benefit to the public. Benefit to an individual that results harm to the community is not justice. The sharī'ah takes the whole community in consideration for its ruling. In contrast to the civil laws implemented and practiced in any country, the scope of sharī'ah is vast. The spirit of Sharī'ah is not only to improve the life on this earth, but also to earn the members of the community a rewarding life in the Hereafter.

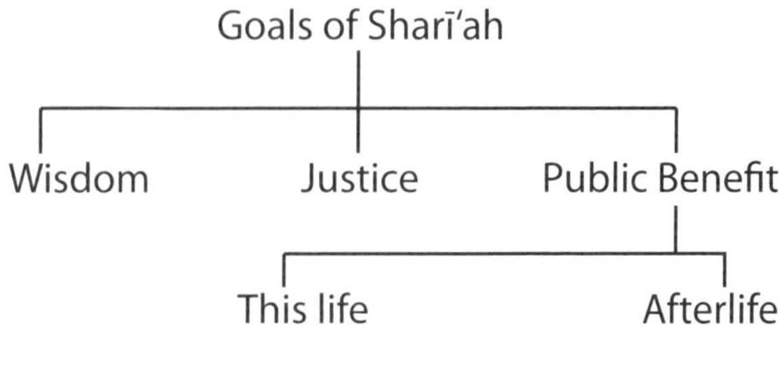

19th and 20th century trends: The laws based on *fiqh, ijmā'* and *qiyās* were develop by human interpretation, these also faced significant changes in the 19th and 20th century. During these two centuries, the West emerged as a global power and colonized large part of the world, including many Muslim territories. Due to rapid industrialization, the society changed from agricultural to industrial society. New social models emerged. Many Muslim territories saw State laws started replacing traditional laws. Sometimes Western countries compelled Muslim states to change their traditional laws. Islamic legal scholarship retained their authority in the matter of ritual, worship, spiritual matter but lost many of the control of the state and politics. As a result of all of these trends, different Muslim countries began to interpret the sharī'ah law differently. Even today such difference in opinion persists.

Contemporary sharī'ah in the world: Muslim world is facing tremendous variance in interpretation and implementation of Islamic law. Muslim thinkers have questioned the relevance and applicability of sharī'ah law from a variety of angles. Predominantly Muslim countries like Bangladesh, Indonesia, Pakistan have largely secular constitution and laws with few Islamic laws. At times sharī'ah laws are separately administered outside the state laws. India, where Muslims are a minority, have separate Muslim civil laws established by Muslim Personal Law board, which is based on sharī'ah law, but in the matter of criminal affair, the state laws prevail.

Many of the Middle Eastern and North African Muslim countries maintain dual system of secular and religious courts. The religious courts administer personal, marriage and moral issues of people. Countries like Saudi Arabia and Iran follow religious courts for civil and criminal matters and they have religious police to ensure compliance. Some countries have severe forms of sharī'ah laws and have harsh punishment for civil offence that are not dictated by the Qur'ān and Sunnah but developed by early jurisprudence based on *ijmā'* and *qiyas*.

Criticism: Many liberal thinkers and the West consider the punishments prescribed by the sharī'ah law are barbaric and cruel. Islamic thinkers have argued in favor of sharī'ah law as well as against its strict implementation. Many Islamic scholars argue that if sharī'ah law is implemented properly, it would deter additional crimes. They believe strict sharī'ah law maintains law and order and prevents many social crimes and moral sins. Statistics shows crime and moral sin in the West, where there are no sharī'ah law, are high. On the other hand in Muslim countries where there is sharī'ah law, the incidence of crime and moral sins are low.

Western media usually creates sensation when strict sharī'ah law is applied in a Muslim country in the matter of crime, adultery or women's education. Some of the sensational verdicts are based on a *fatwā,* and usually not a ruling from the Qur'ān and the Sunnah. We should remember that the rulings from the Qur'ān and the Sunnah are the standard by which all other man-made rulings should be judged. From the other viewpoint, Western laws may be sensational to observers from other countries.

homework**weekend 27**

1. What is the literal meaning of sharīʿah as given in this lesson?

....

2. What are the four basis of *ijtihād?*

a. .... b. ....

c. .... d. ....

3. How does *ijtihād* differ from *fatwā*?

....

....

....

4. What are the three goals of Sharīʿah ?

a. ....

b. ....

c. ....

5. Some off the following changes took place in Muslim territories during the 19th and 20th century. Mark ☑ if the statement is correct, and mark ☒ if it is wrong.

a. The West continued to occupy or colonize Muslim territories. ☐
b. Society moved from agricultural to industrial society. ☐
c. Authority of Islamic scholars was limited to spirituality and rituals. ☐
d. Traditional laws were gradually replaced by State laws. ☐

6. In page 157, a figure is given to classify Sharīʿah in two different ways. What is the primary difference in these two classifications?

....

7. Which of the following is an example of human activity that are covered by sharīʻah law but not covered by the Western concept of law.

   a. Sale of a property.
   b. Cleanliness.
   c. Crime of murder.
   d. Crime of theft.
   e. Death penalty.

8. What are the five categories of action that sharīʻah law covers, but English concept of "law" does not cover?

   a. ....

   b. ....

   c. ....

   d. ....

   e. ....

classwork**weekend 28**

Justice in Islam

Objective of the Lesson:

One of the most prominent Islamic value system teaches us to be just with everything, everybody. One need not be a trained judge to do justice. In this lesson selected Qur'ānic verses are picked to demonstrate why justice is important in Islam and how we can always uphold justice even if we are dealing with our near and dear ones.

The five pillars of Islam help shape our life, as the pillars stand for the five fundamental faiths and practice upon which all Muslims dwell. Just as a house has many other structures that support its overall framework and beauty, Islam too has many other structures that give its unique identity. After establishing the pillars in a house, we also need a roof over it to make the house livable. In Islam that roof is provided by two other components —Peace and Justice.

The concept of peace and justice are interrelated. There cannot be peace unless there is justice. Peace is a condition of security and orderliness, free of disturbance, and is in harmony and quietness. The unity or *Tawhid* of God is also reflected in harmony and balance in the universe. Injustice breaks the harmony, upsets the balance and provokes disorder. For this reason justice is one of the most important tenets in Islam. Peace and justice are central to Allāh's creative design and these two tenets will continue to be the key factors during the Day of Judgment.

Allāh's qualifying names: Allāh's qualifying names indicate His emphasis on justice. One of His most-beautiful names is *Al-'Adl* which means the Just. His another beautiful name is *al-Hakam*, which means the Judge. Yet another name is *al-Muqsīt*, which means the Equitable One. These names recognize Allāh as a Just, Equitable Judge. Of particular importance is the root word of *hakama* (ح ك م) from which words like *hukum* (judgment) is derived. The same root word also gives rise to words like *ahkam* meaning one who is most-Knowing or Wise, and *hikmat*, which means wisdom. Yet another beautiful name is *al-Hakīm*.

Justice and wisdom are closely related. A judge has to be wise and full of insight. Justice cannot be blind, although the word sometimes implies justice must be impartial. Allāh is most wise Judge because He has the best wisdom. A wise judge, based on his inner strength and insight, will not make mistake and will not fall into subjective ruling. Prophet Sulaimān (A) was a wise judge and his rulings were legendary.[21:78-79] His father Dāwūd (A) was also a just ruler.[38:26]

Establishment of justice: Allāh has commanded us to establish justice. Upholding justice is an obligation upon all Muslims and practice of injustice, therefore, is forbidden. We do not need not be in the authority of a judge to uphold justice. It is true, those who have the power and administrative roles have the higher responsibility to promote and maintain justice. Others also must uphold and maintain justice at social, political and economic level. The Qur'ān teaches us:

> *Say: "My Rabb enjoins justice. And you keep your countenances upright at every place of prostration, and you call upon Him being sincere to Him in religion." As He brought you forth, so you will return. (7:29)*

> *Surely Allāh commands the doing of justice, and doing good, and giving to the kindred; and He forbids indecencies, and evil, and rebellion. He exhorts you that you may mind. (16:90)*

> *We have indeed revealed to you the Scripture with the truth, so that you may judge between people by means of what Allāh has shown you. And do not become an advocate in favor of the treacherous, (4:105)*

Violation of justice: Usually, we can be just people under normal circumstances. However, under the influence of emotions, many of us lose the sense of justice. The stronger the emotion, the greater is the risk of violating justice. We can identify four emotional circumstances when we are likely to lose the good sense of justice. These are: a) love, b) self-interest, c) hatred and d) revenge. Let us look at each circumstance:

Love obstructs justice: The Qur'ān recognizes sense of love is a strong emotional reality among human being and it is also a weakness in their character. Excessive love towards wealth [89:20; 100:8; 102:1-2] or to our children[63:9] divert us from remembrance of Allāh. Love for this life distracts people from true objective of life.[75:20-21; 76:27]

In verse 4:135, Allāh points out the importance of upholding justice even if our emotional bonds towards our loved ones may misled us.

> *O you who believe! be upholders of justice, bearers of witness for Allāh, even though it be against your own selves, or parents, and relations; if he be rich, or poor, then Allāh is nearer to both of them; therefore do not follow low desires so that you may act equitably. And if you distort, or keep away, then surely Allāh is ever well-Aware of what you do. (4:135)*

The verse clearly shows the importance of upholding justice in every spheres of life. When it comes to giving a testimony, truth cannot be concealed, nor can it be exaggerated or falsified. We should speak the truth even if such testimony would go against oneself, family or social relations. The ties of kinship, love, compassion, favor or fear could hold back someone from giving a truthful testimony, thus seriously obstruct justice; therefore these ties are specially mentioned.

Self-interest obstructs justice: Self-interest is undue concern for one's own interest or advantage. To have self-interest is good as long as such interest does not violate others rights. As long as self-interest is used properly it will benefit the person. For example, a person performs salāt or *sawm* due to self-interest—to increase *taqwa* and to improve the self. When it comes to deliver justice, ignorant people try to preserve their self-interest by becoming unjust to others. They value their self-interest and become blind to the importance of doing justice.

The verse 4:135 that we read above tells us to bring ourselves above the urge to protect self-interest. The verse reminds us that *Allāh is nearer to both of them*, which means Allāh will protect both of them provided that we remain just.

Hatred obstructs justice: If we nurture hatred in our heart it is very likely that our conduct will express hatred. If we harbor hatred against someone, most likely we will be unfair to that person. Therefore, Allāh commands us in the Qur'ān:

> *O you who believe! be upright for Allāh as witness to fair dealing; and let not the hatred of others carry you away and you fail to act justly. Be just, that is nearer to piety. And fear Allāh. Allāh is indeed well-Aware of what you do. (5:8)*

Earlier, verse 4:135 showed us the importance of acting justly even with our near and dear one. Now, the verse 5:8 reminds us the importance of acting justly even towards the enemies. By nature, people are unfair to the enemies. During the period of *jāhilliyyah,* the society used to punish the enemies unfairly. With Islam, such unfair and improper form of justice was rejected.

Revenge obstructs justice: Fourteen hundred years ago Islam rejected another form of improper justice system. The prevailing system allowed improper, unbalanced and brutal retaliation. When a crime was committed by one person, the entire tribe of that person was targeted for retaliation. This was not justice to the innocent people of that tribe.

Islam reformed the system, and allowed retaliation in case of murder only.[2:178] The verse that permits retaliation brilliantly advocates forgiveness and reconciliation.

> *O you who believe! retaliation is prescribed for you in case of murder: the free for the free, and the slave for the slave, and the female for the female. But whoever is given any remission by his brother, the succession should be with fairness and compensation to him handsomely. This is a relaxation from your Rabb and a mercy. But whoever exceeds the limit after this, for him then is a painful punishment. (2:178)*

Muslims are commanded to return good for evil.[13:22; 23:96] The purpose behind such approach is to break the vicious circle of animosity. This teaching was best demonstrated by the Prophet (S) when he conquered Makkah. Earlier the pagan Quraish tried their best to destroy the Muslims, first by attempting to kill the Prophet (S), then forcing him to exile in Madīnah, and then fighting several battles against him. When the Prophet (S) had opportunity, instead of retaliating, he forgave the pagans. A normal justice would dictate their punishment, but forgiveness was a better way solve the animosity. We, Muslim, have greater need to remember this Sunnah of the Prophet (S) in the way we deal with our enemies.

> *And neither good nor evil can become parallel. Repel with whichever is the best; even when between you and him there were enmity as if he would become a warm friend. (41:34)*

Prophets established justice: Justice is not a fourteen hundred year old concept. As Allāh enjoins justice,[7:29] all the previous prophets also advocated justice. The following verse tells that the objective of all prophets and revelations were to establish justice.

> *Certainly We already sent Our Messengers with clear proofs, and We sent down with them the Book, and the balance, that mankind may establish justice... (57:25).*

Other Qur'ānic verses: The Qur'ān places utmost importance to establishing justice. Some other selected verses further illustrate the importance of justice in Islam:

> *...and when you judge among people, you judge with equity... (4:58)*

> *...if you judge, judge between them with justice.... (5:42)*

> *...And when you speak, then observe justice, even though it be concerning a relative.... (6:152)*

> *...therefore judge among people with justice, and do not follow desire, lest it would lead you astray from the way of Allāh...(38:26)*

> *And if two parties of the Believers fight, then make peace between them. But if one of them transgress against the other, then you fight that which transgressed, till they return to the command of Allāh. But when they do return*

then make peace between them with justice, and act equitably. Allāh certainly loves the equitable ones. (49:9)

Allāh does not prohibit you respecting those who have not fought you for the Religion, and who have not turned you out of your homes, that you show them kindness and act justly towards them. Certainly Allāh loves the just people. (60:8)

From our childhood, we have learned to establish the five pillars of Islam in our lives. As we grow up, it is important to put the aspect of justice in the house of Islam. We should practice justice and fairness in every aspect of our lives, even though we may never become a judge in a court of law.

from**hadith**

I have forbidden injustice for myself and made it forbidden among you, so do not oppress each other. (Muslim).

There are seven categories of people whom Allāh will shelter under His shade on the Day when there will be no shade except His. One is these is a just leader. (Muslim).

homework**weekend 28**

1. Explain briefly how peace and justice are correlated?

....

....

2. Write four names of Allāh that indicate His emphasis on justice.

a. .... b. ....

c. .... d. ....

3. What are the four different reasons that people cannot do justice?

a. .... b. ....

c. .... d. ....

4. What is the Islamic principle of justice if our loved ones are involved?

....

....

5. What is the Islamic principle of justice if our enemies are involved?

....

....

6. Mark ☑ if the statement is correct, and mark ☒ if it is wrong.

a. Islam does not allow justice to be swayed for self-interest. ☐
b. A Muslim must always save another Muslim from legal punishment. ☐
c. Islam allows disproportionate violence to control animosity. ☐
d. Forgiveness maybe better than punishment in some situations. ☐
e. Concept of justice started from the time of Muhammad (S). ☐

7. Based on verse 2:178, given in the lesson, if someone exceeds in the retaliation, what is in his fate?

....

8. Read verse 49:9, which is given in the lesson. What should be our step if we find two Muslims are fighting against each other?

....

....

....

9. Read verse 38:26. Then mention the name of the prophet who was addressed here, and briefly write the instruction about justice in this verse.

....

....

....

Outline of Curriculum – Grades 1, 2 and 3

Every year the curriculum begins with a few topics on Allāh, the Qur'ān, the Prophet (S), the Hadīth or Sunnah. In the early years the emphasis is given on the 5-pillars, but each year the emphasis increases. Every year history of some of the prophets is introduced in an age appropriate manner. Each year, several lessons are devoted to Islamic values to make the children grow up with good understanding of Islamic manners, values and morals. All the lessons are followed by homework.

Week	1st Grade	2nd Grade	3rd Grade
1	Allāh	Allāh the Creator	What does Allāh do
2	Islam	Blessings of Allāh	Some names of Allāh
3	Our Faith	The Qur'ān	Allāh : the Merciful
4	Muhammad (S)	Muhammad (S)	Allāh : the Judge
5	Qur'ān	Sunnah and Hadīth	We are Muslims
6	Exam is recommended in this week		
7	5 pillars of Islam	5 pillars of Islam	Other names of the Qur'ān
8	Shahādah	Shahādah	Hadith
9	Salāt and Wūdū	Salāt	Shahādah
10	Fasting	Sawm	Types of salāt
11	Zakah	Charity	Why to do salāt
12	Exam is recommended in this week		
13	Hajj	Hajj	Sawm
14	Saying bismillāh	Wūdū	Charity
15	Angels	Four khalīfas	Hajj
16	Shaitān	Ibrāhīm (A)	Prophet (S) in Makkah
17	Adam (A)	Ya'qūb (A) and Yūsuf (A)	Prophet (S) in Madīnah
18	Nūh (A)	Mūsā (A) and Hārūn (A)	How Rasul (S) treated others
19	Exam is recommended in this week		
20	Ibrāhīm (A)	Yūnus (A)	Ismā'īl (A) and Ishāq (A)
21	Mūsā (A)	Angels	Dāwūd (A)
22	'Isā (A)	Foods that we may eat	'Isā (A)
23	Makkah and Madīnah	Truthfulness	Being kind
24	Good manners	Kindness	Forgiveness
25	Kindness and sharing	Respect	Good deeds
26	Exam is recommended in this week		
27	Allāh rewards good works	Responsibility	Cleanliness
28	Respect	Obedience	Right Path
29	Forgiveness	Cleanliness	Muslim family
30	Love of Allāh	Honesty	Perseverance
31	Eid	Day of Judgment and Hereafter	Punctuality
32	Thanking Allāh	Muslims from different nations	Jinn
33	Exam is recommended in this week		

Outline of Curriculum – Grades 4, 5 and 6

By 5th grade a summarized biography of the Prophet (S) is completed with an understanding of events that shaped his life and early Islam. By 6th grade, the students will have studied the biography of most of the prominent prophets at least once. By now the students will have learned all the fundamental principles and all key concepts of Islam. Even if the students do not come back to weekend schools after 6th grade, still they will have gained significant age-appropriate knowledge about Islam.

Week	4th Grade	5th Grade	6th Grade
1	Rewards of Allāh	Allāh our sole Master	Attributes of Allāh
2	Discipline of Allāh	Why should we worship Allāh	Promise of Allāh
3	Some names of Allāh	Revelation of the Qur'ān	Objective of the Qur'ān
4	Books of Allāh	Characteristics of prophets	Compilation of the Qur'ān
5	Pre-Islamic Arabia	Battle of Badr	Previous Scriptures and the Qur'ān
6	Exam is recommended in this week		
7	The Year of the Elephant	Battle of Uhud	Importance of Shahādah
8	Early life of Muhammad (S)	Battle of Trench	Hadīth, compilation, narrators
9	Life before prophethood	Hudaibiyah Treaty	Nūh (A)
10	Receipt of prophethood	Conquest of Makkah	Talut, Jalut and Dāwūd (A)
11	Makkan period	Adam (A)	Dāwūd (A) and Sulaimān (A)
12	Exam is recommended in this week		
13	Pledges of Aqaba	Ibrāhīm (A) and his arguments	Sulaimān (A) and Queen of Saba
14	Hijrat to Madīnah	Ibrāhīm (A) and idols	Mūsā (A) and Fir'awn
15	Madīnan period	Luqmān (A) and his teachings	Israelites after their rescue
16	Victory of Makkah	Yūsuf (A) – Childhood and life in Aziz's home	Mūsā (A) and Khidir
17	Abū Bakr (R)	Yūsuf (A) – life in prison and his dream interpretation	'Isā (A) and Maryam (ra)
18	'Umar al-Khattāb (R)	Yūsuf (A) - dream fulfills	Khadījah (ra)
19	Exam is recommended in this week		
20	'Uthmān ibn 'Affan (R)	Ayyūb (A)	'A'ishah (ra)
21	'Ali Ibn Abu Tālib (R)	Zakariyyāh (A) and Yahyā (A)	Fātimah (ra)
22	Compilers of Hadīth	Maryam	Awakening
23	Shaitān's mode of action	Major Masjid in the world	Rūh and Nafs
24	Hūd (A)	Upholding truth	Angel and Jinn
25	Sālih (A)	Responsibility and punctuality	Shaitān's strategy
26	Exam is recommended in this week		
27	Mūsā (A)	My mind, my body	Taqwā
28	Sulaimān (A)	Kindness and forgiveness	My friend is Muslim now
29	Truthfulness	Middle Path	Friendship with others / with opposite gender
30	Perseverance	Significance of salāt	Reading salāt vs performing salāt
31	Day of Judgment	Significance of fasting	Muslims around the world
32	'Eid and its significance	Zakāt and sadaqah - significance	People of other faith
33	Exam is recommended in this week		

Outline of Curriculum – Grades 7, 8 and 9

Application of knowledge is gradually emphasized through carefully selected topics. Details about some of the prophets are introduced to highlight the abiding moral in their lives. In 8th grade several battles and early Muslims' struggle are discussed in detail. Depth and emphasis in the lessons require increased attention from the students. Age appropriate moral lessons e.g. gossip, friendship, peer pressure, dating, indecency, enjoining good and forbidding evil, etc. are covered.

Week	7th Grade	8th Grade	9th Grade
1	Why Islam, what is Islam	Divine Names	Signs of Allāh in nature
2	The Qur'ān - other names	Objective of the Qur'an	Ponder over the Qur'ān
3	Seeking forgiveness of Allāh - Istighfar	Hadīth	Preservation and compilation of the Qur'ān
4	Allāh: Angry or Kind	Madhhab	Ibadat - some easy ways to do it
5	Islamic Greetings	Hope, hopefulness, hopelessness	Why human being are superior
6	Exam is recommended in this week		
7	Adam (A)	Trial	Is Islam a violent religion
8	'Ad and Thamūd	Friends and friendship	Peer pressure
9	Stories of Ibrāhīm (A)-I	Friendship with Non-Muslims	Choices we make
10	Stories of Ibrāhīm (A) -II	Dating in Islam	Dating in Islam
11	Sacrifice of Ibrāhīm (A)	Duties towards Parents	Alcohol and gambling
12	Exam is recommended in this week		
13	Lūt (A)	Islam for middle school student	Permitted and prohibited food
14	Yūsuf (A)- Story of overcoming temptation	Battle of Badr	Food of the People of the Book
15	Dwellers of Cave	Battle of Uhud	Khadījah (ra)
16	Dhul Qurnain	Banu Qaynuka	Prophet's multiple marriages
17	Abū Sufyān	Banu Nadir	Marriage with Zainab (ra)
18	Khālid Ibn Walīd (R)	Battle of Khandaq	The Prophet - a great army general
19	Exam is recommended in this week		
20	How to achieve success	Banu Qurayzah	God's chosen people
21	Character of the prophets	Sūrah Al-Ahzāb on the Battle of Khandaq	Mūsā's personality
22	Prophet's marriages	Hudaibiyah Treaty	Prophecy of Muhammad(S) in Bible
23	Purification	Tabūk Expedition	Shī'ah Muslims
24	Permitted and prohibited	Farewell Pilgrimage	Muslims in North America
25	Lailatul Qadr	Performance of Hajj	Life cycle of truth
26	Exam is recommended in this week		
27	Fasting in Ramadan	Paradise and Hell	How Ramadan makes us better
28	My family is Muslim now	Finality of Prophethood	Indecency
29	Amr bil ma'rūf	Origin and history of Shī'ah	Allegations against the Prophet (S)
30	Guard your tongue	Ummayad DyNāsty	Family values
31	Lessons from past civilizations	Abbasid DyNāsty	Sharī'ah
32	Science in the Qur'ān	Permitted and prohibited food	Justice in Islam
33	Exam is recommended in this week		

Outline of Curriculum – Grades 10, 11 and 12

In 10th, 11th and 12th grades, the topics increasingly prepare the youths to tune their young-adult life. More serious issues are introduced that have real life implications. Application of knowledge continues to be emphasized. Age appropriate moral lessons like righteousness in Islam, marriage, dowry issues, divorce process, music in Islam, jihād etc. are introduced.

Week	10th Grade	11th Grade	12th Grade
1	History of Allāh	"Discovering" God	Our God, their God
2	An analysis of Fātiha	Kalam of Allāh	Loving Allāh
3	Fātiha vs. Lord's Prayer	Precedence of mercy in Allāh	Literal interpretation of the Qur'ān
4	Muhkam Mutashabihat verses	Importance of the Qur'ān in life	Management 101 - from the Prophet's life
5	Being Khalīfa on earth	Succession to Muhammad (S)	Apostasy
6	Exam is recommended in this week		
7	10 Companions - Ashara Mubashirin	Victory comes from apparent setback	Husband and wife - garment for each other
8	The Bible and the Qur'ān	Accountability	Dowry process
9	Adam and Eve in the Garden	Righteousness in Islam	Divorce process
10	Natural calamities	10 years of life changing foundation	Lian verses
11	Racism in Islam	Light upon the Light	Hijab verses
12	Exam is recommended in this week		
13	Superstition	Ruh, Nafs, Spirit, Bodies	Marital relations of the Prophet (S)
14	Al-Asr - timing of the Day	Responsibilities in married life	Men are head of household
15	Position of women in Islam	Divorce	Flogging an adulterer
16	Marriage with Non-Muslims	Balancing faith amid diversity	Why two women witness
17	Distinctive females in Qur'ān	Importance of keeping the "trust"	Hur in Heaven
18	Women's rights in Islam	Music in Islam	Is Islam a violent religion
19	Exam is recommended in this week		
20	Establishing salāt- Institutionalize it	Fitra - Innate human nature	Jihād verses
21	Goodly loan	Heedlessness in human being	Hajj - understanding the significance
22	Fiqh	Importance of tolerance	"Beating thy wife"
23	Death	Guidance and misguidance	"Part time Muslim"
24	Turmoil in early Islam	Stages of life and death	Muslim youths in the US
25	Public finance in early Islam	This world and next world	MSA - An introduction
26	Exam is recommended in this week		
27	Business ethics	How to enjoy life Islamic way	Islamophobia - how to deal with it
28	Balance in life	Wrongdoings - how to identify and avoid them	Future Muslims
29	Islam in America	How to pray Janaza prayer	Independent project
30	Islam in India	Understanding Judaism	Independent project
31	Islam in Spain	Judaism, Christianity and Islam	Independent project
32	Islam in Turkey	Dependence, independence	Independent project
33	Exam is recommended in this week		

Steps of Salāh

The description provided in these pages are the commonly accepted ways of performing salāt in Hanafi madhhab. There may be minor variations, which are allowed. All the variations should have supporting proof that RasulAllāh (S) had occasionally practised that variation. The teacher/parents are requested to show the ideal practice according to their madhhab. The salāh has to be made in Arabic language only.

Physical preparation for salāh:

Physical cleanliness: Before performing salāh, make sure you have a clean body. You must have completed *wudu*, and be in the state of *wudu*. At any time during the salāh, do not look sideways, do not look at others, do not talk to others in the middle of the salāh. Do not make unnecessary movements. Do not scratch, yawn, laugh or smile. If you must sneeze or cough, that is Okay, but try to minimize it.

Clean clothes: Your clothes should be clean and should cover the body. For boys, the cloth should cover at least from the naval to the knees. For girls, the cloth should cover from the neck to the ankle, and to the wrist. The head is covered, while face can remain uncovered. Clothes should be non-see through. Avoid any clothing that has pictures of people, animals or bad writings.

Clean place: You should find a clean place to make your salāh. A prayer rug is not necessary. A prayer rug is always kept clean, and ensures a clean place when you are praying on it.

Direction: You will be facing *Qiblah*, which is the direction of Ka'bah in Makkah.

Time: *Fard* (compulsory) prayers are performed at the proper and appointed time. It is preferable to perform the prayer as soon as the *Adhan* (call to prayer) is announced.

Mental preparation: We will begin the prayer with full mental and physical attention. During *salāh*, we are directly talking to Allāh, therefore we must show total attention. Avoid any place or object that can divert your attention.

What is a raka'ah? Each salāh can be divided into cycles of physical postures or raka'at. Each raka'ah involves position of *qiyam* (standing), *ruku* (bowing), *sujud* (prostration), *jalsa* (seated), and again a *sujud* (prostration), and associated recitations. Following are the specified raka'at in the five daily salāh. Some variation on the number of Sunnah prayer exist among the madhhab.

	Sunnah raka'at before Fard raka'at	Fard raka'at	Sunnah raka'at after Fard raka'at
Fajr	2	2	
Dhuhr	4	4	2
'Asr	4	4	
Maghrib		3	2
'Isha	4	4	2, then 3 (wajib)

Description for a salāh of two raka'at:

Following description is for a salāh of two raka'at (e.g. Fard prayer of Fajr). At the end the description, there is a brief note on how to perform 3 or 4 raka'at of salāh.

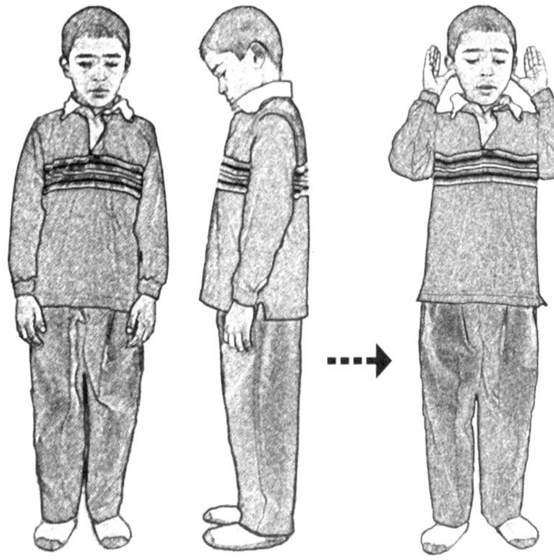

Figure 1

Step 1 (Figure 1)

Make an intention to perform the salāh for the sake of Allāh. Say to yourself (in any language) that you intend to offer this *Salāh* (*Fajr, Dhuhr, Asr, Maghrib* or *Isha*), *Fard*, *Sunnat* or *Witr*, and the number of raka'ahs (example—"I intend to offer two *raka'ah* of *Fard*, *Fajr* prayer for Allāh").

Position: *Qiyam*. You are standing upright. Raise both hands up to the ears (palms facing the *Qiblah*, —the direction to Ka'bah).

What to say: *"Allāhu Akbar"* (Allāh is the Greatest).

Step 2 (Figure 2)

Position: Place your left hand over your stomach, and then place your right hand on top of the left hand, and make a grip around the wrist of the left hand.

What to say:

1. *"Subhanaka Allāhumma wa bihamdika, wa tabārakasmuka, wa ta'āla jadduka, wa lā ilāha ghairuka"*. (This part is known as *thana*. It means "Glory be to you O

Figure 2

Allāh, and praise to You. Blessed be Your Name, exalted be Your Majesty and Glory. There is no god but You").

2. *"A'ūdu billāhi mina ash-Shaytānir rajim"* (I seek protection of Allāh against Shaitān, the condemned)

3. *"Bismillāhir rahmānir rahīm"* (In the Name of Allāh, Most Gracious, Most Merciful).

4. We will recite Sūrah Al-Fātihah now. It is a must that we recite Sūrah Al-Fātihah in each raka'ah. A salāh is not valid if Sūrah Al-Fātihah is not recited if praying alone.

"Al humdu li-llahi rabbi-l 'alamīn. Ar-rahmāni-r rahīm. Māliki yawmi-d dīn. Iyyāka na'budu wa iyyāka Nāsta'īn. Ihdina-s sirāta-l mustaqīm. Sirātal ladhīna an'amta 'alaihim, ghairil maghdūbi 'alaihim, wa la-d dāllīn. (Āmīn)"

(The Praise belong to Allāh, The Rabb of all the worlds; the Rahman; the Rahim. Malik of the Day of Judgment. You alone do we serve, and to You alone we seek for help. Guide us on the Right Path, —the path of those upon whom You have bestowed favors; not of those upon whom wrath is brought down, nor those gone-astray.)

5. After reciting sūrah Fātihah, we will now recite any short sūrah or a few verses from the Holy Qur'ān. This additional recitation of a part of the Qur'ān is done in the first two *raka'ah* only. We should recite the sections in the order that they appear in the Qur'ān, e.g. if you are going to recite Sūrah Falaq and Sūrah Nās in your prayer, you will recite Sūrah Falaq in the first *raka'ah*, and Sūrah Nās in the second raka'ah. It is always good to memorize as many sūrah as you can, as you will recite them in your *salāh*.

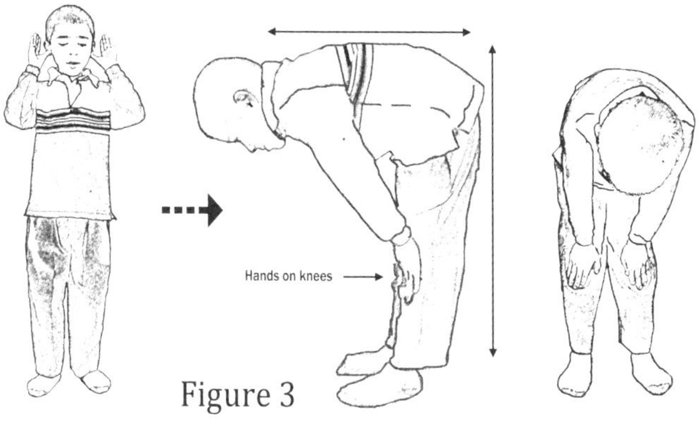

Figure 3

Step 3 (Figure 3)

What to say: *"Allāhu Akbar."*

Position: This position is called *ruku*. First raise your hands up to your ears, then bow with your back perpendicular to your legs. Put your hands on the knees. Do not bend the knees.

What to say: *"Subhana rabbiyal 'Adhīm"* (say it 3 times) (Glorified is my Rabb, the Great).

Figure 4

Step 4 (Figure 4)

While going back to *qiyam* (upright) position,

What to say: *"Samia Allāhu liman hamidah"* (Allāh listens to him who praises Him).

Position: In *qiyam* position.

What to say: *"Rabbanā wa laka al hamd"* ("Our Rabb, praise be for You only").

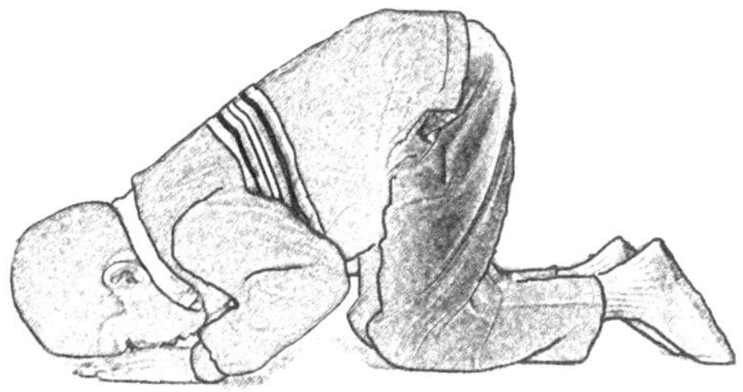

Figure 5

Step 5 (Figure 5)

What to say: While going to the next position of *sujud*, say *"Allāhu Akbar."*

Position: This position is *sujud*. Your will place your both knees on the floor. Try not to move the position of your feet, i.e. you will not step your feet away from the position of *qiyam*. After placing the knees, then you will place your two hands on the ground, with palms touching the ground. Do not glide your hands on the ground. Your elbow is away from the floor. The hands will be sufficiently apart to give space for your head. Now you will place your forehead on the floor. Both your nose and forehead should touch the ground. Your hands are on the side of your head. Your stomach will not touch the floor. You should be most humble in this position.

The most powerful part of our body is our brain, the site of our intelligence. We submit our full selves, with full understanding, to Almighty Allāh. We realize that our strength, power, wealth, everything that we have is from Allāh only. To confirm this physical and spiritual humbleness, we will repeat the *sujud* again in Step 7.

What to say: *"Subhana rabbiyal A'ala"* (say it 3 times) (Glory be to Allāh, the Exalted).

Figure 6

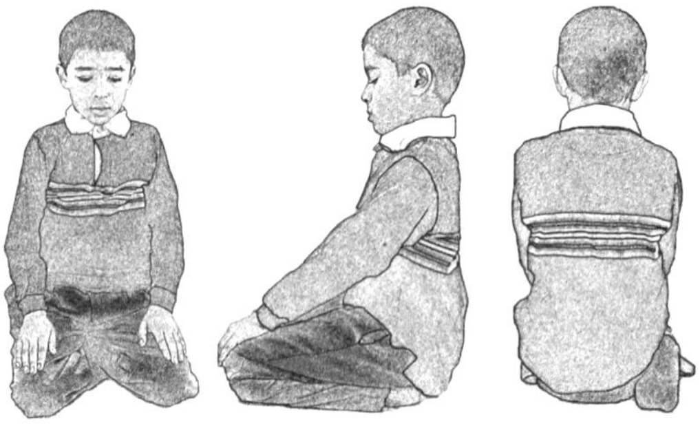

Step 6 (Figure 6)

The next position is *jalsa*.

What to say: While going to the *jalsa* position, say *"Allāhu Akbar."*

Position: To go to *jalsa* position, rise from *sujud*. First you will raise your head off the floor, then you will raise your hands. Now you are sitting on the floor, this posture is called *jalsa*.

What to say: *"Rabbi-ghfir lī wa rhamnī"* (O my Rabb, forgive me and have mercy on me).

Step 7 (Figure 5)

We will repeat the *sujud* again. Every *raka'ah* has two *sujud*.

What to say: While going to the position of *sujud*, say *"Allāhu Akbar."*

Position: *Sujud*. Place your palms on the floor, then place your forehead. Both the nose and the forehead should be touching the floor.

What to say: *"Subhāna rabbiyal A'ala"* (say it 3 times) (Glory to Allāh, the Exalted").

This completes one raka'ah

Beginning of second raka'ah

Step 8 (Figures 1 and 2)

You will rise to *qiyam* (upright) position. The movement should be in a systematic, graceful manner. First your will raise your forehead from the floor, then you will raise your hands off the ground, then you will raise your knees. Try not to move your feet, i.e., the position of your feet should be in the same place as it was in the first *raka'ah*.

What to say: While going up to the position of *qiyam*, say *"Allāhu Akbar."*

Position: You are standing upright. Hold the left hand with the right hand on top.

What to say: 1. Sūrah Al-Fātihah, and 2. Any short sūrah or some verses of the Holy Qur'ān.

Step 9 (Figure 3)

What to say: *"Allāhu Akbar."*

Position: *Ruku*. Raise your both hands up to the ear, palm facing the *Qiblah*. Bow with your back perpendicular to your legs. Put your hands on knee.

What to say: *"Subhāna rabbiyal 'Adhīm"* (say it 3 times).

Step 10 (Figure 4)

Position: While going back to *qiyam* (upright) position,

What to say: *"Sami'a Allāhu liman hamidah."*

Position: In *qiyam* position. You are upright.

What to say: "Rabbanā wa lakal hamd."

Step 11 (Figure 5)

What to say: While going to the next position of *sujud*, say *"Allāhu Akbar."*

Position: *Sujud*. Follow the sequence as in Step 5.

What to say: *"Subhāna Rabbiyal A'ala"* (say it 3 times).

Step 12 (Figure 6)

What to say: While going to the next position of *jalsa*, say *"Allāhu Akbar."*

Position: Rise from the *sujud* position. Now you are sitting in *jalsa* position.

What to say: "*'Rabbi-ghfir lī wa rhamnī*" (O my Rabb, forgive me and have Mercy on me).

Step 13 (Figure 5)

What to say: While going to the next position of sujud, say *"Allāhu Akbar."*

Position: *Sujud*. Place your hands, and then place your forehead on the floor.

What to say: *"Subhāna Rabbiyal A'ala"* (say it 3 times).

Step 14 (Figure 6)

What to say: While going to the next position of *jalsa*, say *"Allāhu Akbar."*

Position: Rise from the *sujud* position. Now you are sitting on *jalsa* position.

What to say: You will say *Tashahud, Durūd* and a short prayer, as follows:

"At-tahiyātu lillahi was-salawātu wattaiyibātu. Assalāmu 'alayka ayyuhan-nabiyu wa rahmatullāhi wa barakātuhu. Assalāmu 'alainā wa 'ala 'ibadi-llāhis-sālihīn. Ashhadu an lā ilāha illallāhu wa ashhadu anna Muhammadan 'abduhu wa rasūluhu."

(All the salutations, prayers and nice things are for Allāh. Peace be on you O Prophet, and the blessings of Allāh, and His grace. Peace on us and on all the righteous servants of Allāh. I bear witness that none but Allāh is worthy of worship and bear witness that Muhammad is the servant and messenger of Allāh.) This is known as *Tashahud.*

Position: raise your right index finger up while reciting the last part of this prayer.

Then you will recite the *Durūd.*

"Allāhumma salli 'ala Muhammadin wa 'ala āli Muhummadin, kamā sallayta 'ala Ibrāhima, wa ala āli Ibrāhima, innaka hamidun majid. Allāhumma barik 'ala Muhammadin wa 'ala āli Muhummadin, kama barakta ala Ibrāhima, wa 'ala āli Ibrahīm, innaka hamīdun majīd".

(O Allāh, send your Mercy on Muhammad and his posterity as you sent Your mercy on Ibrāhīm and his posterity. You are the Most Praised, The Most Glorious. O Allāh, send your Blessings on Muhammad and his posterity as you have blessed Ibrāhīm and his posterity. You are the Most praised, The Most Glorious.)

You may add a short prayer, such as:

"Rabbanā ātinā fi-d dunyā hasanatan wa fi-l ākhirati hasanatan, wa qinā 'adhāban nār"

(Our Rabb, give us the good of this world, and good in the Hereafter and save us from the chastisement of Fire.)

Step 15 (Figure 7)

Position: Slowly turn the face to the right. This is called *salam.*

Figure 7

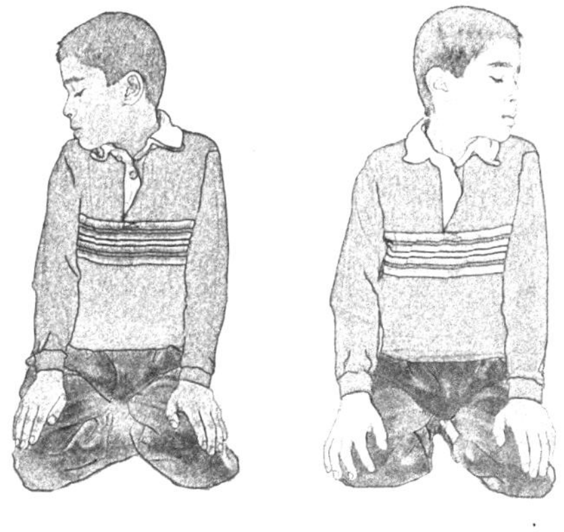

What to say: *"As-salāmu 'alaikum wa rahmatullāh"* (Peace and mercy of Allāh be on you).

Step 16 (Figure 7)

Position: Slowly turn the face to the left. This is called salam.

What to say: *"As-salāmu 'alaikum wa rahmatullāh."*

This completes the two raka'at of salāh.

How to pray three raka'ats (Maghrib)

In order to perform a three raka'at Salāh, all the postures and the prayers are the same up to step 13. But this time in on step 14, recite up to *"At-tahiyātu lillahi was-salawātu wattaiyibātu. Assalāmu 'alayka ayyuhan-nabiyu wa rahmatullāhi wa barakātuhu. Assalāmu 'alainā wa 'ala 'ibadi-llāhis-sālihīn. Ashhadu an lā ilāha illallāhu wa ashhadu anna Muhammadan 'abduhu wa rasūluhu."* This is known as *Tashahud.* Saying *Allāhu akbar,* return back to the *qiyam* position, step 8. This time only *Al-Fātihah,* (in step 8) alone will be recited without adding any sūrah of the Holy Qur'ān. Then all prayers and postures are the same as shown from step 9 - 16.

How to pray four raka'ats (Dhuhr, 'Asr and 'Isha)

In order to perform a four raka'at prayer, all the postures and the prayers are the same up to step 13. In Step 14 only the prayer of *"Tashahud* will be recited, and the *qiyam* position, step 8, will be resumed. In position 8 only *Al-Fātihah,* alone will be recited without adding any sūrah. Step 8 - 13, completes the third raka'ah. The *qiyam* position, step 8, will be re-assumed. In position 8 only *Al-Fātihah,* will be recited without adding any sūrah. Step 8 - 16, completes the fourth raka'ah.

Other useful books from weekendLearning

Arabic Writing Workbook

96 pages $10.00

Teach students how to write Arabic with easy to follow instructions. Practice alphabets are given in shaded and dotted form, followed by blank lines to polish writing skills. Plenty of pages for year-long practice writing.

21 Du'ā for Children: Supplication from Al-Qur'ān

28 pages $2.00

Allāh wants us to always make du'ā to Him for everything. The finest du'ā are those taught by Allāh in the Qur'ān. Use this booklet to teach 21 finest du'ā and many more. Give one copy to each student in your school. It is a life long companion and a great learning tool.

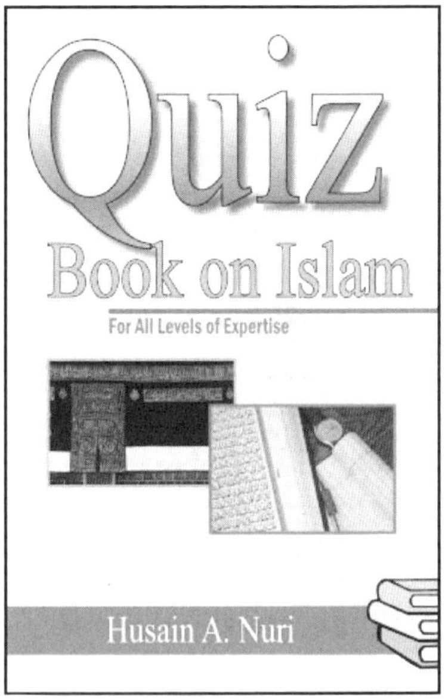

Quiz Book on Islam: For All Levels of Expertise (2nd ed)

160 pages $10.00

Written by the Quiz Master of an Interstate Quiz Bowl, the book will boost Islamic knowledge of children. Adults will equally enjoy the book. Over 1600 questions cover more than 100 topics. Questions become harder as you progress from basic to intermediate and finally to advanced section. Many questions have explanatory answers. Turn to this book to quickly learn a variety of facts about Islam.

Juz 'Amma for School Students

216 pages $12.00

The book is a student friendly presentation of the 30th Part of the Qur'ān. The book contains large and clear Arabic text, transliteration and translation in three-column format. Each sūrah starts with an introduction, followed by explanation of the verses. A "word to know" section provides root and derivatives of several key words. This is followed by a word-to-word meaning of the entire sūrah. Each chapter ends with some teachings in the sūrah that the children can apply in their everyday life. A short question section reinforces the materials learned.